NON SANZ DROICT.

A
PLEASANT
Conceited Comedie
CALLED,
Loues labors loſt.

As it vvas preſented before her Highnes
this laſt Chriſtmas.

Newly correＣted and augmented
By W. Shakeſpere.

Imprinted at London by *W.W.*
for *Cutbert Burby.*
1598.

Title page of the earliest edition of *Love's Labor's Lost*. Also in 1598
the title pages of the second editions of *Richard II* and *Richard III*
name Shakespeare as the author, but *Love's Labor's Lost* is the first
new play whose title page names Shakespeare.

William Shakespeare

Love's Labor's Lost

With New and Updated
Critical Essays
and a Revised Bibliography

Edited by John Arthos

THE SIGNET CLASSICS SHAKESPEARE
General Editor: Sylvan Barnet

SIGNET CLASSICS

SIGNET CLASSICS
Published by New American Library, a division of
Penguin Group (USA) Inc., 375 Hudson Street,
New York, New York 10014, U.S.A.
Penguin Books Ltd, 80 Strand,
London WC2R 0RL, England
Penguin Books Australia Ltd, 250 Camberwell Road,
Camberwell, Victoria 3124, Australia
Penguin Books Canada Ltd, 10 Alcorn Avenue,
Toronto, Ontario, Canada M4V 3B2
Penguin Books (NZ), cnr Airborne and Rosedale Roads,
Albany, Auckland 1310, New Zealand

Penguin Books Ltd, Registered Offices:
80 Strand, London WC2R 0RL, England

Published by Signet Classics, an imprint of New American Library,
a division of Penguin Group (USA) Inc.

First Signet Classics Printing (Second Revised Edition), September 2004
10 9 8 7 6 5 4 3 2 1

Contents

Shakespeare: An Overview

Biographical Sketch

Between the record of his baptism in Stratford on 26 April 1564 and the record of his burial in Stratford on 25 April 1616, some forty official documents name Shakespeare, and many others name his parents, his children, and his grandchildren. Further, there are at least fifty literary references to him in the works of his contemporaries. More facts are known about William Shakespeare than about any other playwright of the period except Ben Jonson. The facts should, however, be distinguished from the legends. The latter, inevitably more engaging and better known, tell us that the Stratford boy killed a calf in high style, poached deer and rabbits, and was forced to flee to London, where he held horses outside a playhouse. These traditions are only traditions; they may be true, but no evidence supports them, and it is well to stick to the facts.

Mary Arden, the dramatist's mother, was the daughter of a substantial landowner; about 1557 she married John Shakespeare, a tanner, glove-maker, and trader in wool, grain, and other farm commodities. In 1557 John Shakespeare was a member of the council (the governing body of Stratford), in 1558 a constable of the borough, in 1561 one of the two town chamberlains, in 1565 an alderman (entitling him to the appellation of "Mr."), in 1568 high bailiff—the town's highest political office, equivalent to mayor. After 1577, for an unknown reason he drops out of local politics. What *is* known is that he had to mortgage his wife's property, and that he was involved in serious litigation.

The birthday of William Shakespeare, the third child and the eldest son of this locally prominent man, is unrecorded, but the Stratford parish register records that the infant was baptized on 26 April 1564. (It is quite possible that he was born on 23 April, but this date has probably been assigned by tradition because it is the date on which, fifty-two years later, he died, and perhaps because it is the feast day of St. George, patron saint of England.) The attendance records of the Stratford grammar school of the period are not extant, but it is reasonable to assume that the son of a prominent local official attended the free school—it had been established for the purpose of educating males precisely of his class—and received substantial training in Latin. The masters of the school from Shakespeare's seventh to fifteenth years held Oxford degrees; the Elizabethan curriculum excluded mathematics and the natural sciences but taught a good deal of Latin rhetoric, logic, and literature, including plays by Plautus, Terence, and Seneca.

On 27 November 1582 a marriage license was issued for the marriage of Shakespeare and Anne Hathaway, eight years his senior. The couple had a daughter, Susanna, in May 1583. Perhaps the marriage was necessary, but perhaps the couple had earlier engaged, in the presence of witnesses, in a formal "troth plight" which would render their children legitimate even if no further ceremony were performed. In February 1585, Anne Hathaway bore Shakespeare twins, Hamnet and Judith.

That Shakespeare was born is excellent; that he married and had children is pleasant; but that we know nothing about his departure from Stratford to London or about the beginning of his theatrical career is lamentable and must be admitted. We would gladly sacrifice details about his children's baptism for details about his earliest days in the theater. Perhaps the poaching episode is true (but it is first reported almost a century after Shakespeare's death), or perhaps he left Stratford to be a schoolmaster, as another tradition holds; perhaps he was moved (like Petruchio in *The Taming of the Shrew*) by

> Such wind as scatters young men through the world,
> To seek their fortunes farther than at home
> Where small experience grows.   (1.2.49–51)

In 1592, thanks to the cantankerousness of Robert Greene, we have our first reference, a snarling one, to Shakespeare as an actor and playwright. Greene, a graduate of St. John's College, Cambridge, had become a playwright and a pamphleteer in London, and in one of his pamphlets he warns three university-educated playwrights against an actor who has presumed to turn playwright:

> There is an upstart crow, beautified with our feathers, that with his *tiger's heart wrapped in a player's hide* supposes he is as well able to bombast out a blank verse as the best of you, and being an absolute Johannes-factotum [i.e., jack-of-all-trades] is in his own conceit the only Shake-scene in a country.

The reference to the player, as well as the allusion to Aesop's crow (who strutted in borrowed plumage, as an actor struts in fine words not his own), makes it clear that by this date Shakespeare had both acted and written. That Shakespeare is meant is indicated not only by *Shake-scene* but also by the parody of a line from one of Shakespeare's plays, *3 Henry VI*: "O, tiger's heart wrapped in a woman's hide" (1.4.137). If in 1592 Shakespeare was prominent enough to be attacked by an envious dramatist, he probably had served an apprenticeship in the theater for at least a few years.

In any case, although there are no extant references to Shakespeare between the record of the baptism of his twins in 1585 and Greene's hostile comment about "Shake-scene" in 1592, it is evident that during some of these "dark years" or "lost years" Shakespeare had acted and written. There are a number of subsequent references to him as an actor. Documents indicate that in 1598 he is a "principal comedian," in 1603 a "principal tragedian," in 1608 he is one of the "men players." (We do not have, however, any solid information about which roles he may have played; later traditions say he played Adam in *As You Like It* and the ghost in *Hamlet*, but nothing supports the assertions. Probably his role as dramatist came to supersede his role as actor.) The profession of actor was not for a gentleman, and it occasionally drew the scorn of university men like Greene who resented writing speeches for persons less educated than themselves, but it was respectable enough; players, if prosperous, were in effect members of the bourgeoisie, and there is nothing to suggest that Stratford considered William Shakespeare less than a solid citizen. When, in 1596, the Shakespeares were granted a coat of arms—i.e., the right to be considered gentlemen—the grant was made to Shakespeare's father, but probably William Shakespeare had arranged the matter on his own behalf. In subsequent transactions he is occasionally styled a gentleman.

Although in 1593 and 1594 Shakespeare published two narrative poems dedicated to the Earl of Southampton, *Venus and Adonis* and *The Rape of Lucrece*, and may well have written most or all of his sonnets in the middle nineties, Shakespeare's literary activity seems to have been almost entirely devoted to the theater. (It may be significant that the two narrative poems were written in years when the plague closed the theaters for several months.) In 1594 he was a charter member of a theatrical company called the Chamberlain's Men, which in 1603 became the royal company, the King's Men, making Shakespeare the king's playwright. Until he retired to Stratford (about 1611, apparently), he was with this remarkably stable company. From 1599 the company acted primarily at the Globe theater, in which Shakespeare held a one-tenth interest. Other Elizabethan dramatists are known to have acted, but no other is known also to have been entitled to a share of the profits.

Shakespeare's first eight published plays did not have his name on them, but this is not remarkable; the most popular play of the period, Thomas Kyd's *The Spanish Tragedy*, went through many editions without naming Kyd, and Kyd's authorship is known only because a book on the profession of acting happens to quote (and attribute to Kyd) some lines on the interest of Roman emperors in the drama. What is remarkable is that after 1598 Shakespeare's name commonly appears on printed plays—some of which are not his. Presumably his name was a drawing card, and publishers used it to attract potential buyers. Another indication of his popularity comes from Francis Meres, author of *Palladis Tamia: Wit's Treasury* (1598). In this anthology of snippets accompanied by an essay on literature, many playwrights are mentioned, but Shakespeare's name occurs

more often than any other, and Shakespeare is the only playwright whose plays are listed.

From his acting, his playwriting, and his share in a
playhouse, Shakespeare seems to have made considerable
money. He put it to work, making substantial investments in
Stratford real estate. As early as 1597 he bought New Place,
the second-largest house in Stratford. His family moved in
soon afterward, and the house remained in the family until a
granddaughter died in 1670. When Shakespeare made his
will in 1616, less than a month before he died, he sought
to leave his property intact to his descendants. Of small
bequests to relatives and to friends (including three actors,
Richard Burbage, John Heminges, and Henry Condell), that
to his wife of the second-best bed has provoked the most
comment. It has sometimes been taken as a sign of an
unhappy marriage (other supposed signs are the apparently hasty marriage, his wife's seniority of eight years, and
his residence in London without his family). Perhaps the
second-best bed was the bed the couple had slept in, the best
bed being reserved for visitors. In any case, had Shakespeare
not excepted it, the bed would have gone (with the rest of his
household possessions) to his daughter and her husband.

On 25 April 1616 Shakespeare was buried within the
chancel of the church at Stratford. An unattractive monu-
ment to his memory, placed on a wall near the grave, says
that he died on 23 April. Over the grave itself are the lines,
perhaps by Shakespeare, that (more than his literary fame)
have kept his bones undisturbed in the crowded burial
ground where old bones were often dislodged to make way
for new:

> Good friend, for Jesus' sake forbear
> To dig the dust enclosed here.
> Blessed be the man that spares these stones
> And cursed be he that moves my bones.

A Note on the Anti-Stratfordians, Especially Baconians and Oxfordians

Not until 1769—more than a hundred and fifty years
after Shakespeare's death—is there any record of anyone

expressing doubt about Shakespeare's authorship of the plays and poems. In 1769, however, Herbert Lawrence nominated Francis Bacon (1561–1626) in *The Life and Adventures of Common Sense*. Since then, at least two dozen other nominees have been offered, including Christopher Marlowe, Sir Walter Raleigh, Queen Elizabeth I, and Edward de Vere, 17th earl of Oxford. The impulse behind all anti-Stratfordian movements is the scarcely concealed snobbish opinion that "the man from Stratford" simply could not have written the plays because he was a country fellow without a university education and without access to high society. Anyone, the argument goes, who used so many legal terms, medical terms, nautical terms, and so forth, and who showed some familiarity with classical writing, must have attended a university, and anyone who knew so much about courtly elegance and courtly deceit must himself have moved among courtiers. The plays do indeed reveal an author whose interests were exceptionally broad, but specialists in any given field—law, medicine, arms and armor, and so on—soon find that the plays do not reveal deep knowledge in specialized matters; indeed, the playwright often gets technical details wrong.

The claim on behalf of Bacon, forgotten almost as soon as it was put forth in 1769, was independently reasserted by Joseph C. Hart in 1848. In 1856 it was reaffirmed by W. H. Smith in a book, and also by Delia Bacon in an article; in 1857 Delia Bacon published a book, arguing that Francis Bacon had directed a group of intellectuals who wrote the plays.

Francis Bacon's claim has largely faded, perhaps because it was advanced with such evident craziness by Ignatius Donnelly, who in *The Great Cryptogram* (1888) claimed to break a code in the plays that proved Bacon had written not only the plays attributed to Shakespeare but also other Renaissance works, for instance the plays of Christopher Marlowe and the essays of Montaigne.

Consider the last two lines of the Epilogue in *The Tempest*:

As you from crimes would pardoned be,
Let your indulgence set me free.

What was Shakespeare—sorry, Francis Bacon, Baron Verulam—*really* saying in these two lines? According to Baconians, the lines are an anagram reading, "Tempest of Francis Bacon, Lord Verulam; do ye ne'er divulge me, ye words." Ingenious, and it is a pity that in the quotation the letter *a* appears only twice in the cryptogram, whereas in the deciphered message it appears three times. Oh, no problem; just alter "Verulam" to "Verul'm" and it works out very nicely.

Most people understand that with sufficient ingenuity one can torture any text and find in it what one wishes. For instance: Did Shakespeare have a hand in the King James Version of the Bible? It was nearing completion in 1610, when Shakespeare was forty-six years old. If you look at the 46th Psalm and count forward for forty-six words, you will find the word *shake*. Now if you go to the end of the psalm and count backward forty-six words, you will find the word *spear*. Clear evidence, according to some, that Shakespeare slyly left his mark in the book.

Bacon's candidacy has largely been replaced in the twentieth century by the candidacy of Edward de Vere (1550–1604), 17th earl of Oxford. The basic ideas behind the Oxford theory, advanced at greatest length by Dorothy and Charlton Ogburn in *This Star of England* (1952, rev. 1955), a book of 1297 pages, and by Charlton Ogburn in *The Mysterious William Shakespeare* (1984), a book of 892 pages, are these: (1) The man from Stratford could not possibly have had the mental equipment and the experience to have written the plays—only a courtier could have written them; (2) Oxford had the requisite background (social position, education, years at Queen Elizabeth's court); (3) Oxford did not wish his authorship to be known for two basic reasons: writing for the public theater was a vulgar pursuit, and the plays show so much courtly and royal disreputable behavior that they would have compromised Oxford's position at court. Oxfordians offer countless details to support the claim. For example, Hamlet's phrase "that ever I was born to set it right" (1.5.89) barely conceals "E. Ver, I was born to set it right," an unambiguous announcement of de Vere's authorship, according to *This Star of England* (p. 654). A second example: Consider Ben

Jonson's poem entitled "To the Memory of My Beloved Master William Shakespeare," prefixed to the first collected edition of Shakespeare's plays in 1623. According to Oxfordians, when Jonson in this poem speaks of the author of the plays as the "swan of Avon," he is alluding not to William Shakespeare, who was born and died in Stratford-on-Avon and who throughout his adult life owned property there; rather, he is alluding to Oxford, who, the Ogburns say, used "William Shakespeare" as his pen name, and whose manor at Bilton was on the Avon River. Oxfordians do not offer any evidence that Oxford took a pen name, and they do not care that Oxford had sold the manor in 1581, forty-two years before Jonson wrote his poem. Surely a reference to the Shakespeare who was born in Stratford, who had returned to Stratford, and who had died there only seven years before Jonson wrote the poem is more plausible. And exactly why Jonson, who elsewhere also spoke of Shakespeare as a playwright, and why Heminges and Condell, who had acted with Shakespeare for about twenty years, should speak of Shakespeare as the author in their dedication in the 1623 volume of collected plays is never adequately explained by Oxfordians. Either Jonson, Heminges and Condell, and numerous others were in on the conspiracy, or they were all duped—equally unlikely alternatives. Another difficulty in the Oxford theory is that Oxford died in 1604, and some of the plays are clearly indebted to works and events later than 1604. Among the Oxfordian responses are: At his death Oxford left some plays, and in later years these were touched up by hacks, who added the material that points to later dates. *The Tempest*, almost universally regarded as one of Shakespeare's greatest plays and pretty clearly dated to 1611, does indeed date from a period after the death of Oxford, but it is a crude piece of work that should not be included in the canon of works by Oxford.

The anti-Stratfordians, in addition to assuming that the author must have been a man of rank and a university man, usually assume two conspiracies: (1) a conspiracy in Elizabethan and Jacobean times, in which a surprisingly large number of persons connected with the theater knew that the actor Shakespeare did not write the plays attributed to him but for some reason or other pretended that he did; (2) a conspiracy of today's Stratfordians, the professors who teach Shakespeare in the colleges and universities, who are said to have a vested interest in preserving Shakespeare as the author of the plays they teach. In fact, (1) it is inconceivable that the secret of Shakespeare's nonauthorship could have been preserved by all of the people who supposedly were in on the conspiracy, and (2) academic fame awaits any scholar today who can disprove Shakespeare's authorship.

The Stratfordian case is convincing not only because hundreds or even thousands of anti-Stratford arguments—of the sort that say "ever I was born" has the secret double meaning "E. Ver, I was born"—add up to nothing at all but also because irrefutable evidence connects the man from Stratford with the London theater and with the authorship of particular plays. The anti-Stratfordians do not seem to understand that it is not enough to dismiss the Stratford case by saying that a fellow from the provinces simply couldn't have written the plays. Nor do they understand that it is not enough to dismiss all of the evidence connecting Shakespeare with the plays by asserting that it is perjured.

The Shakespeare Canon

We return to William Shakespeare. Thirty-seven plays as well as some nondramatic poems are generally held to constitute the Shakespeare canon, the body of authentic works. The exact dates of composition of most of the works are highly uncertain, but evidence of a starting point and/or of a final limiting point often provides a framework for informed guessing. For example, *Richard II* cannot be earlier than 1595, the publication date of some material to which it is indebted; *The Merchant of Venice* cannot be later than 1598, the year Francis Meres mentioned it. Sometimes arguments for a date hang on an alleged topical allusion, such as the lines about the unseasonable weather in *A Midsummer Night's Dream*, 2.1.81–117, but such an allusion, if indeed it is an allusion to an event in the real world, can be variously interpreted, and in any case there is always the possibility that a topical allusion was inserted years later, to bring the play up to date. (The issue of alterations in a text between the time that Shakespeare drafted it and the time that it was printed—alterations due to censorship or playhouse practice or Shakespeare's own second thoughts—will be discussed in "The Play Text as a Collaboration" later in this overview.) Dates are often attributed on the basis of style, and although conjectures about style usually rest on other conjectures (such as Shakespeare's development as a playwright, or the appropriateness of lines to character), sooner or later one must rely on one's literary sense. There is no documentary proof, for example, that *Othello* is not as early as *Romeo and Juliet*, but one feels that *Othello* is a later, more mature work, and because the first record of its performance is 1604, one is glad enough to set its composition at that date and not push it back into Shakespeare's early years. (*Romeo and Juliet* was first published in 1597, but evidence suggests that it was written a little earlier.) The following chronology, then, is indebted not only to facts but also to informed guesswork and sensitivity. The dates, necessarily imprecise for some works, indicate something like a scholarly consensus concerning the time of original composition. Some plays show evidence of later revision.

Plays. The first collected edition of Shakespeare, published in 1623, included thirty-six plays. These are all accepted as Shakespeare's, though for one of them, *Henry VIII*, he is thought to have had a collaborator. A thirty-seventh play, *Pericles*, published in 1609 and attributed to Shakespeare on the title page, is also widely accepted as being partly by Shakespeare even though it is not included in the 1623 volume. Still another play not in the 1623 volume, *The Two Noble Kinsmen*, was first published in 1634, with a title page attributing it to John Fletcher and Shakespeare. Probably most students of the subject now believe that Shakespeare did indeed have a hand in it. Of the remaining plays attributed at one time or another to Shakespeare, only one, *Edward III*, anonymously published in 1596, is now regarded by some scholars as a serious candidate. The prevailing opinion, however, is that this rather simple-minded play is not Shakespeare's; at most he may have revised some passages, chiefly scenes with the Countess of

Salisbury. We include *The Two Noble Kinsmen* but do not include *Edward III* in the following list.

1588–94	*The Comedy of Errors*
1588–94	*Love's Labor's Lost*
1589–91	*2 Henry VI*
1590–91	*3 Henry VI*
1589–92	*1 Henry VI*
1592–93	*Richard III*
1589–94	*Titus Andronicus*
1593–94	*The Taming of the Shrew*
1592–94	*The Two Gentlemen of Verona*
1594–96	*Romeo and Juliet*
1595	*Richard II*
1595–96	*A Midsummer Night's Dream*
1596–97	*King John*
1594–96	*The Merchant of Venice*
1596–97	*1 Henry IV*
1597	*The Merry Wives of Windsor*
1597–98	*2 Henry IV*
1598–99	*Much Ado About Nothing*
1598–99	*Henry V*
1599	*Julius Caesar*
1599–1600	*As You Like It*
1599–1600	*Twelfth Night*
1600–1601	*Hamlet*
1601–1602	*Troilus and Cressida*
1602–1604	*All's Well That Ends Well*
1603–1604	*Othello*
1604	*Measure for Measure*
1605–1606	*King Lear*
1605–1606	*Macbeth*
1606–1607	*Antony and Cleopatra*
1605–1608	*Timon of Athens*
1607–1608	*Coriolanus*
1607–1608	*Pericles*
1609–10	*Cymbeline*
1610–11	*The Winter's Tale*
1611	*The Tempest*

| 1612–13 | *Henry VIII* |
| 1613 | *The Two Noble Kinsmen* |

Poems. In 1989 Donald W. Foster published a book in which he argued that "A Funeral Elegy for Master William Peter," published in 1612, ascribed only to the initials W.S., *may* be by Shakespeare. Foster later published an article in a scholarly journal, *PMLA* 111 (1996), in which he asserted the claim more positively. The evidence begins with the initials, and includes the fact that the publisher and the printer of the elegy had published Shakespeare's *Sonnets* in 1609. But such facts add up to rather little, especially because no one has found any connection between Shakespeare and William Peter (an Oxford graduate about whom little is known, who was murdered at the age of twenty-nine). The argument is based chiefly on statistical examinations of word patterns, which are said to correlate with Shakespeare's known work. Despite such correlations, however, many readers feel that the poem does not sound like Shakespeare. True, Shakespeare has a great range of styles, but his work is consistently imaginative and interesting. Many readers find neither of these qualities in "A Funeral Elegy."

1592–93	*Venus and Adonis*
1593–94	*The Rape of Lucrece*
1593–1600	*Sonnets*
1600–1601	*The Phoenix and the Turtle*

Shakespeare's English

1. Spelling and Pronunciation. From the philologist's point of view, Shakespeare's English is modern English. It requires footnotes, but the inexperienced reader can comprehend substantial passages with very little help, whereas for the same reader Chaucer's Middle English is a foreign language. By the beginning of the fifteenth century the chief grammatical changes in English had taken place, and the final unaccented -*e* of Middle English had been lost (though

it survives even today in spelling, as in *name*); during the fifteenth century the dialect of London, the commercial and
political center, gradually displaced the provincial dialects,
at least in writing; by the end of the century, printing had
helped to regularize and stabilize the language, especially
spelling. Elizabethan spelling may seem erratic to us (there
were dozens of spellings of *Shakespeare*, and a simple word
like *been* was also spelled *beene* and *bin*), but it had much in
common with our spelling. Elizabethan spelling was conser-
vative in that for the most part it reflected an older pronunciation (Middle English) rather than the sound of the
language as it was then spoken, just as our spelling continues
to reflect medieval pronunciation—most obviously in the
now silent but formerly pronounced letters in a word such as
knight. Elizabethan pronunciation, though not identical with
ours, was much closer to ours than to that of the Middle
Ages. Incidentally, though no one can be certain about what
Elizabethan English sounded like, specialists tend to believe
it was rather like the speech of a modern stage Irishman
(*time* apparently was pronounced *toime*, *old* pronounced
awld, *day* pronounced *die*, and *join* pronounced *jine*) and not
at all like the Oxford speech that most of us think it was.

An awareness of the difference between our pronunciation and Shakespeare's is crucial in three areas—in accent,
or number of syllables (many metrically regular lines may
look irregular to us); in rhymes (which may not look like
rhymes); and in puns (which may not look like puns).
Examples will be useful. Some words that were at least on
occasion stressed differently from today are *aspèct*, *còm-
plete*, *fòrlorn*, *revènue*, and *sepùlcher*. Words that sometimes had an additional syllable are *emp[e]ress*, *Hen[e]ry*,
mon[e]th, and *villain* (three syllables, *vil-lay-in*). An additional syllable is often found in possessives, like *moon's*
(pronounced *moones*), and in words ending in *-tion* or *-sion*.
Words that had one less syllable than they now have are
needle (pronounced *neel*) and *violet* (pronounced *vilet*).
Among rhymes now lost are *one* with *loan*, *love* with *prove*,
beast with *jest*, *eat* with *great*. (In reading, trust your sense
of metrics and your ear, more than your eye.) An example of
a pun that has become obliterated by a change in pronunciation is Falstaff's reply to Prince Hal's "Come, tell us your

reason" in *1 Henry IV*: "Give you a reason on compulsion? If reasons were as plentiful as blackberries, I would give no man a reason upon compulsion, I" (2.4.237–40). The *ea* in *reason* was pronounced rather like a long *a*, like the *ai* in *raisin*, hence the comparison with blackberries.

Puns are not merely attempts to be funny; like metaphors they often involve bringing into a meaningful relationship areas of experience normally seen as remote. In *2 Henry IV*, when Feeble is conscripted, he stoically says, "I care not. A man can die but once. We owe God a death" (3.2.242–43), punning on *debt,* which was the way *death* was pronounced. Here an enormously significant fact of life is put into simple commercial imagery, suggesting its commonplace quality. Shakespeare used the same pun earlier in *1 Henry IV,* when Prince Hal says to Falstaff, "Why, thou owest God a death," and Falstaff replies, " 'Tis not due yet: I would be loath to pay him before his day. What need I be so forward with him that calls not on me?" (5.1.126–29).

Sometimes the puns reveal a delightful playfulness; sometimes they reveal aggressiveness, as when, replying to Claudius's "But now, my cousin Hamlet, and my son," Hamlet says, "A little more than kin, and less than kind!" (1.2.64–65). These are Hamlet's first words in the play, and we already hear him warring verbally against Claudius. Hamlet's "less than kind" probably means (1) Hamlet is not of Claudius's family or nature, *kind* having the sense it still has in our word *mankind*; (2) Hamlet is not kindly (affectionately) disposed toward Claudius; (3) Claudius is not naturally (but rather unnaturally, in a legal sense incestuously) Hamlet's father. The puns evidently were not put in as sops to the groundlings; they are an important way of communicating a complex meaning.

2. *Vocabulary.* A conspicuous difficulty in reading Shakespeare is rooted in the fact that some of his words are no longer in common use—for example, words concerned with armor, astrology, clothing, coinage, hawking, horsemanship, law, medicine, sailing, and war. Shakespeare had a large vocabulary—something near thirty thousand words—but it was not so much a vocabulary of big words as a vocabulary drawn from a wide range of life, and it is partly

his ability to call upon a great body of concrete language that gives his plays the sense of being in close contact with life. When the right word did not already exist, he made it up. Among words thought to be his coinages are *accommodation, all-knowing, amazement, bare-faced, countless, dexterously, dislocate, dwindle, fancy-free, frugal, indistinguishable, lackluster, laughable, overawe, premeditated, sea change, star-crossed*. Among those that have not survived are the verb *convive*, meaning to feast together, and *smilet*, a little smile.

Less overtly troublesome than the technical words but more treacherous are the words that seem readily intelligible to us but whose Elizabethan meanings differ from their modern ones. When Horatio describes the Ghost as an "erring spirit," he is saying not that the ghost has sinned or made an error but that it is wandering. Here is a short list of some of the most common words in Shakespeare's plays that often (but not always) have a meaning other than their most usual modern meaning:

'a	he
abuse	deceive
accident	occurrence
advertise	inform
an, and	if
annoy	harm
appeal	accuse
artificial	skillful
brave	fine, splendid
censure	opinion
cheer	(1) face (2) frame of mind
chorus	a single person who comments on the events
closet	small private room
competitor	partner
conceit	idea, imagination
cousin	kinsman
cunning	skillful
disaster	evil astrological influence
doom	judgment
entertain	receive into service

envy	malice
event	outcome
excrement	outgrowth (of hair)
fact	evil deed
fancy	(1) love (2) imagination
fell	cruel
fellow	(1) companion (2) low person (often an insulting term if addressed to someone of approximately equal rank)
fond	foolish
free	(1) innocent (2) generous
glass	mirror
hap, haply	chance, by chance
head	army
humor	(1) mood (2) bodily fluid thought to control one's psychology
imp	child
intelligence	news
kind	natural, acting according to nature
let	hinder
lewd	base
mere(ly)	utter(ly)
modern	commonplace
natural	a fool, an idiot
naughty	(1) wicked (2) worthless
next	nearest
nice	(1) trivial (2) fussy
noise	music
policy	(1) prudence (2) stratagem
presently	immediately
prevent	anticipate
proper	handsome
prove	test
quick	alive
sad	serious
saw	proverb
secure	without care, incautious
silly	innocent

sensible	capable of being perceived by the senses
shrewd	sharp
so	provided that
starve	die
still	always
success	that which follows
tall	brave
tell	count
tonight	last night
wanton	playful, careless
watch	keep awake
will	lust
wink	close both eyes
wit	mind, intelligence

All glosses, of course, are mere approximations; sometimes one of Shakespeare's words may hover between an older meaning and a modern one, and as we have seen, his words often have multiple meanings.

3. Grammar. A few matters of grammar may be surveyed, though it should be noted at the outset that Shakespeare sometimes made up his own grammar. As E. A. Abbott says in *A Shakespearian Grammar,* "Almost any part of speech can be used as any other part of speech": a noun as a verb ("he childed as I fathered"); a verb as a noun ("She hath made compare"); or an adverb as an adjective ("a seldom pleasure"). There are hundreds, perhaps thousands, of such instances in the plays, many of which at first glance would not seem at all irregular and would trouble only a pedant. Here are a few broad matters.

Nouns: The Elizabethans thought the *-s* genitive ending for nouns (as in *man's*) derived from *his*; thus the line " 'gainst the count his galleys I did some service," for "the count's galleys."

Adjectives: By Shakespeare's time adjectives had lost the endings that once indicated gender, number, and case. About the only difference between Shakespeare's adjectives and ours is the use of the now redundant *more* or *most* with the comparative ("some more fitter place") or superlative

("This was the most unkindest cut of all"). Like double comparatives and double superlatives, double negatives were acceptable; Mercutio "will not budge for no man's pleasure."

Pronouns: The greatest change was in pronouns. In Middle English *thou, thy,* and *thee* were used among familiars and in speaking to children and inferiors; *ye, your,* and *you* were used in speaking to superiors (servants to masters, nobles to the king) or to equals with whom the speaker was not familiar. Increasingly the "polite" forms were used in all direct address, regardless of rank, and the accusative *you* displaced the nominative *ye*. Shakespeare sometimes uses *ye* instead of *you,* but even in Shakespeare's day *ye* was archaic, and it occurs mostly in rhetorical appeals.

Thou, thy, and *thee* were not completely displaced, however, and Shakespeare occasionally makes significant use of them, sometimes to connote familiarity or intimacy and sometimes to connote contempt. In *Twelfth Night* Sir Toby advises Sir Andrew to insult Cesario by addressing him as *thou:* "If thou thou'st him some thrice, it shall not be amiss" (3.2.46–47). In *Othello* when Brabantio is addressing an unidentified voice in the dark he says, "What are you?" (1.1.91), but when the voice identifies itself as the foolish suitor Roderigo, Brabantio uses the contemptuous form, saying, "I have charged thee not to haunt about my doors" (93). He uses this form for a while, but later in the scene, when he comes to regard Roderigo as an ally, he shifts back to the polite *you,* beginning in line 163, "What said she to you?" and on to the end of the scene. For reasons not yet satisfactorily explained, Elizabethans used *thou* in addresses to God—"O God, thy arm was here," the king says in *Henry V* (4.8.108)—and to supernatural characters such as ghosts and witches. A subtle variation occurs in *Hamlet.* When Hamlet first talks with the Ghost in 1.5, he uses *thou,* but when he sees the Ghost in his mother's room, in 3.4, he uses *you,* presumably because he is now convinced that the Ghost is not a counterfeit but is his father.

Perhaps the most unusual use of pronouns, from our point of view, is the neuter singular. In place of our *its, his* was often used, as in "How far that little candle throws *his* beams." But the use of a masculine pronoun for a neuter noun came to seem unnatural, and so *it* was used for the possessive as well as the nominative: "The hedge-sparrow fed the cuckoo so long / That it had it head bit off by it young." In the late sixteenth century the possessive form *its* developed, apparently by analogy with the *-s* ending used to indicate a genitive noun, as in *book*'s, but *its* was not yet common usage in Shakespeare's day. He seems to have used *its* only ten times, mostly in his later plays. Other usages, such as "you have seen Cassio and she together" or the substitution of *who* for *whom,* cause little problem even when noticed.

Verbs, Adverbs, and Prepositions: Verbs cause almost no difficulty: The third person singular present form commonly ends in *-s,* as in modern English (e.g., "He blesses"), but sometimes in *-eth* (Portia explains to Shylock that mercy "blesseth him that gives and him that takes"). Broadly speaking, the *-eth* ending was old-fashioned or dignified or "literary" rather than colloquial, except for the words *doth, hath,* and *saith.* The *-eth* ending (regularly used in the King James Bible, 1611) is very rare in Shakespeare's dramatic prose, though not surprisingly it occurs twice in the rather formal prose summary of the narrative poem *Lucrece.* Sometimes a plural subject, especially if it has collective force, takes a verb ending in *-s,* as in "My old bones aches." Some of our strong or irregular preterites (such as *broke*) have a different form in Shakespeare (*brake*); some verbs that now have a weak or regular preterite (such as *helped*) in Shakespeare have a strong or irregular preterite (*holp*). Some adverbs that today end in *-ly* were not inflected: "grievous sick," "wondrous strange." Finally, prepositions often are not the ones we expect: "We are such stuff as dreams are made on," "I have a king here to my flatterer."

Again, none of the differences (except meanings that have substantially changed or been lost) will cause much difficulty. But it must be confessed that for some elliptical passages there is no widespread agreement on meaning. Wise editors resist saying more than they know, and when they are uncertain they add a question mark to their gloss.

Shakespeare's Theater

In Shakespeare's infancy, Elizabethan actors performed wherever they could—in great halls, at court, in the courtyards of inns. These venues implied not only different audiences but also different playing conditions. The innyards must have made rather unsatisfactory theaters: on some days they were unavailable because carters bringing goods to London used them as depots; when available, they had to be rented from the innkeeper. In 1567, presumably to avoid such difficulties, and also to avoid regulation by the Common Council of London, which was not well disposed toward theatricals, one John Brayne, brother-in-law of the carpenter turned actor James Burbage, built the Red Lion in an eastern suburb of London. We know nothing about its shape or its capacity; we can say only that it may have been the first building in Europe constructed for the purpose of giving plays since the end of antiquity, a thousand years earlier. Even after the building of the Red Lion theatrical activity continued in London in makeshift circumstances, in marketplaces and inns, and always uneasily. In 1574 the Common Council required that plays and playing places in London be licensed because

> sundry great disorders and inconveniences have been found to ensue to this city by the inordinate haunting of great multitudes of people, specially youth, to plays, interludes, and shows, namely occasion of frays and quarrels, evil practices of incontinency in great inns having chambers and secret places adjoining to their open stages and galleries.

The Common Council ordered that innkeepers who wished licenses to hold performance put up a bond and make contributions to the poor.

The requirement that plays and innyard theaters be licensed, along with the other drawbacks of playing at inns and presumably along with the success of the Red Lion, led James Burbage to rent a plot of land northeast of the city walls, on property outside the jurisdiction of the city. Here he built England's second playhouse, called simply the Theatre. About all that is known of its construction is that it was wood. It soon had imitators, the most famous being the Globe (1599), essentially an amphitheater built across the Thames (again outside the city's jurisdiction), constructed with timbers of the Theatre, which had been dismantled when Burbage's lease ran out.

Admission to the theater was one penny, which allowed spectators to stand at the sides and front of the stage that jutted into the yard. An additional penny bought a seat in a covered part of the theater, and a third penny bought a more comfortable seat and a better location. It is notoriously difficult to translate prices into today's money, since some things that are inexpensive today would have been expensive in the past and vice versa—a pipeful of tobacco (imported, of course) cost a lot of money, about three pennies, and an orange (also imported) cost two or three times what a chicken cost—but perhaps we can get some idea of the low cost of the penny admission when we realize that a penny could also buy a pot of ale. An unskilled laborer made about five or sixpence a day, an artisan about twelve pence a day, and the hired actors (as opposed to the sharers in the company, such as Shakespeare) made about ten pence a performance. A printed play cost five or sixpence. Of course a visit to the theater (like a visit to a baseball game today) usually cost more than the admission since the spectator probably would also buy food and drink. Still, the low entrance fee meant that the theater was available to all except the very poorest people, rather as movies and most athletic events are today. Evidence indicates that the audience ranged from apprentices who somehow managed to scrape together the minimum entrance fee and to escape from their masters for a few hours, to prosperous members of the middle class and aristocrats who paid the additional fee for admission to the galleries. The exact proportion of men to women cannot be determined, but women of all classes certainly were present. Theaters were open every afternoon but Sundays for much of the year, except in times of plague, when they were closed because of fear of infection. By the way, no evidence suggests the presence of toilet facilities. Presumably the patrons relieved themselves by making a quick trip to the fields surrounding the playhouses.

There are four important sources of information about the

structure of Elizabethan public playhouses—drawings, a contract, recent excavations, and stage directions in the plays. Of drawings, only the so-called de Witt drawing (c. 1596) of the Swan—really his friend Aernout van Buchell's copy of Johannes de Witt's drawing—is of much significance. The drawing, the only extant representation of the interior of an Elizabethan theater, shows an amphitheater of three tiers, with a stage jutting from a wall into the yard or

Johannes de Witt, a Continental visitor to London, made a drawing of the Swan theater in about the year 1596. The original drawing is lost; this is Aernout van Buchell's copy of it.

center of the building. The tiers are roofed, and part of the stage is covered by a roof that projects from the rear and is supported at its front on two posts, but the groundlings, who paid a penny to stand in front of the stage or at its sides, were exposed to the sky. (Performances in such a playhouse were held only in the daytime; artificial illumination was not used.) At the rear of the stage are two massive doors; above the stage is a gallery.

The second major source of information, the contract for the Fortune (built in 1600), specifies that although the Globe (built in 1599) is to be the model, the Fortune is to be square, eighty feet outside and fifty-five inside. The stage is to be forty-three feet broad, and is to extend into the middle of the yard, i.e., it is twenty-seven and a half feet deep.

The third source of information, the 1989 excavations of the Rose (built in 1587), indicate that the Rose was fourteen-sided, about seventy-two feet in diameter with an inner yard almost fifty feet in diameter. The stage at the Rose was about sixteen feet deep, thirty-seven feet wide at the rear, and twenty-seven feet wide downstage. The relatively small dimensions and the tapering stage, in contrast to the rectangular stage in the Swan drawing, surprised theater historians and have made them more cautious in generalizing about the Elizabethan theater. Excavations at the Globe have not yielded much information, though some historians believe that the fragmentary evidence suggests a larger theater, perhaps one hundred feet in diameter.

From the fourth chief source, stage directions in the plays, one learns that entrance to the stage was by the doors at the rear (*"Enter one citizen at one door, and another at the other"*). A curtain hanging across the doorway—or a curtain hanging between the two doorways—could provide a place where a character could conceal himself, as Polonius does, when he wishes to overhear the conversation between Hamlet and Gertrude. Similarly, withdrawing a curtain from the doorway could "discover" (reveal) a character or two. Such discovery scenes are very rare in Elizabethan drama, but a good example occurs in *The Tempest* (5.1.171), where a stage direction tells us, *"Here Prospero discovers Ferdinand and Miranda playing at chess."* There was also some sort of playing space "aloft" or "above" to represent, for instance, the top of a city's walls or a room above the street. Doubtless each theater had its own peculiarities, but perhaps we can talk about a "typical" Elizabethan theater if we realize that no theater need exactly fit the description, just as no mother is the average mother with 2.7 children.

This hypothetical theater is wooden, round, or polygonal (in *Henry V* Shakespeare calls it a "wooden *O*"), capable of holding some eight hundred spectators who stood in the yard around the projecting elevated stage—these spectators were the "groundlings"—and some fifteen hundred additional spectators who sat in the three roofed galleries. The stage, protected by a "shadow" or "heavens" or roof, is entered from two doors; behind the doors is the "tiring house" (attiring house, i.e., dressing room), and above the stage is some sort of gallery that may sometimes hold spectators but can be used (for example) as the bedroom from which Romeo—according to a stage direction in one text—"goeth down." Some evidence suggests that a throne can be lowered onto the platform stage, perhaps from the "shadow"; certainly characters can descend from the stage through a trap or traps into the cellar or "hell." Sometimes this space beneath the stage accommodates a sound-effects man or musician (in *Antony and Cleopatra* "*music of the hautboys* [oboes] *is under the stage*") or an actor (in *Hamlet* the "*Ghost cries under the stage*"). Most characters simply walk on and off through the doors, but because there is no curtain in front of the platform, corpses will have to be carried off (Hamlet obligingly clears the stage of Polonius's corpse, when he says, "I'll lug the guts into the neighbor room"). Other characters may have fallen at the rear, where a curtain on a doorway could be drawn to conceal them.

Such may have been the "public theater," so called because its inexpensive admission made it available to a wide range of the populace. Another kind of theater has been called the "private theater" because its much greater admission charge (sixpence versus the penny for general admission at the public theater) limited its audience to the wealthy or the prodigal. The private theater was basically a large room, entirely roofed and therefore artificially illuminated, with a stage at one end. The theaters thus were distinct in two ways: One was essentially an amphitheater that

catered to the general public; the other was a hall that catered
to the wealthy. In 1576 a hall theater was established in
Blackfriars, a Dominican priory in London that had been
suppressed in 1538 and confiscated by the Crown and thus
was not under the city's jurisdiction. All the actors in this
Blackfriars theater were boys about eight to thirteen years
old (in the public theaters similar boys played female parts;
a boy Lady Macbeth played to a man Macbeth). Near the
end of this section on Shakespeare's theater we will talk at
some length about possible implications in this convention
of using boys to play female roles, but for the moment we
should say that it doubtless accounts for the relative lack of
female roles in Elizabethan drama. Thus, in *A Midsummer
Night's Dream*, out of twenty-one named roles, only four are
female; in *Hamlet*, out of twenty-four, only two (Gertrude
and Ophelia) are female. Many of Shakespeare's characters
have fathers but no mothers—for instance, King Lear's
daughters. We need not bring in Freud to explain the dis-
parity; a dramatic company had only a few boys in it.

To return to the private theaters, in some of which all of
the performers were children—the "eyrie of . . . little eyases"
(nest of unfledged hawks—2.2.347–48) which Rosencrantz
mentions when he and Guildenstern talk with Hamlet. The
theater in Blackfriars had a precarious existence, and ceased
operations in 1584. In 1596 James Burbage, who had already
made theatrical history by building the Theatre, began to
construct a second Blackfriars theater. He died in 1597, and
for several years this second Blackfriars theater was used by
a troupe of boys, but in 1608 two of Burbage's sons and five
other actors (including Shakespeare) became joint operators
of the theater, using it in the winter when the open-air Globe
was unsuitable. Perhaps such a smaller theater, roofed, artificially illuminated, and with a tradition of a wealthy audience, exerted an influence in Shakespeare's late plays.

Performances in the private theaters may well have had
intermissions during which music was played, but in the
public theaters the action was probably uninterrupted,
flowing from scene to scene almost without a break. Actors
would enter, speak, exit, and others would immediately
enter and establish (if necessary) the new locale by a few
properties and by words and gestures. To indicate that the

scene took place at night, a player or two would carry a torch. Here are some samples of Shakespeare establishing the scene:

This is Illyria, lady.   (*Twelfth Night,* 1.2.2)

Well, this is the Forest of Arden.   (*As You Like It,* 2.4.14)

This castle has a pleasant seat; the air
Nimbly and sweetly recommends itself
Unto our gentle senses.   (*Macbeth,* 1.6.1–3)

The west yet glimmers with some streaks of day.
                                          (*Macbeth,* 3.3.5)

Sometimes a speech will go far beyond evoking the minimal setting of place and time, and will, so to speak, evoke the social world in which the characters move. For instance, early in the first scene of *The Merchant of Venice* Salerio suggests an explanation for Antonio's melancholy. (In the following passage, *pageants* are decorated wagons, floats, and *cursy* is the verb "to curtsy," or "to bow.")

Your mind is tossing on the ocean,
There where your argosies with portly sail—
Like signiors and rich burghers on the flood,
Or as it were the pageants of the sea—
Do overpeer the petty traffickers
That cursy to them, do them reverence,
As they fly by them with their woven wings.   (1.1.8–14)

Late in the nineteenth century, when Henry Irving produced the play with elaborate illusionistic sets, the first scene showed a ship moored in the harbor, with fruit vendors and dock laborers, in an effort to evoke the bustling and exotic life of Venice. But Shakespeare's words give us this exotic, rich world of commerce in his highly descriptive language when Salerio speaks of "argosies with portly sail" that fly with "woven wings"; equally important, through Salerio Shakespeare conveys a sense of the orderly, hierarchical society in which the lesser ships, "the petty traffickers," curtsy and thereby "do . . . reverence" to their superiors, the merchant prince's ships, which are "Like signiors and rich burghers."

On the other hand, it is a mistake to think that except for verbal pictures the Elizabethan stage was bare. Although Shakespeare's Chorus in *Henry V* calls the stage an "unworthy scaffold" (Prologue 1.10) and urges the spectators to "eke out our performance with your mind" (Prologue 3.35), there was considerable spectacle. The last act of *Macbeth,* for instance, has five stage directions calling for *"drum and colors,"* and another sort of appeal to the eye is indicated by the stage direction *"Enter Macduff, with Macbeth's head."* Some scenery and properties may have been substantial; doubtless a throne was used, but the pillars supporting the roof would have served for the trees on which Orlando pins his poems in *As You Like It.*

Having talked about the public theater—"this wooden *O*"—at some length, we should mention again that Shakespeare's plays were performed also in other locales. Alvin Kernan, in *Shakespeare, the King's Playwright: Theater in the Stuart Court 1603–1613* (1995), points out that "several of [Shakespeare's] plays contain brief theatrical performances, set always in a court or some noble house. When Shakespeare portrayed a theater, he did not, except for the choruses in *Henry V,* imagine a public theater" (p. 195). (Examples include episodes in *The Taming of the Shrew, A Midsummer Night's Dream, Hamlet,* and *The Tempest.*)

A Note on the Use of Boy Actors in Female Roles

Until fairly recently, scholars were content to mention that the convention existed; they sometimes also mentioned that it continued the medieval practice of using males in female roles, and that other theaters, notably in ancient Greece and in China and Japan, also used males in female roles. (In classical Noh drama in Japan, males still play the female roles.) Prudery may have been at the root of the academic failure to talk much about the use of boy actors, or maybe there really is not much more to say than that it was a convention of a male-centered culture (Stephen Greenblatt's view, in *Shakespearean Negotiations* [1988]). Further, the very nature of a convention is that it is not thought about: Hamlet is a Dane and Julius Caesar is a Roman, but in Shakespeare's plays they speak English, and we in the audience never give this odd fact a thought. Similarly, a character may speak in the presence of others and we understand, again without thinking about it, that he or she is not heard by the figures on the stage (the aside); a character alone on the stage may speak (the soliloquy), and we do not take the character to be unhinged; in a realistic (box) set, the fourth wall, which allows us to see what is going on, is miraculously missing. The no-nonsense view, then, is that the boy actor was an accepted convention, accepted unthinkingly—just as today we know that Kenneth Branagh is not Hamlet, Al Pacino is not Richard III, and Denzel Washington is not the Prince of Aragon. In this view, the audience takes the performer for the role, and that is that; such is the argument we now make for race-free casting, in which African-Americans and Asians can play roles of persons who lived in medieval Denmark and ancient Rome. But gender perhaps is different, at least today. It is a matter of abundant academic study: The Elizabethan theater is now sometimes called a transvestite theater, and we hear much about cross-dressing.

Shakespeare himself in a very few passages calls attention to the use of boys in female roles. At the end of *As You Like It* the boy who played Rosalind addresses the audience, and says, "O men, . . . if I were a woman, I would kiss as many of you as had beards that pleased me." But this is in the Epilogue; the plot is over, and the actor is stepping out of the play and into the audience's everyday world. A second reference to the practice of boys playing female roles occurs in *Antony and Cleopatra*, when Cleopatra imagines that she and Antony will be the subject of crude plays, her role being performed by a boy:

> The quick comedians
> Extemporally will stage us, and present
> Our Alexandrian revels: Antony
> Shall be brought drunken forth, and I shall see
> Some squeaking Cleopatra boy my greatness.   (5.2.216–20)

In a few other passages, Shakespeare is more indirect. For instance, in *Twelfth Night* Viola, played of course by a boy, disguises herself as a young man and seeks service in the house of a lord. She enlists the help of a Captain, and (by way of explaining away her voice and her beardlessness) says,

> I'll serve this duke
> Thou shalt present me as an eunuch to him.   (1.2.55–56)

In *Hamlet*, when the players arrive in 2.2, Hamlet jokes with the boy who plays a female role. The boy has grown since Hamlet last saw him: "By'r Lady, your ladyship is nearer to heaven than when I saw you last by the altitude of a chopine" (a lady's thick-soled shoe). He goes on: "Pray God your voice . . . be not cracked" (434–38).

Exactly how sexual, how erotic, this material was and is, is now much disputed. Again, the use of boys may have been unnoticed, or rather not thought about—an unexamined convention—by most or all spectators most of the time, perhaps *all* of the time, except when Shakespeare calls the convention to the attention of the audience, as in the passages just quoted. Still, an occasional bit seems to invite erotic thoughts. The clearest example is the name that Rosalind takes in *As You Like It*, Ganymede—the beautiful youth whom Zeus abducted. Did boys dressed to play female roles carry homoerotic appeal for straight men (Lisa Jardine's view, in *Still Harping on Daughters* [1983]), or for gay men, or for some or all women in the audience? Further, when the boy actor played a woman who (for the purposes of the plot) disguised herself as a male, as Rosalind, Viola, and Portia do—so we get a boy playing a woman playing a man—what sort of appeal was generated, and for what sort of spectator?

Some scholars have argued that the convention empowered women by letting female characters display a freedom unavailable in Renaissance patriarchal society; the convention, it is said, undermined rigid gender distinctions. In this view, the convention (along with plots in which female characters for a while disguised themselves as young men) allowed Shakespeare to say what some modern gender critics say: Gender is a constructed role rather than a bio-logical given, something we make, rather than a fixed binary opposition of male and female (see Juliet Dusinberre, in *Shakespeare and the Nature of Women* [1975]). On the other hand, some scholars have maintained that the male disguise assumed by some female characters serves only to reaffirm traditional social distinctions since female characters who don male garb (notably Portia in *The Merchant of Venice* and Rosalind in *As You Like It*) return to their female garb and at least implicitly (these critics say) reaffirm the status quo. (For this last view, see Clara Claiborne Park, in an essay in *The Woman's Part*, ed. Carolyn Ruth Swift Lenz et al. [1980].) Perhaps no one answer is right for all plays; in *As You Like It* cross-dressing empowers Rosalind, but in *Twelfth Night* cross-dressing comically traps Viola.

Shakespeare's Dramatic Language: Costumes, Gestures and Silences; Prose and Poetry

Because Shakespeare was a dramatist, not merely a poet, he worked not only with language but also with costume, sound effects, gestures, and even silences. We have already discussed some kinds of spectacle in the preceding section, and now we will begin with other aspects of visual language; a theater, after all, is literally a "place for seeing." Consider the opening stage direction in *The Tempest*, the first play in the first published collection of Shakespeare's plays: *"A tempestuous noise of thunder and Lightning heard: Enter a Ship-master, and a Boteswain."*

Costumes: What did that shipmaster and that boatswain wear? Doubtless they wore something that identified them as men of the sea. Not much is known about the costumes that Elizabethan actors wore, but at least three points are clear: (1) many of the costumes were splendid versions of contemporary Elizabethan dress; (2) some attempts were made to approximate the dress of certain occupations and of antique or exotic characters such as Romans, Turks, and Jews; (3) some costumes indicated that the wearer was supernatural. Evidence for elaborate Elizabethan clothing can be found in the plays themselves and in contemporary comments about the "sumptuous" players who wore the discarded clothing of noblemen, as well as in account books that itemize such things as "a scarlet cloak with two broad gold laces, with gold buttons down the sides."

The attempts at approximation of the dress of certain occupations and nationalities also can be documented from the plays themselves, and it derives additional confirmation from a drawing of the first scene of Shakespeare's *Titus Andronicus*—the only extant Elizabethan picture of an identifiable episode in a play. (See pp. xxxviii–xxxix.) The drawing, probably done in 1594 or 1595, shows Queen Tamora pleading for mercy. She wears a somewhat medieval-looking robe and a crown; Titus wears a toga and a wreath, but two soldiers behind him wear costumes fairly close to Elizabethan dress. We do not know, however, if the drawing represents an actual stage production in the public theater, or perhaps a private production, or maybe only a reader's visualization of an episode. Further, there is some conflicting evidence: In *Julius Caesar* a reference is made to Caesar's doublet (a close-fitting jacket), which, if taken literally, suggests that even the protagonist did not wear Roman clothing; and certainly the lesser characters, who are said to wear hats, did not wear Roman garb.

It should be mentioned, too, that even ordinary clothing can be symbolic: Hamlet's "inky cloak," for example, sets him apart from the brightly dressed members of Claudius's court and symbolizes his mourning; the fresh clothes that are put on King Lear partly symbolize his return to sanity. Consider, too, the removal of disguises near the end of some plays. For instance, Rosalind in *As You Like It* and Portia and Nerissa in *The Merchant of Venice* remove their male attire, thus again becoming fully themselves.

Gestures and Silences: Gestures are an important part of a dramatist's language. King Lear kneels before his daughter Cordelia for a benediction (4.7.57–59), an act of humility that contrasts with his earlier speeches banishing her and that contrasts also with a comparable gesture, his ironic

kneeling before Regan (2.4.153–55). Northumberland's failure to kneel before King Richard II (3.3.71–72) speaks volumes. As for silences, consider a moment in *Coriolanus*: Before the protagonist yields to his mother's entreaties (5.3.182), there is this stage direction: *"Holds her by the hand, silent."* Another example of "speech in dumbness" occurs in *Macbeth*, when Macduff learns that his wife and children have been murdered. He is silent at first, as Malcolm's speech indicates: "What, man! Ne'er pull your hat upon your brows. Give sorrow words" (4.3.208–9). (For a discussion of such moments, see Philip C. McGuire's *Speechless Dialect: Shakespeare's Open Silences* [1985].)

Of course when we think of Shakespeare's work, we think primarily of his language, both the poetry and the prose.

Prose: Although two of his plays (*Richard II* and *King John*) have no prose at all, about half the others have at least one quarter of the dialogue in prose, and some have notably more: *1 Henry IV* and *2 Henry IV*, about half; *As You Like It*

and *Twelfth Night*, a little more than half; *Much Ado About Nothing*, more than three quarters; and *The Merry Wives of Windsor*, a little more than five sixths. We should remember that despite Molière's joke about M. Jourdain, who was amazed to learn that he spoke prose, most of us do not speak prose. Rather, we normally utter repetitive, shapeless, and often ungrammatical torrents; prose is something very different—a sort of literary imitation of speech at its most coherent.

Today we may think of prose as "natural" for drama; or even if we think that poetry is appropriate for high tragedy we may still think that prose is the right medium for comedy. Greek, Roman, and early English comedies, however, were written in verse. In fact, prose was not generally considered a literary medium in England until the late fifteenth century; Chaucer tells even his bawdy stories in verse. By the end of the 1580s, however, prose had established itself on the English comic stage. In tragedy, Marlowe made some use of prose, not simply in the speeches of clownish servants but even in the speech of a tragic hero, Doctor Faustus. Still, before Shakespeare, prose normally was used in the theater only for special circumstances: (1) letters and proclamations, to set them off from the poetic dialogue; (2) mad characters, to indicate that normal thinking has become disordered; and (3) low comedy, or speeches uttered by clowns even when they are not being comic. Shakespeare made use of these conventions, but he also went far beyond them. Sometimes he begins a scene in prose and then shifts into verse as the emotion is heightened; or conversely, he may shift from verse to prose when a speaker is lowering the emotional level, as when Brutus speaks in the Forum.

Shakespeare's prose usually is not prosaic. Hamlet's prose includes not only small talk with Rosencrantz and Guildenstern but also princely reflections on "What a piece of work is a man" (2.2.312). In conversation with Ophelia, he shifts from light talk in verse to a passionate prose denunciation of women (3.1.103), though the shift to prose here is perhaps also intended to suggest the possibility of madness. (Consult Brian Vickers, *The Artistry of Shakespeare's Prose* [1968].)

Poetry: Drama in rhyme in England goes back to the Middle Ages, but by Shakespeare's day rhyme no longer dominated poetic drama; a finer medium, blank verse (strictly speaking, unrhymed lines of ten syllables, with the stress on every second syllable) had been adopted. But before looking at unrhymed poetry, a few things should be said about the chief uses of rhyme in Shakespeare's plays. (1) A couplet (a pair of rhyming lines) is sometimes used to convey emotional heightening at the end of a blank verse speech; (2) characters sometimes speak a couplet as they leave the stage, suggesting closure; (3) except in the latest plays, scenes fairly often conclude with a couplet, and sometimes, as in *Richard II*, 2.1.145–46, the entrance of a new character within a scene is preceded by a couplet, which wraps up the earlier portion of that scene; (4) speeches of two characters occasionally are linked by rhyme, most notably in *Romeo and Juliet*, 1.5.95–108, where the lovers speak a sonnet between them; elsewhere a taunting reply occasionally rhymes with the previous speaker's last line; (5) speeches with sententious or gnomic remarks are sometimes in rhyme, as in the duke's speech in *Othello* (1.3.199–206); (6) speeches of sardonic mockery are sometimes in rhyme—for example, Iago's speech on women in *Othello* (2.1.146–58)—and they sometimes conclude with an emphatic couplet, as in Bolingbroke's speech on comforting words in *Richard II* (1.3.301–2); (7) some characters are associated with rhyme, such as the fairies in *A Midsummer Night's Dream*; (8) in the early plays, especially *The Comedy of Errors* and *The Taming of the Shrew*, comic scenes that in later plays would be in prose are in jingling rhymes; (9) prologues, choruses, plays-within-the-play, inscriptions, vows, epilogues, and so on are often in rhyme, and the songs in the plays are rhymed.

Neither prose nor rhyme immediately comes to mind when we first think of Shakespeare's medium: It is blank verse, unrhymed iambic pentameter. (In a mechanically exact line there are five iambic feet. An iambic foot consists of two syllables, the second accented, as in *away*; five feet make a pentameter line. Thus, a strict line of iambic pentameter contains ten syllables, the even syllables being stressed more heavily than the odd syllables. Fortunately, Shakespeare usually varies the line somewhat.) The first speech in *A Midsummer Night's Dream*, spoken by Duke Theseus to his betrothed, is an example of blank verse:

> Now, fair Hippolyta, our nuptial hour
> Draws on apace. Four happy days bring in
> Another moon; but, O, methinks, how slow
> This old moon wanes! She lingers my desires,
> Like to a stepdame, or a dowager,
> Long withering out a young man's revenue.   (1.1.1–6)

As this passage shows, Shakespeare's blank verse is not mechanically unvarying. Though the predominant foot is the iamb (as in *apace* or *desires*), there are numerous variations. In the first line the stress can be placed on "fair," as the regular metrical pattern suggests, but it is likely that "Now" gets almost as much emphasis; probably in the second line "Draws" is more heavily emphasized than "on," giving us a trochee (a stressed syllable followed by an unstressed one); and in the fourth line each word in the phrase "This old moon wanes" is probably stressed fairly heavily, conveying by two spondees (two feet, each of two stresses) the oppressive tedium that Theseus feels.

In Shakespeare's early plays much of the blank verse is end-stopped (that is, it has a heavy pause at the end of each line), but he later developed the ability to write iambic pentameter verse paragraphs (rather than lines) that give the illusion of speech. His chief techniques are (1) enjambing, i.e., running the thought beyond the single line, as in the first three lines of the speech just quoted; (2) occasionally replacing an iamb with another foot; (3) varying the position of the chief pause (the caesura) within a line; (4) adding an occasional unstressed syllable at the end of a line, traditionally called a feminine ending; and (5) beginning or ending a speech with a half line.

Shakespeare's mature blank verse has much of the rhythmic flexibility of his prose; both the language, though richly figurative and sometimes dense, and the syntax seem natural. It is also often highly appropriate to a particular character. Consider, for instance, this speech from *Hamlet*, in which Claudius, King of Denmark ("the Dane"), speaks to Laertes:

> And now, Laertes, what's the news with you?
> You told us of some suit. What is't, Laertes?
> You cannot speak of reason to the Dane
> And lose your voice. What wouldst thou beg, Laertes,
> That shall not be my offer, not thy asking?　　　(1.2.42–46)

Notice the short sentences and the repetition of the name "Laertes," to whom the speech is addressed. Notice, too, the shift from the royal "us" in the second line to the more intimate "my" in the last line, and from "you" in the first three lines to the more intimate "thou" and "thy" in the last two lines. Claudius knows how to ingratiate himself with Laertes.

For a second example of the flexibility of Shakespeare's blank verse, consider a passage from *Macbeth*. Distressed by the doctor's inability to cure Lady Macbeth and by the imminent battle, Macbeth addresses some of his remarks to the doctor and others to the servant who is arming him. The entire speech, with its pauses, interruptions, and irresolution (in "Pull't off, I say," Macbeth orders the servant to remove the armor that the servant has been putting on him), catches Macbeth's disintegration. (In the first line, *physic* means "medicine," and in the fourth and fifth lines, *cast the water* means "analyze the urine.")

> Throw physic to the dogs, I'll none of it.
> Come, put mine armor on. Give me my staff.
> Seyton, send out.—Doctor, the thanes fly from me.—
> Come, sir, dispatch. If thou couldst, doctor, cast
> The water of my land, find her disease
> And purge it to a sound and pristine health,
> I would applaud thee to the very echo,
> That should applaud again.—Pull't off, I say.—
> What rhubarb, senna, or what purgative drug,
> Would scour these English hence? Hear'st thou of them?
>
> (5.3.47–56)

Blank verse, then, can be much more than unrhymed iambic pentameter, and even within a single play Shakespeare's blank verse often consists of several styles, depending on the speaker and on the speaker's emotion at the moment.

The Play Text as a Collaboration

Shakespeare's fellow dramatist Ben Jonson reported that the actors said of Shakespeare, "In his writing, whatsoever he penned, he never blotted out line," i.e., never crossed out material and revised his work while composing. None of Shakespeare's plays survives in manuscript (with the possible exception of a scene in *Sir Thomas More*), so we cannot fully evaluate the comment, but in a few instances the published work clearly shows that he revised his manuscript. Consider the following passage (shown here in facsimile) from the best early text of *Romeo and Juliet*, the Second Quarto (1599):

> *Ro.* Would I were sleepe and peace so sweet to rest
> The grey eyde morne smiles on the frowning night,
> Checkring the Easterne Clouds with streaks of light,
> And darknesse fleckted like a drunkard reeles,
> From forth daies pathway, made by *Tytans* wheeles.
> Hence will I to my ghostly Friers close cell,
> His helpe to craue, and my deare hap to tell.
>
> *Exit.*
>
> *Enter Frier alone with a basket.*   (night,
> *Fri.* The grey-eyed morne smiles on the frowning
> Checking the Easterne clowdes with streaks of light:
> And fleckeld darknesse like a drunkard reeles,
> From forth daies path, and *Titans* burning wheeles:
> Now erethe sun aduance his burning eie,

Romeo rather elaborately tells us that the sun at dawn is dispelling the night (morning is smiling, the eastern clouds are checked with light, and the sun's chariot—Titan's wheels—advances), and he will seek out his spiritual father, the Friar. He exits and, oddly, the Friar enters and says pretty much the same thing about the sun. Both speakers say that "the gray-eyed morn smiles on the frowning night," but there are small differences, perhaps having more to do with the business of printing the book than with the author's composition: For Romeo's "checkring," "fleckted," and "pathway," we get the Friar's "checking," "fleckeld," and "path." (Notice, by the way, the inconsistency in Elizabethan spelling: Romeo's "clouds" become the Friar's "clowdes.")

Both versions must have been in the printer's copy, and it seems safe to assume that both were in Shakespeare's manuscript. He must have written one version—let's say he first wrote Romeo's closing lines for this scene—and then he decided, no, it's better to give this lyrical passage to the Friar, as the opening of a new scene, but he neglected to delete the first version. Editors must make a choice, and they may feel that the reasonable thing to do is to print the text as Shakespeare intended it. But how can we know what he intended? Almost all modern editors delete the lines from

Romeo's speech, and retain the Friar's lines. They don't do this because they know Shakespeare's intention, however. They give the lines to the Friar because the first published version (1597) of *Romeo and Juliet* gives only the Friar's version, and this text (though in many ways inferior to the 1599 text) is thought to derive from the memory of some actors, that is, it is thought to represent a performance, not just a script. Maybe during the course of rehearsals Shakespeare—an actor as well as an author—unilaterally decided that the Friar should speak the lines; if so (remember that we don't know this to be a fact) his final intention was to give the speech to the Friar. Maybe, however, the actors talked it over and settled on the Friar, with or without Shakespeare's approval. On the other hand, despite the 1597 version, one might argue (if only weakly) on behalf of giving the lines to Romeo rather than to the Friar, thus: (1) Romeo's comment on the coming of the daylight emphasizes his separation from Juliet, and (2) the figurative language seems more appropriate to Romeo than to the Friar. Having said this, in the Signet edition we have decided in this instance to draw on the evidence provided by earlier text and to give the lines to the Friar, on the grounds that since Q1 reflects a production, in the theater (at least on one occasion) the lines were spoken by the Friar.

A playwright sold a script to a theatrical company. The script thus belonged to the company, not the author, and author and company alike must have regarded this script not as a literary work but as the basis for a play that the actors would create on the stage. We speak of Shakespeare as the author of the plays, but readers should bear in mind that the texts they read, even when derived from a single text, such as the First Folio (1623), are inevitably the collaborative work not simply of Shakespeare with his company—doubtless during rehearsals the actors would suggest alterations—but also with other forces of the age. One force was governmental censorship. In 1606 parliament passed "an Act to restrain abuses of players," prohibiting the utterance of oaths and the name of God. So where the earliest text of *Othello* gives us "By heaven" (3.3.106), the first Folio gives "Alas," presumably reflecting the compliance of stage practice with the law. Similarly, the 1623 version of *King Lear* omits the oath "Fut" (probably from "By God's foot") at 1.2.142, again presumably reflecting the line as it was spoken on the stage. Editors who seek to give the reader the play that Shakespeare initially conceived—the "authentic" play conceived by the solitary Shakespeare—probably will restore the missing oaths and references to God. Other editors, who see the play as a collaborative work, a construction made not only by Shakespeare but also by actors and compositors and even government censors, may claim that what counts is the play as it was actually performed. Such editors regard the censored text as legitimate, since it is the play that was (presumably) finally put on. A performed text, they argue, has more historical reality than a text produced by an editor who has sought to get at what Shakespeare initially wrote. In this view, the text of a play is rather like the script of a film; the script is not the film, and the play text is not the performed play. Even if we want to talk about the play that Shakespeare "intended," we will find ourselves talking about a script that he handed over to a company with the intention that it be implemented by actors. The "intended" play is the one that the actors—we might almost say "society"—would help to construct.

Further, it is now widely held that a play is also the work of readers and spectators, who do not simply receive meaning, but who create it when they respond to the play. This idea is fully in accord with contemporary poststructuralist critical thinking, notably Roland Barthes's "The Death of the Author," in *Image-Music-Text* (1977) and Michel Foucault's "What Is an Author?", in *The Foucault Reader* (1984). The gist of the idea is that an author is not an isolated genius; rather, authors are subject to the politics and other social structures of their age. A dramatist especially is a worker in a collaborative project, working most obviously with actors—parts may be written for particular actors—but working also with the audience. Consider the words of Samuel Johnson, written to be spoken by the actor David Garrick at the opening of a theater in 1747:

> The stage but echoes back the public voice;
> The drama's laws, the drama's patrons give,
> For we that live to please, must please to live.

The audience—the public taste as understood by the playwright—helps to determine what the play is. Moreover, even members of the public who are not part of the playwright's immediate audience may exert an influence through censorship. We have already glanced at governmental censorship, but there are also other kinds. Take one of Shakespeare's most beloved characters, Falstaff, who appears in three of Shakespeare's plays, the two parts of *Henry IV* and *The Merry Wives of Windsor*. He appears with this name in the earliest printed version of the first of these plays, *1 Henry IV*, but we know that Shakespeare originally called him (after an historical figure) Sir John Oldcastle. Oldcastle appears in Shakespeare's source (partly reprinted in the Signet edition of *1 Henry IV*), and a trace of the name survives in Shakespeare's play, 1.2.43–44, where Prince Hal punningly addresses Falstaff as "my old lad of the castle." But for some reason—perhaps because the family of the historical Oldcastle complained—Shakespeare had to change the name. In short, the play as we have it was (at least in this detail) subject to some sort of censorship. If we think that a text should present what we take to be the author's intention, we probably will want to replace *Falstaff* with *Oldcastle*. But if we recognize that a play is a collaboration, we may welcome the change, even if it was forced on Shakespeare. Somehow *Falstaff*, with its hint of *false-staff*, i.e., inadequate prop, seems just right for this fat knight who, to our delight, entertains the young prince with untruths. We can go as far as saying that, at least so far as a play is concerned, an insistence on the author's original intention (even if we could know it) can sometimes impoverish the text.

The tiny example of Falstaff's name illustrates the point that the text we read is inevitably only a version—something in effect produced by the collaboration of the playwright with his actors, audiences, compositors, and editors—of a fluid text that Shakespeare once wrote, just as the *Hamlet* that we see on the screen starring Kenneth Branagh is not the *Hamlet* that Shakespeare saw in an open-air playhouse starring Richard Burbage. *Hamlet* itself, as we shall note in a moment, also exists in several versions. It is not surprising that there is now much talk about the *instability* of Shakespeare's texts.

Because he was not only a playwright but was also an actor and a shareholder in a theatrical company, Shakespeare probably was much involved with the translation of the play from a manuscript to a stage production. He may or may not have done some rewriting during rehearsals, and he may or may not have been happy with cuts that were made. Some plays, notably *Hamlet* and *King Lear*, are so long that it is most unlikely that the texts we read were acted in their entirety. Further, for both of these plays we have more than one early text that demands consideration. In *Hamlet*, the Second Quarto (1604) includes some two hundred lines not found in the Folio (1623). Among the passages missing from the Folio are two of Hamlet's reflective speeches, the "dram of evil" speech (1.4.13–38) and "How all occasions do inform against me" (4.4.32–66). Since the Folio has more numerous and often fuller stage directions, it certainly looks as though in the Folio we get a theatrical version of the play, a text whose cuts were probably made—this is only a hunch, of course—not because Shakespeare was changing his conception of Hamlet but because the playhouse demanded a modified play. (The problem is complicated, since the Folio not only cuts some of the Quarto but adds some material. Various explanations have been offered.)

Or take an example from *King Lear*. In the First and Second Quarto (1608, 1619), the final speech of the play is given to Albany, Lear's surviving son-in-law, but in the First Folio version (1623), the speech is given to Edgar. The Quarto version is in accord with tradition—usually the highest-ranking character in a tragedy speaks the final words. Why does the Folio give the speech to Edgar? One possible answer is this: The Folio version omits some of Albany's speeches in earlier scenes, so perhaps it was decided (by Shakespeare? by the players?) not to give the final lines to so pale a character. In fact, the discrepancies are so many between the two texts, that some scholars argue we do not simply have texts showing different theatrical productions. Rather, these scholars say, Shakespeare substantially revised the play, and we really have two versions of *King Lear* (and of *Othello* also, say some)—two different plays—not simply two texts, each of which is in some ways imperfect.

In this view, the 1608 version of *Lear* may derive from Shakespeare's manuscript, and the 1623 version may derive from his later revision. The Quartos have almost three hundred lines not in the Folio, and the Folio has about a hundred lines not in the Quartos. It used to be held that all the texts were imperfect in various ways and from various causes— some passages in the Quartos were thought to have been set from a manuscript that was not entirely legible, other passages were thought to have been set by a compositor who was new to setting plays, and still other passages were thought to have been provided by an actor who misremembered some of the lines. This traditional view held that an editor must draw on the Quartos and the Folio in order to get Shakespeare's "real" play. The new argument holds (although not without considerable strain) that we have two authentic plays, Shakespeare's early version (in the Quarto) and Shakespeare's—or his theatrical company's—revised version (in the Folio). Not only theatrical demands but also Shakespeare's own artistic sense, it is argued, called for extensive revisions. Even the titles vary: Q1 is called *True Chronicle Historie of the life and death of King Lear and his three Daughters*, whereas the Folio text is called *The Tragedie of King Lear*. To combine the two texts in order to produce what the editor thinks is the play that Shakespeare intended to write is, according to this view, to produce a text that is false to the history of the play. If the new view is correct, and we do have texts of two distinct versions of *Lear* rather than two imperfect versions of one play, it supports in a textual way the poststructuralist view that we cannot possibly have an unmediated vision of (in this case) a play by Shakespeare; we can only recognize a plurality of visions.

Editing Texts

Though eighteen of his plays were published during his lifetime, Shakespeare seems never to have supervised their publication. There is nothing unusual here; when a playwright sold a play to a theatrical company he surrendered his ownership to it. Normally a company would not publish the play, because to publish it meant to allow competitors to acquire the piece. Some plays did get published: Apparently hard-up actors sometimes pieced together a play for a publisher; sometimes a company in need of money sold a play; and sometimes a company allowed publication of a play that no longer drew audiences. That Shakespeare did not concern himself with publication is not remarkable; of his contemporaries, only Ben Jonson carefully supervised the publication of his own plays.

In 1623, seven years after Shakespeare's death, John Heminges and Henry Condell (two senior members of Shakespeare's company, who had worked with him for about twenty years) collected his plays—published and unpublished—into a large volume, of a kind called a folio. (A folio is a volume consisting of large sheets that have been folded once, each sheet thus making two leaves, or four pages. The size of the page of course depends on the size of the sheet—a folio can range in height from twelve to sixteen inches, and in width from eight to eleven; the pages in the 1623 edition of Shakespeare, commonly called the First Folio, are approximately thirteen inches tall and eight inches wide.) The eighteen plays published during Shakespeare's lifetime had been issued one play per volume in small formats called quartos. (Each sheet in a quarto has been folded twice, making four leaves, or eight pages, each page being about nine inches tall and seven inches wide, roughly the size of a large paperback.)

Heminges and Condell suggest in an address "To the great variety of readers" that the republished plays are presented in better form than in the quartos:

> Before you were abused with diverse stolen and surreptitious copies, maimed and deformed by the frauds and stealths of injurious impostors that exposed them; even those, are now offered to your view cured and perfect of their limbs, and all the rest absolute in their numbers, as he [i.e., Shakespeare] conceived them.

There is a good deal of truth to this statement, but some of the quarto versions are better than others; some are in fact preferable to the Folio text.

Whoever was assigned to prepare the texts for publication

in the first Folio seems to have taken the job seriously and yet not to have performed it with uniform care. The sources of the texts seem to have been, in general, good unpublished copies or the best published copies. The first play in the collection, *The Tempest*, is divided into acts and scenes, has unusually full stage directions and descriptions of spectacle, and concludes with a list of the characters, but the editor was not able (or willing) to present all of the succeeding texts so fully dressed. Later texts occasionally show signs of carelessness: in one scene of *Much Ado About Nothing* the names of actors, instead of characters, appear as speech prefixes, as they had in the Quarto, which the Folio reprints; proofreading throughout the Folio is spotty and apparently was done without reference to the printer's copy; the pagination of *Hamlet* jumps from 156 to 257. Further, the proofreading was done while the presses continued to print, so that each play in each volume contains a mix of corrected and uncorrected pages.

Modern editors of Shakespeare must first select their copy; no problem if the play exists only in the Folio, but a considerable problem if the relationship between a Quarto and the Folio—or an early Quarto and a later one—is unclear. In the case of *Romeo and Juliet*, the First Quarto (Q1), published in 1597, is vastly inferior to the Second (Q2), published in 1599. The basis of Q1 apparently is a version put together from memory by some actors. Not surprisingly, it garbles many passages and is much shorter than Q2. On the other hand, occasionally Q1 makes better sense than Q2. For instance, near the end of the play, when the parents have assembled and learned of the deaths of Romeo and Juliet, in Q2 the Prince says (5.3.208–9),

> Come, *Montague;* for thou art early vp
> To see thy sonne and heire, now earling downe.

The last three words of this speech surely do not make sense, and many editors turn to Q1, which instead of "now earling downe" has "more early downe." Some modern editors take only "early" from Q1, and print "now early down"; others take "more early," and print "more early down." Further, Q1 (though, again, quite clearly a garbled and abbreviated text) includes some stage directions that are not found in Q2, and today many editors who base their text on Q2 are glad to add these stage directions, because the directions help to give us a sense of what the play looked like on Shakespeare's stage. Thus, in 4.3.58, after Juliet drinks the potion, Q1 gives us this stage direction, not in Q2: *"She falls upon her bed within the curtains."*

In short, an editor's decisions do not end with the choice of a single copy text. First of all, editors must reckon with Elizabethan spelling. If they are not producing a facsimile, they probably modernize the spelling, but ought they to preserve the old forms of words that apparently were pronounced quite unlike their modern forms—*lanthorn, alablaster*? If they preserve these forms are they really preserving Shakespeare's forms or perhaps those of a compositor in the printing house? What is one to do when one finds *lanthorn* and *lantern* in adjacent lines? (The editors of this series in general, but not invariably, assume that words should be spelled in their modern form, unless, for instance, a rhyme is involved.) Elizabethan punctuation, too, presents problems. For example, in the First Folio, the only text for the play, Macbeth rejects his wife's idea that he can wash the blood from his hand (2.2.60–62):

> No: this my Hand will rather
> The multitudinous Seas incarnardine,
> Making the Greene one, Red.

Obviously an editor will remove the superfluous capitals, and will probably alter the spelling to "incarnadine," but what about the comma before "Red"? If we retain the comma, Macbeth is calling the sea "the green one." If we drop the comma, Macbeth is saying that his bloody hand will make the sea ("the Green") *uniformly* red.

An editor will sometimes have to change more than spelling and punctuation. Macbeth says to his wife (1.7.46–47):

> I dare do all that may become a man,
> Who dares no more, is none.

For two centuries editors have agreed that the second line is unsatisfactory, and have emended "no" to "do": "Who dares do more is none." But when in the same play (4.2.21–22) Ross says that fearful persons

> Floate vpon a wilde and violent Sea
> Each way, and moue,

need we emend the passage? On the assumption that the compositor misread the manuscript, some editors emend "each way, and move" to "and move each way"; others emend "move" to "none" (i.e., "Each way and none"). Other editors, however, let the passage stand as in the original. The editors of the Signet Classic Shakespeare have restrained themselves from making abundant emendations. In their minds they hear Samuel Johnson on the dangers of emendation: "I have adopted the Roman sentiment, that it is more honorable to save a citizen than to kill an enemy." Some departures (in addition to spelling, punctuation, and lineation) from the copy text have of course been made, but the original readings are listed in a note following the play, so that readers can evaluate the changes for themselves.

Following tradition, the editors of the Signet Classic Shakespeare have prefaced each play with a list of characters, and throughout the play have regularized the names of the speakers. Thus, in our text of *Romeo and Juliet*, all speeches by Juliet's mother are prefixed "Lady Capulet," although the 1599 Quarto of the play, which provides our copy text, uses at various points seven speech tags for this one character: *Capu. Wi.* (i.e., Capulet's wife), *Ca. Wi., Wi., Wife, Old La.* (i.e., Old Lady), *La.,* and *Mo.* (i.e., Mother). Similarly, in *All's Well That Ends Well*, the character whom we regularly call "Countess" is in the Folio (the copy text) variously identified as *Mother, Countess, Old Countess, Lady,* and *Old Lady.* Admittedly there is some loss in regularizing, since the various prefixes may give us a hint of the way Shakespeare (or a scribe who copied Shakespeare's manuscript) was thinking of the character in a particular scene—for instance, as a mother, or as an old lady. But too much can be made of these differing prefixes, since the social relationships implied are *not* always relevant to the given scene.

We have also added line numbers and in many cases act and scene divisions as well as indications of locale at the beginning of scenes. The Folio divided most of the plays into acts and some into scenes. Early eighteenth-century editors increased the divisions. These divisions, which provide a convenient way of referring to passages in the plays, have been retained, but when not in the text chosen as the basis for the Signet Classic text they are enclosed within square brackets, [ ], to indicate that they are editorial additions. Similarly, though no play of Shakespeare's was equipped with indications of the locale at the heads of scene divisions, locales have here been added in square brackets for the convenience of readers, who lack the information that costumes, properties, gestures, and scenery afford to spectators. Spectators can tell at a glance they are in the throne room, but without an editorial indication the reader may be puzzled for a while. It should be mentioned, incidentally, that there are a few authentic stage directions—perhaps Shakespeare's, perhaps a prompter's—that suggest locales, such as *"Enter Brutus in his orchard,"* and *"They go up into the Senate house."* It is hoped that the bracketed additions in the Signet text will provide readers with the sort of help provided by these two authentic directions, but it is equally hoped that the reader will remember that the stage was not loaded with scenery.

Shakespeare on the Stage

Each volume in the Signet Classic Shakespeare includes a brief stage (and sometimes film) history of the play. When we read about earlier productions, we are likely to find them eccentric, obviously wrongheaded—for instance, Nahum Tate's version of *King Lear*, with a happy ending, which held the stage for about a century and a half, from the late seventeenth century until the end of the first quarter of the nineteenth. We see engravings of David Garrick, the greatest actor of the eighteenth century, in eighteenth-century garb as King Lear, and we smile, thinking how absurd the production must have been. If we are more thoughtful, we say, with the English novelist L. P. Hartley, "The past is a foreign country: they do things differently there." But if the eighteenth-century staging is a foreign country, what of the plays of the late sixteenth and seventeenth centuries? A foreign language, a foreign theater, a foreign audience.

Probably all viewers of Shakespeare's plays, beginning with Shakespeare himself, at times have been unhappy with the plays on the stage. Consider three comments about production that we find in the plays themselves, which suggest Shakespeare's concerns. The Chorus in *Henry V* complains that the heroic story cannot possibly be adequately staged:

> But pardon, gentles all,
> The flat unraisèd spirits that hath dared
> On this unworthy scaffold to bring forth
> So great an object. Can this cockpit hold
> The vasty fields of France? Or may we cram
> Within this wooden *O* the very casques
> That did affright the air at Agincourt?
>
> . . . .
>
> Piece out our imperfections with your thoughts.
>
> (Prologue 1.8–14,23)

Second, here are a few sentences (which may or may not represent Shakespeare's own views) from Hamlet's longish lecture to the players:

> Speak the speech, I pray you, as I pronounced it to you, trippingly on the tongue. But if you mouth it, as many of our players do, I had as lief the town crier spoke my lines. . . . O, it offends me to the soul to hear a robustious periwig-pated fellow tear a passion to tatters, to very rags, to split the ears of the groundlings. . . . And let those that play your clowns speak no more than is set down for them, for there be of them that will themselves laugh, to set on some quantity of barren spectators to laugh too, though in the meantime some necessary question of the play be then to be considered. That's villainous and shows a most pitiful ambition in the fool that uses it. (3.2.1–47)

Finally, we can quote again from the passage cited earlier in this introduction, concerning the boy actors who played the female roles. Cleopatra imagines with horror a theatrical version of her activities with Antony:

> The quick comedians
> Extemporally will stage us, and present
> Our Alexandrian revels: Antony
> Shall be brought drunken forth, and I shall see
> Some squeaking Cleopatra boy my greatness
> I' th' posture of a whore.   (5.2.216–21)

It is impossible to know how much weight to put on such passages—perhaps Shakespeare was just being modest about his theater's abilities—but it is easy enough to think that he was unhappy with some aspects of Elizabethan production. Probably no production can fully satisfy a playwright, and for that matter, few productions can fully satisfy *us;* we regret this or that cut, this or that way of costuming the play, this or that bit of business.

One's first thought may be this: Why don't they just do "authentic" Shakespeare, "straight" Shakespeare, the play as Shakespeare wrote it? But as we read the plays—words written to be performed—it sometimes becomes clear that we do not know *how* to perform them. For instance, in *Antony and Cleopatra* Antony, the Roman general who has succumbed to Cleopatra and to Egyptian ways, says, "The nobleness of life / Is to do thus" (1.1.36–37). But what is "thus"? Does Antony at this point embrace Cleopatra? Does he embrace and kiss her? (There are, by the way, very few scenes of kissing on Shakespeare's stage, possibly because boys played the female roles.) Or does he make a sweeping gesture, indicating the Egyptian way of life?

This is not an isolated example; the plays are filled with lines that call for gestures, but we are not sure what the gestures should be. *Interpretation* is inevitable. Consider a passage in *Hamlet*. In 3.1, Polonius persuades his daughter, Ophelia, to talk to Hamlet while Polonius and Claudius eavesdrop. The two men conceal themselves, and Hamlet encounters Ophelia. At 3.1.131 Hamlet suddenly says to her, "Where's your father?" Why does Hamlet, apparently out of nowhere—they have not been talking about Polonius—ask this question? Is this an example of the "antic disposition" (fantastic behavior) that Hamlet earlier (1.5.172) had told Horatio and others—including us—he would display? That is, is the question about the whereabouts of her father a seemingly irrational one, like his earlier question (3.1.103) to Ophelia, "Ha, ha! Are you honest?" Or, on the other hand, has Hamlet (as in many productions) suddenly glimpsed Polonius's foot protruding from beneath a drapery at the rear? That is, does Hamlet ask the question because he has suddenly seen something suspicious and now is testing Ophelia? (By the way, in productions that do give Hamlet a physical cue, it is almost always Polonius rather than Claudius who provides the clue. This itself is an act of interpretation on the part of the director.) Or (a third possibility) does Hamlet get a clue from Ophelia, who inadvertently betrays the spies by nervously glancing at their place of hiding? This is the interpretation used in the BBC television version, where Ophelia glances in fear toward the hiding place just after Hamlet says "Why wouldst thou be a breeder of sinners?" (121–22). Hamlet, realizing that he is being observed, glances here and there *before* he asks "Where's your father?" The question thus is a climax to what he has been doing while speaking the preceding lines. Or (a fourth interpretation) does Hamlet suddenly, without the aid of any clue whatsoever, intuitively (insightfully, mysteriously, wonderfully) sense that someone is spying? Directors must decide, of course—and so must readers.

Recall, too, the preceding discussion of the texts of the plays, which argued that the texts—though they seem to be before us in permanent black on white—are unstable. The Signet text of *Hamlet*, which draws on the Second Quarto (1604) and the First Folio (1623) is considerably longer than any version staged in Shakespeare's time. Our version, even if spoken very briskly and played without any intermission, would take close to four hours, far beyond "the two hours' traffic of our stage" mentioned in the Prologue to *Romeo and Juliet*. (There are a few contemporary references to the duration of a play, but none mentions more than three hours.) Of Shakespeare's plays, only *The Comedy of Errors*, *Macbeth*, and *The Tempest* can be done in less than three hours without cutting. And even if we take a play that exists only in a short text, *Macbeth*, we cannot claim that we are experiencing the very play that Shakespeare conceived, partly because some of the Witches' songs almost surely are non-Shakespearean additions, and partly because we are not willing to watch the play performed without an intermission and with boys in the female roles.

Further, as the earlier discussion of costumes mentioned, the plays apparently were given chiefly in contemporary, that is, in Elizabethan dress. If today we give them in the costumes that Shakespeare probably saw, the plays seem not contemporary but curiously dated. Yet if we use our own dress, we find lines of dialogue that are at odds with what we see; we may feel that the language, so clearly not our own, is inappropriate coming out of people in today's dress. A common solution, incidentally, has been to set the plays in the nineteenth century, on the grounds that this attractively distances the plays (gives them a degree of foreignness, allowing for interesting costumes) and yet doesn't put them into a museum world of Elizabethan England.

Inevitably our productions are adaptations, *our* adaptations, and inevitably they will look dated, not in a century but in twenty years, or perhaps even in a decade. Still, we cannot escape from our own conceptions. As the director Peter Brook has said, in *The Empty Space* (1968):

> It is not only the hair-styles, costumes and make-ups that look dated. All the different elements of staging—the shorthands of behavior that stand for emotions; gestures, gesticulations and tones of voice—are all fluctuating on an invisible stock exchange all the time. . . . A living theatre that thinks it can stand aloof from anything as trivial as fashion will wilt. (p. 16)

As Brook indicates, it is through today's hairstyles, costumes, makeup, gestures, gesticulations, tones of voice—this includes our *conception* of earlier hairstyles, costumes, and so forth if we stage the play in a period other than our own—that we inevitably stage the plays.

It is a truism that every age invents its own Shakespeare, just as, for instance, every age has invented its own classical world. Our view of ancient Greece, a slave-holding society in which even free Athenian women were severely circum-scribed, does not much resemble the Victorians' view of ancient Greece as a glorious democracy, just as, perhaps, our view of Victorianism itself does not much resemble theirs. We cannot claim that the Shakespeare on our stage is the true Shakespeare, but in our stage productions we find a Shakespeare that speaks to us, a Shakespeare that our ances-tors doubtless did not know but one that seems to us to be the true Shakespeare—at least for a while.

Our age is remarkable for the wide variety of kinds of staging that it uses for Shakespeare, but one development deserves special mention. This is the now common practice of race-blind or color-blind or nontraditional casting, which allows persons who are not white to play in Shakespeare. Previously blacks performing in Shakespeare were limited to a mere three roles, Othello, Aaron (in *Titus Andronicus*), and the Prince of Morocco (in *The Merchant of Venice*), and there were no roles at all for Asians. Indeed, African-Americans rarely could play even one of these three roles, since they were not welcome in white companies. Ira Aldridge (c.1806–1867), a black actor of undoubted talent, was forced to make his living by performing Shakespeare in England and in Europe, where he could play not only Othello but also—in whiteface—other tragic roles such as King Lear. Paul Robeson (1898–1976) made theatrical his-tory when he played Othello in London in 1930, and there was some talk about bringing the production to the United States, but there was more talk about whether American audiences would tolerate the sight of a black man—a real black man, not a white man in blackface—kissing and then killing a white woman. The idea was tried out in summer stock in 1942, the reviews were enthusiastic, and in the fol-lowing year Robeson opened on Broadway in a production that ran an astounding 296 performances. An occasional all-black company sometimes performed Shakespeare's plays, but otherwise blacks (and other minority members) were in effect shut out from performing Shakespeare. Only since about 1970 has it been common for nonwhites to play major roles along with whites. Thus, in a 1996–97 production of *Antony and Cleopatra*, a white Cleopatra, Vanessa Red-grave, played opposite a black Antony, David Harewood.

Multiracial casting is now especially common at the New York Shakespeare Festival, founded in 1954 by Joseph Papp, and in England, where even siblings such as Claudio and Isabella in *Measure for Measure* or Lear's three daughters may be of different races. Probably most viewers today soon stop worrying about the lack of realism, and move beyond the color of the performers' skin to the quality of the performance.

Nontraditional casting is not only a matter of color or race; it includes sex. In the past, occasionally a distinguished woman of the theater has taken on a male role—Sarah Bernhardt (1844–1923) as Hamlet is perhaps the most famous example—but such performances were widely regarded as eccentric. Although today there have been some performances involving cross-dressing (a drag *As You Like It* staged by the National Theatre in England in 1966 and in the United States in 1974 has achieved considerable fame in the annals of stage history), what is more interesting is the casting of women in roles that traditionally are male but that need not be. Thus, a 1993–94 English production of *Henry V* used a woman—*not* cross-dressed—in the role of the governor of Harfleur. According to Peter Holland, who reviewed the production in *Shakespeare Survey* 48 (1995), "having a female Governor of Harfleur feminized the city and provided a direct response to the horrendous threat of rape and murder that Henry had offered, his language and her body in direct connection and opposition" (p. 210). Ten years from now the device may not play so effectively, but today it speaks to us. Shakespeare, born in the Elizabethan Age, has been dead nearly four hundred years, yet he is, as Ben Jonson said, "not of an age but for all time." We must understand, however, that he is "for all time" precisely because each age finds in his abundance something for itself and something of itself.

And here we come back to two issues discussed earlier in this introduction—the instability of the text and, curiously, the Bacon/Oxford heresy concerning the authorship of the plays. *Of course* Shakespeare wrote the plays, and we should daily fall on our knees to thank him for them—and yet there is something to the idea that he is not their only author. Every editor, every director and actor, and every reader to some degree shapes them, too, for when we edit, direct, act, or read, we inevitably become Shakespeare's collaborator and re-create the plays. The plays, one might say, are so cunningly contrived that they guide our responses, tell us how we ought to feel, and make a mark on us, but (for better or for worse) we also make a mark on them.

—SYLVAN BARNET
Tufts University

Introduction

Love's Labor's Lost is one of Shakespeare's earliest and happiest comedies. It is excellently formed, moving easily towards its conclusion in a masque and a song, at the end recapitulating in all the stage's beauty the courting warfare of the young noblemen and ladies that has made up the chief part of the play, the sparrings and the surrenders and the victories. The play makes the point the theater seems to live to make, that sooner or later love conquers all, and although the title tells us that love's labor is lost, this we know is joking: the happy outcome is certain, and love and long life—as we learn at the end from what G. L. Kittredge called one of the best songs in the world—define the happy prospect.

In this Boccaccio-like setting another comic action plays its part, a comedy about the falsely learned and the grotesquely loving, partly contrasting with and partly parallel to the main story. The king and his lords, moved by the love of philosophy and virtue, have fallen into a most unphilosophical absurdity in supposing that the claims of love can easily be put aside. The foolish scholars light up the folly of the wise ones in still other ways, even as their own courting is mocked by the love-making of the others. As in so many of the later plays, it is all there—the multiple plot, the ranging between high and low minds, and love's challenge to every power in the world. All there, and as fluent in its display as in a dance.

The date of the play's composition must be guessed. The 1598 quarto title page mentions a performance of the play before her Highness "this last Christmas," and it adds the phrase, "Newly corrected and augmented." This, taken along with the evidence of revisions in the text, and with the known dates of certain historical occurrences, leads to pretty substantial arguments for the composition of the play in

1593 or 1594. It should be said, however, that in the past the play was thought to be earlier than this; Coleridge, for example, believed it to be Shakespeare's first play because he thought Shakespeare was bringing into it part of the life he had just left, exploiting his experience as a schoolmaster while the memory of it was still fresh to him. This might push the writing back as far as 1589. More recently Alfred Harbage* has returned to a similar line of reasoning. Likenesses to Lyly's plays in the 1580s and certain considerations making for the possibility that the play was produced by child actors in either a private or public theater, lead him to suggest 1589 or even earlier as the time of performance.

The arguments for a later date point to a general friendliness in England for Henry of Navarre until he reverted to the Church of Rome in July 1593; the beginning of the investigation in 1594 into the atheism of men associated with Sir Walter Raleigh, a group perhaps identified in the play (in 4.3.254) as "the school of night"; the use of language that suggests the *Venus and Adonis* of 1593, the *Lucrece* of 1594, and sonnets of presumably the same period. And, of course, a number of topical allusions.†

The occasion of the play's first production is not known, but it was surely meant for a private performance—the house of the Earl of Southampton has been suggested—perhaps in 1593. As such it would have been part of festivities in which music and dancing would naturally be called for. The first printed text of the play alludes to a performance before the Queen at Christmas, either in 1597 or 1598, and the play's immediately succeeding stage history establishes the special suitability of the work for a courtly audience. The substance of the play also makes this clear enough—the initiating idea of learned gentlemen in the company of their monarch retiring from the life of power, the better to perfect their lives; the abjuring the society of women in serious as well as fantastic aspiration, following the directions of the most fashionable writers out of Italy; the mockery of literary men and most particularly of courtiers with ambitions in lit-

---

* "*Love's Labor's Lost* and the Early Shakespeare," *Philological Quarterly*, XLI (1962), 18–36.
† The basic discussion of the play's composition is in Rupert Taylor, *The Date of "Love's Labor's Lost"* (New York: AMS Press, 1966).

erature; the battles between the sexes conducted with the most elaborate and sensitive protocol. In large and small matters alike the play seems to be taking something directly out of the life of the court of Elizabeth (wisely enough under another name), making what it takes into something more than life-size. It gives the audience of lords and ladies a mirror in which they will see themselves in all the wit, imagining, beauty and fun they are absorbed in.

The idea of nobility sets the tone for it all. It begins in the king's first speech, it is taken up more than once by the princess, and, ironically, it is finally triumphant in Berowne, the railer at both love and philosophy, so dangerously close in his disposition to the discarding of all values, himself in the end the defender of an aspiration as passionately felt as it is truly thought.

When the king speaks of retiring to the learned academy, we feel the genuine love of learning and of virtue in his words:

> Navarre shall be the wonder of the world;
> Our court shall be a little academe,
> Still and contemplative in living art.
>
> (1.1.12–14)

And the chief critic of the idea is no philistine. He is high-spirited and he is tired of going to school, but he has his wisdom, too, and we judge he has the experience to support it:

> So study evermore is overshot.
> While it doth study to have what it would,
> It doth forget to do the thing it should.
>
> (141–43)

And so we immediately perceive that in the conflicts that are to rage in the play the sparks of thought will be flying everywhere. The issue is to be granted its proper dignity, whatever the comic emphasis, and in the end love will be allowed to break up the academy not only because it is strong but because it may claim a special worth, and because the temper of these noble persons is deeply founded in the cultivation of the best of everything the world offers.

The princess' first scene gives us so beautiful a picture of a woman that it carries all before it as if it were the very praise of womankind. The first words to tell us this come from one of her lords, advising her on her approach to the king:

> Be now as prodigal of all dear grace
> As Nature was in making graces dear
> When she did starve the general world beside,
> And prodigally gave them all to you.
>
> (2.1.9–12)

On the other side, the king is acknowledged as "the sole inheritor/Of all perfections that a man may owe" (5–6). The bounty of the woman and the perfection of the man, these are the qualities that set the tone, and these are the persons to lead the dancing interplay, the parrying and the reversals and the resolutions that are to come. They themselves are the matter of love's labors, the union of nobility and bounty, like some splendid foreshadowing of the masque of Ceres in *The Tempest*.

Nature has its austerity, and love has its temperance, and the princess' chiding of the busy old lord Boyet for his flattery is a still more telling criticism of the affectations and grossness of another kind of courtly love—

> my beauty, though but mean,
> Needs not the painted flourish of your praise.
>
> (13–14)

Armado with his affectations brought from Spain and Italy, and the courtiers with their sonnets, are abusing "the heart's still rhetoric" (229). False speaking conforms to warped natures, and the play never loses sight of the idea of inherent excellence in manhood and womanhood and of the importance of true expression in love. Whatever the follies of the great as well as lesser characters, and whatever the ironies whereby nobility and the taking of oaths are made to seem like tinder before the fires of love, the decorum of the truly courtly prevails as the basis of the play's beauty.

The comic ideas also are as alive with intellectuality as the play's most serious affirmations. When the ladies call to mind and comment on the lords who accompany the king—men in the past they had encountered only briefly—praising them as it appears they deserve to be praised, we discover that all of them are in love before they know it. The audience enters into a kind of conspiracy with Shakespeare, schooled, as we are certain he was, by literature and the conventions of the stage, agreeing in advance that the great and noble always love the beautiful, and the beautiful the brave. Since this is the stage, we know that all these must be paired no matter what the claims of study. And so, won not only by the beauty and youth but by the wit of the ladies, we anticipate with pleasure the defeat of the men. We have seen the signs of love in the first words of each of the women as she sizes up her choice, and while we know enough of the men to know they will put up a kind of fight, we cannot be sorry at the prospect of a surrender they themselves will not regret.

The intermingling of the two plots is as expert as the rest. After the king has announced the program he means to follow and Berowne has had his say about it, we meet a clown, Costard, and a fop, Armado. They are showing off, and Shakespeare mocks both the clown's wenching and the fop's romancing. The scene is dramatically focused when the two confront each other in the presence of the one they are both taken with, the country maid, Jaquenetta. Costard, who has been misbehaving, is put into the custody of Armado, who is to guarantee his good behavior. The contrast is in itself pleasing—the fool who from time to time blunders into sense, and the most affected of courtiers who is yet not all fool. And in their folly as in their sense we see that they are being made to pose different versions of the questions the other characters are also asking—what has learning to do with love? and what has love to do with learning? As the plots proceed, the various lovers fall into many absurdities, but the questions themselves continually receive thoughtful answers, or thoughtful mockery. The varieties of the questioning, from such different kinds of lovers, require and get complex and significant answers, and the confusions of Costard and Armado prepare for the resolution Berowne will finally discover.

Meanwhile, the lords about the king are made to show

their folly. One after another, subdued to his lady, takes to
poetry, and one after another passes across the stage, sonnet
in hand, or under his hat, or tucked into his belt—a snow of
sonnets. The mockery is so lavish it adds the beauty of a
pageant to the absurdity. The noble lords demean themselves in becoming poets, and they glory in their humiliation
since they imagine it is pleasing to the ladies. This is indeed
what the ladies require of those they favor, but they also
require more than words. They require, as Rosaline says of
her own lover,

> That he should be my fool, and I his fate.
>
> (5.2.68)

The play will spell this out. Subjecting themselves to such
cruel and whimsical tyrants, the men become as funny as
Armado and Moth. Shakespeare lays it on with a trowel—

> To see a king transformèd to a gnat!
> To see great Hercules whipping a gig,
> And profound Solomon to tune a jig,
> And Nestor play at push-pin with the boys,
> And critic Timon laugh at idle toys!
>
> (4.3.165–69)

At the end they will endure still greater transformations, but
already they are well schooled in the doctrine that love is
madness, and that that madness redeems all. As the song
jubilantly declares of one lady:

> Thou for whom Jove would swear
> Juno but an Ethiop were.
>
> (116–17)

The beautiful lyric is part of the singing of the whole play,
the beauty love worships is the beauty the play is celebrating. All the changes it is ringing on the courting of high
and low, on absurdity and exaggeration, on grossness and
refinement, are subdued to the grave and splendid beauty
that conquers even Jove.

The secondary plot continues the mockery of false ideas

of learning and it also brings before us the sight of other kinds of lovemaking. The most obvious point to the mockery of pedantry is as an abuse of what the academy stands for. Holofernes, the walking dictionary, may represent John Florio, or Thomas Harriot. The name Armado brings the Spanish Armada to mind, and so it has been argued that Armado is a portrayal of Sir Walter Raleigh, the man who defeated the Armada. (If this were to be substantiated, it might strengthen the argument of those who think the play was produced shortly after the defeat of the Armada in 1588). Or the character may be thought to represent a quite different person, the arrogant and tedious Gabriel Harvey. Moth may be Thomas Nashe. But however much the possibility of such identifications causes the characters to jump out of their parts, the parts they do play are plainly so much more interesting to the audience for the comments they provide on the characters in the main action. The characters of the minor plot are strangers to the nobility of the others, and in their ambitions and pretensions they are illustrating not only the follies of the court but its essential superiority. The king values learning because it serves the noblest purposes in life; the ideas of the pedants are ignoble. For them it is always the letter at the expense of the spirit, and pride in learning at the expense of its good use.

The point is also being made that the abuse of learning is like the stupidity of affectation in love. The true power of love as well as the true worth of learning is lost upon the low characters, not only in their grossness but in their false refinement too. In the fun Shakespeare is making of them he strikes at everyone, but most of all he means to preserve our esteem for the truer men. They want glory for learning, for the academy, glory that will outlast death, because they want learning to be a light for those who will come after them. It is such men, no mere inkpots, who are love's true targets. In different ways, then, both plots are reinforcing the teaching that love belongs properly to the gentle heart.

Heightening and enriching this doctrine is the idea of the divinity of love. Character after character speaks of love as if it were a presence as well as a power. The play's title names love as the power at work in the play, and in every turn of the story we are shown events as if they were indeed the manipulations of a god—Eros, although unseen, yet surely directing and effecting all, showing his strength and enforcing his laws. As much as in *All's Well That Ends Well,* those who strive against him strive in vain.

Love's "labor" is a bringing to birth. The remembrances of ancient meetings come fast upon the courtiers and the ladies:

> Did not I dance with you in Brabant once?
>
> (2.1.114)

and in one after the other the seed burgeons. Part of the poetry as well as the comedy is that this growing of love goes on as it were in isolation. Cutting themselves off from so much of society, from the cares of power as well as from the entanglements with women, the lords are the more defenseless in their idleness. The king himself, treating of the matter the princess has come to negotiate on behalf of her sick father, even as he begins to talk of business finds that his heart is moved. Boyet notes this instantly:

> Why, all his behaviors did make their retire
> To the court of his eye, peeping thorough desire.
> His heart, like an agate with your print impressed,
> Proud with his form, in his eye pride expressed.
>
> (234–37)

Already love is at work, in the highest as in the lowest, sometimes beautifully and sometimes grotesquely, but always irresistibly.

This leads to the truly inspired idea in the extraordinary, not to say unlikely, happenings presumably only to be accounted for by a god's workings—that all the lovers should from the beginning have had no doubt who were to be their partners. In the masquing, the ladies switched their lords' favors in order to trick their lovers into another perjury, like Portia and Nerissa in *The Merchant of Venice,* merry in forging other chains for their slaves. So this time the lords will swear again, but to the wrong partners—as if another Puck were at work—and the ladies can mock the men until, as Berowne says, they are "dry-beaten" (5.2.264)—the very blood leaves their faces.

They are driven off, and it is no comfort to them to learn finally that they have now forsworn themselves twice. Shakespeare has had his fun with the idea of inexorable destiny in love at first sight, and he makes more fun of it still by asking another question: What is it that love sees?

Love's working and love's presence—a very god—come into full sight in Berowne's great speech, wherein the railer at love and wisdom, himself now enslaved, mocks himself:

> O, and I, forsooth, in love!
> I, that have been love's whip,
> A very beadle to a humorous sigh,
> A critic, nay, a night-watch constable,
> A domineering pedant o'er the boy,
> Than whom no mortal so magnificent!
> This wimpled, whining, purblind, wayward boy,
> This senior-junior, giant-dwarf, Dan Cupid,
> Regent of love-rhymes, lord of folded arms,
> Th' anointed sovereign of sighs and groans . . .
> And I to be a corporal of his field.
>
> (3.1.175–89)

To make it worse, he is in love with the one he says is the least beautiful of the ladies, the most wanton, the one who would escape a guardian with a hundred eyes. But he accepts his fate.

> Some men must love my lady, and some Joan.
>
> (207)

This time Touchstone is a gentleman, and so somewhat more love's fool. But finally he will say more in praise of love than any other will, and however light in touch his words substantiate what the others must now acknowledge:

> From women's eyes this doctrine I derive. . . .
> They are the books, the arts, the academes,
> That show, contain, and nourish all the world;
> Else none at all in aught proves excellent.
>
> (4.3.349–53)

With this conclusion the play moves towards its end. The haughty must change their tactics. There is the call to arms and the embrace of battle:

> Advance your standards, and upon them, lords!
>
> (366)

And so they dance, recapitulating in their motions the warring that has made the play, the advances and retreats, the defeats and victories, the strivings, and capitulations, and the final treaties.

For the play's last words there is a song sung by allegorical personages, Spring and Winter, fantastic figures out of the world of musical entertainment and Renaissance allegory. It speaks of flowers and countrymaids and ploughmen, of love and marriage and cuckoldry, of spring and winter, of idleness and of hard work, of nature when it is kind and when it is cruel, of life by the hearth. It is a song about love making peace with life, with things as they are. It provides the most brilliant of comments on all that has been fanciful in the beauty of the play and in the ideas of these fine people. In the perfection and balance of the contrast with all that has gone before, this song sung by the personifications of time is the true culmination of the play, the marriage of sophistication and reality, of the stage and its glory and the strength of love's endurance outside it. The song celebrates the poetry of life as it is, and it is one of Shakespeare's most glorious inspirations that he has it sung by the deities of "curds and flowers," magnificently adorned, without doubt, as the Renaissance imagined gods would be.

The song follows the princess' farewell as she and the ladies leave Navarre, postponing the marriages. The lords are meanwhile to prove themselves by the most strenuous and demanding discipline, for the courtship has been

> A time, methinks, too short
> To make a world-without-end bargain in.
>
> (5.2.789–90)

The words of wisdom are indeed harsh after the music of the god of poetry, as the comment that ends the play says, words that may be given to Armado. They are words that sustain us as the play sustains us, and as the marvelous song does. And the reflection to which the last scene leads us is that love, like learning, is but a part of life, and what the whole of it is there is no one to say—there is only the testing, and good hope.

—JOHN ARTHOS
University of Michigan

*Love's
Labor's Lost*

Love's Labor's Lost

[ACT 1

Scene 1. *The park of the King of Navarre.*]

Enter Ferdinand King of Navarre, Berowne, Long-aville, and Dumaine.

King. Let fame, that all hunt after in their lives,
    Live regist'red upon our brazen tombs
    And then grace us in the disgrace°¹ of death,
    When, spite of cormorant° devouring time,
    Th' endeavor of this present breath may buy   5
    That honor which shall bate° his scythe's keen edge
    And make us heirs of all eternity.
    Therefore, brave conquerors—for so you are
    That war against your own affections
    And the huge army of the world's desires—   10
    Our late edict shall strongly stand in force:
    Navarre shall be the wonder of the world;
    Our court shall be a little academe,°
    Still and contemplative in living art.°

---

1 The degree sign (°) indicates a footnote, which is keyed to the
text by line number. Text references are printed in **boldface** type;
the annotation follows in roman type. 1.1.3 **disgrace** degradation
4 **cormorant** ravenous 6 **bate** make dull 13 **academe** academy
14 **Still . . . art** continually studying the art of living

15 You three, Berowne, Dumaine, and Longaville,
    Have sworn for three years' term to live with me,
    My fellow scholars, and to keep those statutes
    That are recorded in this schedule here.
    Your oaths are passed; and now subscribe your
        names,
20 That his own hand may strike his honor down
    That violates the smallest branch herein.
    If you are armed° to do as sworn to do,
    Subscribe to your deep oaths, and keep it too.

    Longaville. I am resolved. 'Tis but a three years' fast.
25 The mind shall banquet though the body pine.
    Fat paunches have lean pates, and dainty bits
    Make rich the ribs, but bankrout° quite the wits.

    Dumaine. My loving lord, Dumaine is mortified.°
    The grosser manner of these world's delights
30 He throws upon the gross world's baser slaves.
    To love, to wealth, to pomp, I pine and die,
    With all these living in philosophy.

    Berowne. I can but say their protestation over°—
    So much, dear liege, I have already sworn,
35 That is, to live and study here three years.
    But there are other strict observances:
    As not to see a woman in that term—
    Which I hope well is not enrollèd there;
    And one day in a week to touch no food,
40 And but one meal on every day beside—
    The which I hope is not enrollèd there;
    And then to sleep but three hours in the night,
    And not be seen to wink of° all the day
    (When I was wont to think no harm all night
45 And make a dark night too of half the day)—
    Which I hope well is not enrollèd there.
    O, these are barren tasks, too hard to keep,
    Not to see ladies, study, fast, not sleep!

---

22 **armed** resolved   27 **bankrout** bankrupt   28 **mortified** dead to
worldly pleasures   33 **say their protestation over** repeat their solemn
declarations   43 **wink of** close the eyes during

King. Your oath is passed, to pass away from these.

Berowne. Let me say no, my liege, and if° you please.   50
 I only swore to study with your Grace
 And stay here in your court for three years' space.

Longaville. You swore to that, Berowne, and to the
 rest.

Berowne. By yea and nay,° sir, then I swore in jest.
 What is the end of study, let me know?   55

King. Why, that to know which else we should not
 know.

Berowne. Things hid and barred, you mean, from
 common sense?

King. Ay, that is study's godlike recompense.

Berowne. Come on then, I will swear to study so,
 To know the thing I am forbid to know: 60
 As thus—to study where I well may dine
 When I to feast expressly am forbid;
 Or study where to meet some mistress fine
 When mistresses from common sense are hid;
 Or having sworn too hard-a-keeping oath,   65
 Study to break it and not break my troth.°
 If study's gain be thus, and this be so,
 Study knows that which yet it doth not know.
 Swear me to this, and I will ne'er say no.

King. These be the stops° that hinder study quite   70
 And train° our intellects to vain delight.

Berowne. Why, all delights are vain, but that most
 vain
 Which, with pain purchased, doth inherit pain:
 As, painfully to pore upon a book,
 To seek the light of truth, while truth the while   75
 Doth falsely° blind the eyesight of his look.

---

50 **and if** if   54 **By yea and nay** in all earnestness   66 **troth** faith
70 **stops** obstructions   71 **train** entice   76 **falsely** treacherously

Light seeking light doth light of light beguile;°
So, ere you find where light in darkness lies,
Your light grows dark by losing of your eyes.
80 Study me how to please the eye indeed
By fixing it upon a fairer eye,
Who dazzling so, that eye shall be his heed°
And give him light that it was blinded by.
Study is like the heaven's glorious sun,
85 That will not be deep-searched with saucy looks.
Small have continual plodders ever won
Save base authority from others' books.
These earthly godfathers° of heaven's lights,
That give a name to every fixèd star
90 Have no more profit of their shining nights
Than those that walk and wot° not what they are.
Too much to know is to know nought but fame;°
And every godfather can give a name.

King. How well he's read to reason against reading!

Dumaine. Proceeded° well, to stop all good proceed-
95   ing!

Longaville. He weeds the corn,° and still lets grow the
weeding.°

Berowne. The spring is near, when green geese° are
a-breeding.

Dumaine. How follows that?

Berowne.   Fit in his place and time.

Dumaine. In reason nothing.

Berowne.   Something then in rhyme.

100 *King.* Berowne is like an envious sneaping° frost
That bites the first-born infants of the spring.

---

77 **Light . . . beguile** i.e., eyes in seeking truth lose their sight in too
much seeking   82 **heed** protector   88 **earthly godfathers** i.e., as-
tronomers   91 **wot** know   92 **fame** report   95 **Proceeded** took a
degree at the university   96 **corn** wheat   96 **weeding** weeds   97
green geese geese born the previous autumn   100 **sneaping** nipping
(Berowne's "rhyme" is taken as "rime" or frost)

Berowne. Well, say I am! Why should proud summer
      boast
   Before the birds have any cause to sing?
   Why should I joy in an abortive birth?
   At Christmas I no more desire a rose   *105*
   Than wish a snow in May's new-fangled shows,
   But like of each thing that in season grows.
   So you—to study now it is too late—
   Climb o'er the house to unlock the little gate.

King. Well, sit you out. Go home, Berowne. Adieu.   *110*

Berowne. No, my good lord, I have sworn to stay with
      you;
   And though I have for barbarism° spoke more
   Than for that angel knowledge you can say,
   Yet confident I'll keep what I have swore,
   And bide the penance of each three years' day.°   *115*
   Give me the paper, let me read the same,
   And to the strictest decrees I'll write my name.

King. How well this yielding rescues thee from shame!

Berowne. [*Reads.*] "Item. That no woman shall come
   within a mile of my court—" Hath this been pro-   *120*
   claimed?

Longaville. Four days ago.

Berowne. Let's see the penalty. [*Reads.*] "—on pain of
   losing her tongue." Who devised this penalty?

Longaville. Marry,° that did I.

Berowne.   Sweet lord, and why?   *125*

Longaville. To fright them hence with that dread penalty.

Berowne. A dangerous law against gentility!°
   [*Reads*] "Item. If any man be seen to talk with a
   woman within the term of three years, he shall

112 **barbarism** philistinism   115 **each three years' day** each day of
the three years   125 **Marry** By Mary (mild oath)   127 **gentility**
good manners

130   endure such public shame as the rest of the court
       can possibly devise."
       This article, my liege, yourself must break;
       For well you know here comes in embassy
       The French king's daughter with yourself to speak,
135   A maid of grace and complete majesty,
       About surrender up of Aquitaine
       To her decrepit, sick, and bed-rid father.
       Therefore this article is made in vain,
       Or vainly comes th' admirèd princess hither.

140 *King.* What say you, lords? Why, this was quite forgot.

Berowne. So study evermore is overshot.°
       While it doth study to have what it would,
       It doth forget to do the thing it should;
       And when it hath the thing it hunteth most,
145   'Tis won as towns with fire°—so won, so lost.

King. We must of force° dispense with this decree.
       She must lie° here on mere° necessity.

Berowne. Necessity will make us all forsworn
       Three thousand times within this three years' space:
150   For every man with his affects° is born,
       Not by might mast'red, but by special grace.
       If I break faith, this word shall speak for me,
       I am forsworn "on mere necessity."
       So to the laws at large I write my name;

                                        [*Subscribes.*]
155   And he that breaks them in the least degree
       Stands in attainder of° eternal shame.
       Suggestions° are to other as to me,
       But I believe, although I seem so loath,°
       I am the last that will last keep his oath.
160   But is there no quick recreation granted?

King. Ay, that there is. Our court, you know, is
       haunted

141   **overshot** wide of the mark   145 **won as towns with fire** destroyed
in being won   146 **of force** of necessity   147 **lie** lodge   147 **mere**
simple   150 **affects** passions   156 **in attainder of** to be condemned
to   157 **Suggestions** temptations   158 **loath** reluctant

With a refinèd traveler of Spain,
A man in all the world's new fashion planted,
That hath a mint of phrases in his brain;
One who the music of his own vain tongue　　　165
Doth ravish like enchanting harmony;
A man of complements,° whom right and wrong
Have chose as umpire of their mutiny.
This child of fancy, that Armado hight,°
For interim° to our studies shall relate　　　170
In high-born words the worth of many a knight
From tawny Spain, lost in the world's debate.
How you delight, my lords, I know not, I,
But, I protest, I love to hear him lie,
And I will use him for my minstrelsy.°　　　175

Berowne. Armado is a most illustrious wight,
A man of fire-new° words, fashion's own knight.

Longaville. Costard the swain° and he shall be our
　　sport;
And so to study three years is but short.

*Enter [Dull,] a Constable, with Costard, [a Clown,]
with a letter.*

Dull. Which is the duke's own person?　　　180

Berowne. This, fellow. What wouldst?

Dull. I myself reprehend° his own person, for I am
　　his Grace's farborough.° But I would see his own
　　person in flesh and blood.

Berowne. This is he.　　　185

Dull. Signior Arm—Arm—commends you. There's
　　villainy abroad. This letter will tell you more.

Costard. Sir, the contempts° thereof are as touching
　　me.

167 **complements** formal manners 169 **hight** is named 170 **in-
terim** interruption 175 **minstrelsy** court entertainer 177 **fire-new**
fresh from the mint 178 **swain** countryman 182 **reprehend** (Dull
means to say, "represent") 183 **farborough** petty constable
188 **contempts** (Costard means the "contents" of the letter)

190 *King.* A letter from the magnificent Armado.

Berowne. How low soever the matter, I hope in God for high words.

Longaville. A high hope for a low heaven. God grant us patience!

195 *Berowne.* To hear, or forbear hearing?

Longaville. To hear meekly, sir, and to laugh moderately, or to forbear both.

Berowne. Well, sir, be it as the style shall give us cause to climb in the merriness.

200 *Costard.* The matter is to me, sir, as concerning Jaquenetta. The manner of it is, I was taken with the manner.°

Berowne. In what manner?

Costard. In manner and form following, sir—all those
205 three: I was seen with her in the manor-house, sitting with her upon the form,° and taken following her into the park; which, put together, is, in manner and form, following. Now, sir, for the manner—it is the manner of a man to speak to a woman.
210 For the form—in some form.

Berowne. For the following, sir?

Costard. As it shall follow in my correction,° and God defend the right!

King. Will you hear this letter with attention?

215 *Berowne.* As we would hear an oracle.

Costard. Such is the simplicity of man to hearken after the flesh.

King. [*Reads.*] "Great deputy, the welkin's vicegerent,°
and sole dominator of Navarre, my soul's earth's
220 God, and body's fost'ring patron—"

201–02 **with the manner** in the act 206 **form** bench 212 **correction**
punishment 218 **welkin's vicegerent** deputy-ruler of heaven

Costard. Not a word of Costard yet.

King. "So it is—"

Costard. It may be so; but if he say it is so, he is, in
telling true, but so.°

King. Peace!   225

Costard. Be to me and every man that dares not fight.

King. No words!

Costard. Of other men's secrets, I beseech you.

King. [*Reads.*] "So it is, besieged with sable-colored
melancholy, I did commend the black-oppressing   230
humor° to the most wholesome physic° of thy
health-giving air; and, as I am a gentleman, betook
myself to walk. The time When? About the sixth
hour; when beasts most graze, birds best peck,
and men sit down to that nourishment which is   235
called supper. So much for the time When. Now
for the ground Which? Which, I mean, I walked
upon. It is ycleped° thy park. Then for the place
Where? Where, I mean, I did encounter that ob-
scene and most preposterous event, that draweth   240
from my snow-white pen° the ebon-colored ink,
which here thou viewest, beholdest, surveyest, or
seest. But to the place Where? It standeth north-
north-east and by east from the west corner of thy
curious-knotted° garden. There did I see that low-   245
spirited swain, that base minnow of thy mirth—"

Costard. Me?

King. "that unlettered° small-knowing soul—"

Costard. Me?

King. "that shallow vassal°—"   250

224 **but so** not worth much   230–31 **black-oppressing humor** fluid in
the body that causes melancholy   231 **physic** treatment   238 **ycleped**
called   241 **snow-white pen** goose-quill   245 **curious-knotted**
flower beds and paths in intricate patterns   248 **unlettered** illiterate
250 **vassal** underling

Costard. Still me!

King. "which, as I remember, hight° Costard—"

Costard. O me!

King. "sorted and consorted, contrary to thy estab-
255   lished proclaimed edict and continent canon,°
       which with—O, with—but with this I passion to
       say wherewith—"

Costard. With a wench.

King. "with a child of our grandmother Eve, a female;
260   or, for thy more sweet understanding, a woman.
       Him I (as my ever-esteemed duty pricks° me on)
       have sent to thee, to receive the meed° of punish-
       ment, by thy sweet Grace's officer, Anthony Dull,
       a man of good repute, carriage, bearing, and esti-
265   mation."

Dull. Me, an 't shall please you: I am Anthony Dull.

King. "For Jaquenetta (so is the weaker vessel°
       called), which I apprehended with the aforesaid
       swain, I keep her as a vessel of thy law's fury, and
270   shall, at the least of thy sweet notice,° bring her
       to trial. Thine in all compliments of devoted and
       heart-burning heat of duty,

                        Don Adriano de Armado."

Berowne. This is not so well as I looked for, but the
275   best that ever I heard.

King. Ay, the best for the worst. But, sirrah,° what
       say you to this?

Costard. Sir, I confess the wench.

King. Did you hear the proclamation?

---

252 **hight** called 255 **continent canon** the decree restraining the
members of the Academy 261 **pricks** spurs 262 **meed** reward
267 **weaker vessel** (general phrase for "womankind") 270 **at the
least . . . notice** at the slightest indication of thy concern 276 **sirrah**
(term of address used to an inferior)

Costard. I do confess much of the hearing it, but little 280
of the marking of it.

King. It was proclaimed a year's imprisonment to be
taken with a wench.

Costard. I was taken with none, sir; I was taken with
a damsel. 285

King. Well, it was proclaimed "damsel."

Costard. This was no damsel neither, sir, she was a
virgin.

King. It is so varied° too, for it was proclaimed
"virgin." 290

Costard. If it were, I deny her virginity. I was taken
with a maid.

King. This maid will not serve your turn, sir.

Costard. This maid will serve my turn,° sir.

King. Sir, I will pronounce your sentence: you shall 295
fast a week with bran and water.

Costard. I had rather pray a month with mutton and
porridge.

King. And Don Armado shall be your keeper.
My Lord Berowne, see him delivered o'er. 300
And go we, lords, to put in practice that
Which each to other hath so strongly sworn.
        [*Exeunt King, Longaville, and Dumaine.*]

Berowne. I'll lay° my head to any good man's hat,
These oaths and laws will prove an idle scorn.
Sirrah, come on. 305

Costard. I suffer for the truth, sir, for true it is I was
taken with Jaquenetta, and Jaquenetta is a true°
girl. And therefore welcome the sour cup of prosperity! Affliction may one day smile again, and till
then sit thee down, sorrow! *Exeunt.* 310

289 **varied** distinguished   294 **turn** (Costard uses the word in a
bawdy sense)   303 **lay** bet   307 **true** honest

[Scene 2. *The park.*]

Enter Armado and Moth,° his Page.

Armado. Boy, what sign is it when a man of great spirit grows melancholy?

Moth. A great sign, sir, that he will look sad.

Armado. Why, sadness is one and the selfsame thing,
5   dear imp.

Moth. No, no, O Lord, sir, no!

Armado. How canst thou part° sadness and melancholy, my tender juvenal?°

Moth. By a familiar demonstration of the working,
10   my tough signor.°

Armado. Why tough signor? Why tough signor?

Moth. Why tender juvenal? Why tender juvenal?

Armado. I spoke it, tender juvenal, as a congruent epitheton° appertaining to thy young days, which
15   we may nominate tender.

Moth. And I, tough signor, as an appertinent title to your old time, which we may name tough.

Armado. Pretty and apt.

Moth. How mean you, sir? I pretty, and my saying
20   apt? Or I apt and my saying pretty?

1.2.s.d. **Moth** (probably pronounced, and with the meaning of, "mote," i.e., speck) 7 **part** distinguish between 8 **juvenal** youth (it may also signify *Juvenal*, the Roman satirist, and allude to the nickname of Thomas Nashe, Elizabethan writer) 10 **signor** (with a pun on "senior") 13–14 **congruent epitheton** appropriate adjective

Armado. Thou pretty, because little.

Moth. Little pretty, because little. Wherefore apt?

Armado. And therefore apt because quick.

Moth. Speak you this in my praise, master?

Armado. In thy condign° praise.   25

Moth. I will praise an eel with the same praise.

Armado. What, that an eel is ingenious?

Moth. That an eel is quick.

Armado. I do say thou art quick in answers. Thou
heat'st my blood.   30

Moth. I am answered, sir.

Armado. I love not to be crossed.

Moth. [*Aside*] He speaks the mere contrary—crosses°
love not him.

Armado. I have promised to study three years with   35
the duke.

Moth. You may do it in an hour, sir.

Armado. Impossible.

Moth. How many is one thrice told?

Armado. I am ill at reck'ning—it fitteth the spirit of   40
a tapster.°

Moth. You are a gentleman and a gamester, sir.

Armado. I confess both. They are both the varnish°
of a complete man.

Moth. Then I am sure you know how much the gross   45
sum of deuce-ace amounts to.

Armado. It doth amount to one more than two.

25 **condign** well-deserved 33 **crosses** coins (so named for the
crosses engraved on them) 41 **tapster** bartender 43 **varnish** outward gloss

Moth. Which the base vulgar do call three.

Armado. True.

50   *Moth.* Why, sir, is this such a piece of study? Now
     here is three studied ere ye'll thrice wink; and how
     easy it is to put "years" to the word "three," and
     study three years in two words, the dancing horse°
     will tell you.

55   *Armado.* A most fine figure.°

     Moth. [*Aside*] To prove you a cipher.

     Armado. I will hereupon confess I am in love, and
     as it is base for a soldier to love, so am I in love
     with a base wench. If drawing my sword against
60   the humor° of affection would deliver me from the
     reprobate thought of it, I would take Desire pris-
     oner and ransom him to any French courtier for
     a new devised cursy.° I think scorn° to sigh: me-
     thinks I should outswear° Cupid. Comfort me, boy.
65   What great men have been in love?

     Moth. Hercules, master.

     Armado. Most sweet Hercules! More authority, dear
     boy, name more; and, sweet my child, let them
     be men of good repute and carriage.

70   *Moth.* Samson, master—he was a man of good car-
     riage, great carriage, for he carried the town-gates
     on his back like a porter, and he was in love.

     Armado. O well-knit Samson, strong-jointed Samson!
     I do excel thee in my rapier as much as thou didst
75   me in carrying gates. I am in love too. Who was
     Samson's love, my dear Moth?

     Moth. A woman, master.

53 **dancing horse** (a performing horse well-known for beating out
numbers) 55 **figure** figure of speech 60 **humor** innate disposition 63 **new devised cursy** novel mannerism 63 **think scorn** dis-
dain 64 **outswear** forswear

Armado. Of what complexion?°

Moth. Of all the four,° or the three, or the two, or
    one of the four.   80

Armado. Tell me precisely of what complexion.

Moth. Of the sea-water green, sir.

Armado. Is that one of the four complexions?

Moth. As I have read, sir, and the best of them too.

Armado. Green° indeed is the color of lovers. But to   85
    have a love of that color, methinks Samson had
    small reason for it. He surely affected her for her
    wit.°

Moth. It was so, sir, for she had a green wit.

Armado. My love is most immaculate white and red.   90

Moth. Most maculate° thoughts, master, are masked
    under such colors.

Armado. Define, define, well-educated infant.

Moth. My father's wit, and my mother's tongue, assist
    me!   95

Armado. Sweet invocation of a child, most pretty and
    pathetical.

Moth. If she be made of white and red,
        Her faults will ne'er be known,
    For blushing cheeks by faults are bred,   100
        And fears by pale white shown.
    Then if she fear or be to blame,
        By this you shall not know,
    For still her cheeks possess the same
        Which native° she doth owe.°   105
  A dangerous rhyme, master, against the reason of
  white and red.

78 **complexion** disposition 79 **all the four** (the four humors or
fluids of the body: blood, phlegm, bile, black bile) 85 **Green** (immature) 88 **wit** mind 91 **maculate** spotted 105 **native** by nature
105 **owe** possess

Armado. Is there not a ballet,° boy, of the King and
the Beggar?

110 *Moth.* The world was very guilty of such a ballet
some three ages since. But I think now 'tis not to
be found, or if it were, it would neither serve for
the writing nor the tune.

Armado. I will have that subject newly writ o'er, that
115 I may example my digression° by some mighty
precedent. Boy, I do love that country girl that I
took in the park with the rational hind,° Costard.
She deserves well.

Moth. [*Aside*] To be whipped—and yet a better love
120 than my master.

Armado. Sing, boy. My spirit grows heavy in love.

Moth. And that's great marvel, loving a light wench.

Armado. I say, sing.

Moth. Forbear till this company be past.

> *Enter [Costard, the] Clown, [Dull, the]*
> *Constable, and [Jaquenetta, a] Wench.*

125 *Dull.* Sir, the duke's pleasure is that you keep Costard
safe, and you must suffer him to take no delight
nor no penance,° but 'a° must fast three days a
week. For this damsel, I must keep her at the park—
she is allowed for the day-woman.° Fare you
130 well.

Armado. I do betray myself with blushing. Maid!

Jaquenetta. Man?

Armado. I will visit thee at the lodge.

Jaquenetta. That's hereby.

---

108 **ballet** ballad 115 **digression** (Armado means to say, "transgression") 117 **rational hind** intelligent yokel 127 **penance** (perhaps Dull means to say "pleasance," meaning pleasure) 127 **'a** he
129 **allowed for the day-woman** admitted as the dairy maid

Armado. I know where it is situate.   135

Jaquenetta. Lord, how wise you are!

Armado. I will tell thee wonders.

Jaquenetta. With that face?

Armado. I love thee.

Jaquenetta. So I heard you say.   140

Armado. And so farewell.

Jaquenetta. Fair weather after you!

Dull. Come, Jaquenetta, away!
                            Exeunt [Dull and Jaquenetta].

Armado. Villain, thou shalt fast for thy offenses ere
    thou be pardoned.   145

Costard. Well, sir, I hope when I do it I shall do it
    on a full stomach.°

Armado. Thou shalt be heavily punished.

Costard. I am more bound to you than your fellows,°
    for they are but lightly rewarded.   150

Armado. Take away this villain. Shut him up.

Moth. Come, you transgressing slave, away!

Costard. Let me not be pent up, sir. I will fast, being
    loose.

Moth. No, sir, that were fast and loose.° Thou shalt 155
    to prison.

Costard. Well, if ever I do see the merry days of des-
    olation that I have seen, some shall see.

Moth. What shall some see?

Costard. Nay, nothing, Master Moth, but what they 160
    look upon. It is not for prisoners to be too silent

_____

147 **on a full stomach** bravely   149 **fellows** servants   155 **fast and
loose** not playing fairly

in their words,° and therefore I will say nothing. I
thank God I have as little patience as another man,
and therefore I can be quiet.   *Exit [with Moth].*

165 *Armado.* I do affect° the very ground (which is base)
where her shoe (which is baser) guided by her foot
(which is basest) doth tread. I shall be forsworn
(which is a great argument of falsehood) if I love.
And how can that be true love which is falsely at-
170 tempted? Love is a familiar;° Love is a devil. There
is no evil angel but Love. Yet was Samson so
tempted, and he had an excellent strength; yet was
Solomon so seduced, and he had a very good wit.
Cupid's butt-shaft° is too hard for Hercules' club,
175 and therefore too much odds for a Spaniard's
rapier. The first and second cause° will not serve
my turn; the *passado*° he respects not, the *duello*°
he regards not. His disgrace is to be called boy, but
his glory is to subdue men. Adieu, valor; rust, ra-
180 pier; be still, drum; for your manager is in love;
yea, he loveth. Assist me some extemporal god of
rhyme,° for I am sure I shall turn sonnet.° Devise,
wit; write, pen; for I am for whole volumes in folio.
                                        Exit.

---

162 **words** (probably with pun on *wards* = cells) 165 **affect** love
170 **familiar** attendant spirit 174 **butt-shaft** unbarbed arrow
176 **first and second cause** (referring to rules governing the conduct
of a duel) 177 **passado** forward thrust 177 **duello** correct way
of dueling 181–82 **extemporal god of rhyme** god of rhymes written on the spur of the moment 182 **turn sonnet** compose a sonnet

[ACT 2

Scene 1. *The park.*]

Enter the Princess of France, with three attending Ladies [Maria, Katharine, Rosaline] and three Lords [one named Boyet].

Boyet. Now, madam, summon up your dearest spirits.°
  Consider who the king your father sends,
  To whom he sends, and what's his embassy:
  Yourself, held precious in the world's esteem,
  To parley with the sole inheritor°   5
  Of all perfections that a man may owe,°
  Matchless Navarre; the plea of no less weight
  Than Aquitaine, a dowry for a queen,
  Be now as prodigal of all dear grace
  As Nature was in making graces dear°   10
  When she did starve the general world beside,
  And prodigally gave them all to you.

Princess. Good Lord Boyet, my beauty, though but mean,
  Needs not the painted flourish° of your praise.
  Beauty is bought by judgment of the eye,   15
  Not utt'red by base sale of chapmen's tongues.°

2.1.1 **dearest spirits** best intelligence   5 **inheritor** possessor   6 **owe** own   10 **graces dear** beauty scarce   14 **painted flourish** elaborate ornament   16 **utt'red ... tongues** put up for sale by hucksters

I am less proud to hear you tell my worth
Than you much willing to be counted wise
In spending your wit in the praise of mine.
20 But now to task the tasker:° good Boyet,
You are not ignorant all-telling fame
Doth noise abroad Navarre hath made a vow,
Till painful study shall outwear three years,
No woman may approach his silent court.
25 Therefore to's seemeth it a needful course,
Before we enter his forbidden gates,
To know his pleasure; and in that behalf,
Bold of your worthiness,° we single you
As our best-moving° fair solicitor.
30 Tell him the daughter of the king of France,
On serious business, craving quick dispatch,
Importunes personal conference with his Grace.
Haste, signify so much while we attend
Like humble-visaged suitors his high will.

35 *Boyet.* Proud of employment, willingly I go.

                                    Exit Boyet.

Princess. All pride is willing pride, and yours is so.
Who are the votaries,° my loving lords,
That are vow-fellows with this virtuous duke?

Lord. Longaville is one.

Princess.   Know you the man?

40 *Maria.* I know him, madam. At a marriage feast
Between Lord Perigort and the beauteous heir
Of Jacques Falconbridge solemnizèd
In Normandy saw I this Longaville.
A man of sovereign parts° he is esteemed,
45 Well fitted in arts, glorious in arms.
Nothing becomes him ill that he would well.°
The only soil of his fair virtue's gloss—

20 **task the tasker** set a task to the one who sets tasks   28 **Bold of your worthiness** confident of your worth   29 **best-moving** most persuasive   37 **votaries** those who have sworn a vow   44 **sovereign parts** lordly qualities   46 **Nothing . . . well** nothing that he values is unbecoming to him

If virtue's gloss will stain with any soil—
Is a sharp wit matched with too blunt a will,
Whose edge hath power to cut, whose will still wills   50
It should none spare that come within his power.

Princess. Some merry mocking lord, belike—is 't so?

Maria. They say so most that most his humors know.

Princess. Such short-lived wits do wither as they grow.
Who are the rest?   55

Katharine. The young Dumaine, a well-accomplished
   youth,
Of all that virtue love for virtue loved;
Most power to do most harm, least knowing ill,
For he hath wit to make an ill shape good,
And shape to win grace though he had no wit.   60
I saw him at the Duke Alençon's once;
And much too little° of that good I saw
Is my report to° his great worthiness.

Rosaline. Another of these students at that time
Was there with him, if I have heard a truth.   65
Berowne they call him; but a merrier man,
Within the limit of becoming mirth,
I never spent an hour's talk withal.°
His eye begets occasion° for his wit;
For every object that the one doth catch   70
The other turns to a mirth-moving jest,
Which his fair tongue (conceit's expositor°)
Delivers in such apt and gracious words,
That agèd ears play truant at his tales,
And younger hearings are quite ravishèd,   75
So sweet and voluble is his discourse.

Princess. God bless my ladies! Are they all in love,
That every one her own hath garnishèd
With such bedecking ornaments of praise?

---

62 **much too little** far short   63 **to** compared to   68 **withal** with
69 **begets occasion** finds opportunity   72 **conceit's expositor** one
who explains an ingenious notion

Lord. Here comes Boyet.

Enter Boyet.

80 *Princess.*   Now, what admittance,° lord?

Boyet. Navarre had notice of your fair approach;
And he and his competitors° in oath
Were all addressed° to meet you, gentle lady,
Before I came. Marry, thus much I have learnt;
85 He rather means to lodge you in the field,
Like one that comes here to besiege his court,
Than seek a dispensation for his oath
To let you enter his unpeopled house.

[The Ladies mask.]

*Enter Navarre, Longaville, Dumaine, and
Berowne [with Attendants].*

Here comes Navarre.

90 *King.* Fair princess, welcome to the court of Navarre.

Princess. "Fair" I give you back again; and "welcome" I have not yet. The roof of this court is too
high to be yours, and welcome to the wide fields
too base to be mine.

95 *King.* You shall be welcome, madam, to my court.

Princess. I will be welcome, then. Conduct me thither.

King. Hear me, dear lady—I have sworn an oath.

Princess. Our Lady help my lord! He'll be forsworn.

King. Not for the world, fair madam, by my will.

Princess. Why, will shall break it, will, and nothing
100 else.

King. Your ladyship is ignorant what it is.

---

80 **admittance** permission to enter   82 **competitors** partners   83 **addressed** ready

Princess. Were my lord so, his ignorance were wise,
    Where now his knowledge must prove ignorance.
    I hear your Grace hath sworn out house-keeping.°
    'Tis deadly sin to keep that oath, my lord,   *105*
    And sin to break it.
    But pardon me, I am too sudden-bold;
    To teach a teacher ill beseemeth me.
    Vouchsafe to read the purpose of my coming,
    And suddenly resolve me° in my suit.   *110*
                    [Gives a paper.]

King. Madam, I will, if suddenly I may.

Princess. You will the sooner that I were away,
    For you'll prove perjured if you make me stay.

Berowne. Did not I dance with you in Brabant once?

Rosaline. Did not I dance with you in Brabant once? *115*

Berowne. I know you did.

Rosaline.   How needless was it then
    To ask the question!

Berowne.   You must not be so quick.

Rosaline. 'Tis long° of you that spur me with such
    questions.

Berowne. Your wit's too hot, it speeds too fast, 'twill
    tire.

Rosaline. Not till it leave the rider in the mire.   *120*

Berowne. What time o' day?

Rosaline. The hour that fools should ask.

Berowne. Now fair befall° your mask!

Rosaline. Fair fall the face it covers!

Berowne. And send you many lovers!   *125*

---

104 **sworn out house-keeping** sworn not to keep house or offer hos-
pitality 110 **suddenly resolve me** quickly give me a decision
118 **long** because 123 **fair befall** good luck to

Rosaline. Amen, so you be none.

Berowne. Nay, then will I be gone.

King. Madam, your father here doth intimate°
          The payment of a hundred thousand crowns,
130   Being but the one half of an entire sum
          Disbursèd by my father in his wars.
          But say that he, or we (as neither have),
          Received that sum, yet there remains unpaid
          A hundred thousand more, in surety of the which,
135   One part of Aquitaine is bound to us,
          Although not valued to the money's worth.
          If then the king your father will restore
          But that one half which is unsatisfied,
          We will give up our right in Aquitaine,
140   And hold fair friendship with his Majesty.
          But that, it seems, he little purposeth,
          For here he doth demand to have repaid
          A hundred thousand crowns; and not demands,
          On payment of a hundred thousand crowns,
145   To have his title live in Aquitaine;
          Which we much rather had depart withal,°
          And have the money by our father lent,
          Than Aquitaine, so gelded° as it is.
          Dear princess, were not his requests so far
150   From reason's yielding, your fair self should make
          A yielding 'gainst some reason in my breast,
          And go well satisfied to France again.

Princess. You do the king my father too much wrong,
          And wrong the reputation of your name,
155   In so unseeming° to confess receipt
          Of that which hath so faithfully been paid.

King. I do protest I never heard of it;
          And if you prove it, I'll repay it back
          Or yield up Aquitaine.

---

128 **intimate** make known   146 **depart withal** give up   148 **gelded**
cut up   155 **unseeming** not appearing

Princess.   We arrest your word.°
　Boyet, you can produce acquittances°   *160*
　For such a sum from special officers
　Of Charles his father.

King.   Satisfy me so.

Boyet. So please your Grace, the packet° is not come
　Where that and other specialties° are bound.
　Tomorrow you shall have a sight of them.   *165*

King. It shall suffice me—at which interview
　All liberal reason I will yield unto.
　Meantime, receive such welcome at my hand
　As honor (without breach of honor) may
　Make tender of° to thy true worthiness.   *170*
　You may not come, fair princess, within my gates;
　But here without you shall be so received
　As you shall deem yourself lodged in my heart,
　Though so denied fair harbor in my house.
　Your own good thoughts excuse me, and farewell. *175*
　Tomorrow shall we visit you again.

Princess. Sweet health and fair desires consort° your
　　Grace.

King. Thy own wish wish I thee in every place.
　　　　　　　　　　　Exit [King and his Train].

Berowne. Lady, I will commend you to mine own
　heart.   *180*

Rosaline. Pray you, do my commendations, I would
　be glad to see it.

Berowne. I would you heard it groan.

Rosaline. Is the fool sick?

Berowne. Sick at the heart.   *185*

Rosaline. Alack, let it blood!°

159 **arrest your word** take your word as security 160 **acquittances**
receipts 163 **packet** package 164 **specialties** particular legal documents 170 **Make tender of** offer 177 **consort** accompany 186 **let it
blood** bleed him

Berowne. Would that do it good?

Rosaline. My physic says ay.

Berowne. Will you prick 't with your eye?

190 *Rosaline.* No point,° with my knife.

Berowne. Now, God save thy life!

Rosaline. And yours from long living!

Berowne. I cannot stay thanksgiving.°   *Exit.*

Enter Dumaine.

Dumaine. Sir, I pray you a word. What lady is that same?

195 *Boyet.* The heir of Alençon, Katharine her name.

Dumaine. A gallant lady. Monsieur, fare you well.

Exit.

[*Enter Longaville.*]

Longaville. I beseech you a word. What is she in the white?

Boyet. A woman sometimes, and° you saw her in the light.

Longaville. Perchance light in the light.° I desire her name.

Boyet. She hath but one for herself. To desire that
200   were a shame.

Longaville. Pray you, sir, whose daughter?

Boyet. Her mother's, I have heard.

Longaville. God's blessing on your beard!

⸴

190 **No point** not at all   193 **stay thanksgiving** stay long enough to
give you proper thanks (for your unkind remark)   198 **and** if
199 **light in the light** wanton if rightly perceived

Boyet. Good sir, be not offended.
  She is an heir of Falconbridge.   205

Longaville. Nay, my choler° is ended.
  She is a most sweet lady.

Boyet. Not unlike, sir; that may be.

                                      Exit Longaville.

                      Enter Berowne.

Berowne. What's her name in the cap?

Boyet. Rosaline, by good hap.   210

Berowne. Is she wedded or no?

Boyet. To her will, sir, or so.°

Berowne. O, you are welcome, sir! Adieu.

Boyet. Farewell to me, sir, and welcome to you.
                                       Exit Berowne.

Maria. That last is Berowne, the merry madcap lord. 215
  Not a word with him but a jest.

Boyet.   And every jest but a word.

Princess. It was well done of you to take him at his
  word.

Boyet. I was as willing to grapple as he was to board.

Katharine. Two hot sheeps, marry!

Boyet.   And wherefore not ships?
  No sheep, sweet lamb, unless we feed on your lips.   220

Katharine. You sheep, and I pasture. Shall that finish
  the jest?

Boyet. So you grant pasture for me.
                                  [*Offers to kiss her.*]

_____

206 **choler** wrath   212 **or so** something like that

Katharine.   Not so, gentle beast.
  My lips are no common,° though several° they be.

Boyet. Belonging to whom?

Katharine.   To my fortunes and me.

Princess. Good wits will be jangling; but, gentles,
225 agree.
  This civil war of wits were much better used
  On Navarre and his book-men, for here 'tis abused.

Boyet. If my observation (which very seldom lies)
  By the heart's still rhetoric disclosèd with eyes
230 Deceive me not now, Navarre is infected.

Princess. With what?

Boyet. With that which we lovers entitle "affected."°

Princess. Your reason?

Boyet. Why, all his behaviors° did make their retire
235 To the court° of his eye, peeping thorough desire.
  His heart, like an agate° with your print impressed,°
  Proud with his form, in his eye pride expressed.
  His tongue, all impatient to speak and not see,°
  Did stumble with haste in his eyesight to be;
240 All senses to that sense did make their repair,
  To feel only looking on fairest of fair.°
  Methought all his senses were locked in his eye,
  As jewels in crystal for some prince to buy;
  Who, tend'ring° their own worth from where they
    were glassed,°
245 Did point° you to buy them, along as you passed.

---

223 **no common** i.e., not like pasture held in common   223 **several**
two (the word also, in this context, signifies "private property")
232 **affected** impassioned   234 **behaviors** expression of his feelings
235 **court** watch-post   236 **agate** (stone used for the engraving of
images)   236 **impressed** imprinted   238 **His tongue . . . see** his
tongue, vexed at having the power of speaking without having the
power of seeing   241 **To feel . . . fair** (sight is translated into feeling
in regarding her)   244 **tend'ring** offering   244 **glassed** enclosed in
glass   245 **point** urge

His face's own margent did quote such amazes
That all eyes saw his eyes enchanted with gazes.°
I'll give you Aquitaine, and all that is his,
And° you give him for my sake but one loving kiss.

Princess. Come to our pavilion. Boyet is disposed.   250

Boyet. But to speak that in words which his eye hath
disclosed.
I only have made a mouth of his eye
By adding a tongue which I know will not lie.

Rosaline. Thou art an old love-monger, and speakest
skillfully.

Maria. He is Cupid's grandfather, and learns news of
him.   255

Katharine. Then was Venus like her mother, for her
father is but grim.

Boyet. Do you hear, my mad wenches?

Rosaline.   No.

Boyet.   What then? Do you see?

Rosaline. Ay, our way to be gone.

Boyet.   You are too hard for me.
                                   Exeunt omnes.°

246–47 **His face's . . . gazes** i.e., the amazement in Navarre's face
drew attention, like comments in a book's margin, to the love in his
eyes   249 **And** if   258s.d. **omnes** all (Latin)

[ACT 3

Scene 1. *The park.*]

Enter [Armado, the] Braggart, and [Moth,] his Boy.

Armado. Warble, child, make passionate my sense of
hearing.

Moth. [*Sings.*] Concolinel.°

Armado. Sweet air! Go, tenderness of years,° take
5   this key, give enlargement° to the swain, bring him
festinately° hither. I must employ him in a letter
to my love.

Moth. Master, will you win your love with a French
brawl?°

10 *Armado.* How meanest thou? Brawling in French?

Moth. No, my complete master; but to jig off a tune
at the tongue's end, canary to it° with your feet,
humor it with turning up your eyelids, sigh a note
and sing a note, sometime through the throat as if
15   you swallowed love with singing love, sometime
through the nose as if you snuffed up love by smelling love, with your hat penthouse-like o'er the shop

---

3.1.3 **Concolinel** (perhaps the name of a song) 4 **tenderness of
years** (affected talk for "young fellow") 5 **enlargement** freedom
6 **festinately** quickly 8–9 **French brawl** French dance 12 **canary
to it** dance in a lively way

of your eyes, with your arms crossed° on your
thin-belly doublet° like a rabbit on a spit, or your
hands in your pocket like a man after the old paint-   20
ing; and keep not too long in one tune, but a snip°
and away. These are complements,° these are humors, these betray nice wenches (that would be
betrayed without these), and make them men of
note—do you note me?—that most are affected   25
to° these.

Armado. How hast thou purchased this experience?

Moth. By my penny of observation.

Armado. But O—but O—

Moth. "The hobby-horse is forgot."°   30

Armado. Call'st thou my love "hobby-horse"?

Moth. No, master. The hobby-horse is but a colt, and
your love perhaps a hackney.° But have you forgot your love?

Armado. Almost I had.   35

Moth. Negligent student, learn her by heart.

Armado. By heart, and in heart, boy.

Moth. And out of heart, master. All those three I will
prove.

Armado. What wilt thou prove?   40

Moth. A man, if I live; and this, by, in, and without,
upon the instant. By heart you love her, because
your heart cannot come by her; in heart you love
her, because your heart is in love with her; and
out of heart you love her, being out of heart that   45
you cannot enjoy her.

18 **arms crossed** (a sign of melancholy) 19 **thin-belly doublet**
garment unpadded in the lower part (across your thin belly) 21 **snip**
snatch 22 **complements** accompaniments 25–26 **affected to** taken
with 30 **"The hobby-horse is forgot"** (perhaps a phrase from an
old song) 32–33 **hobby-horse, colt, hackney** (slang words for
"whore")

Armado. I am all these three.

Moth. [*Aside*] And three times as much more, and yet nothing at all.

50 *Armado.* Fetch hither the swain. He must carry me a letter.

Moth. A message well sympathized°—a horse to be ambassador for an ass.

Armado. Ha, ha, what sayest thou?

55 *Moth.* Marry, sir, you must send the ass upon the horse, for he is very slow-gaited. But I go.

Armado. The way is but short. Away!

Moth. As swift as lead, sir.

Armado. The meaning, pretty ingenious?
60   Is not lead a metal heavy, dull, and slow?

Moth. Minime,° honest master; or rather, master, no.

Armado. I say, lead is slow.

Moth.   You are too swift, sir, to say so.
      Is that lead slow which is fired from a gun?

Armado. Sweet smoke of rhetoric!
65   He reputes me a cannon; and the bullet, that's he:
      I shoot thee at the swain.

Moth.   Thump, then, and I flee.
                              [*Exit.*]

Armado. A most acute juvenal,° voluble and free of grace!
      By thy favor, sweet welkin,° I must sigh in thy face:
      Most rude melancholy, valor gives thee place.°
70   My herald is returned.

52 **well sympathized** in proper accord   61 **Minime** by no means (Latin)   67 **juvenal** (in two senses) young fellow, satirist   68 **welkin** heaven   69 **gives thee place** gives place to you

Enter [Moth, the] Page and [Costard, the] Clown.

Moth. A wonder, master! Here's a costard° broken
in a shin.

Armado. Some enigma, some riddle. Come, thy
l'envoy°—begin.

Costard. No egma, no riddle, no l'envoy; no salve°
in the mail,° sir. O, sir, plantain,° a plain plantain.
No l'envoy, no l'envoy, no salve, sir, but a plantain.   75

Armado. By virtue, thou enforcest laughter; thy silly
thought, my spleen;° the heaving of my lungs pro-
vokes me to ridiculous smiling. O, pardon me, my
stars! Doth the inconsiderate° take salve for
l'envoy, and the word l'envoy for a salve?   80

Moth. Do the wise think them other? Is not l'envoy
a salve?

Armado. No, page; it is an epilogue, or discourse to
make plain
Some obscure precedence° that hath tofore been
sain.°
I will example it: 85
        The fox, the ape, and the humble-bee
        Were still at odds, being but three.
There's the moral. Now the l'envoy.

Moth. I will add the l'envoy. Say the moral again.

Armado. The fox, the ape, and the humble-bee   90
        Were still at odds, being but three.

Moth.   Until the goose came out of door,
        And stayed the odds by adding four.°

---

71 **costard** apple, or head   72 **l'envoy** words ending a composition
by way of leave-taking   73 **salve** (with a pun on *salve*, the Latin
word for "salute")   74 **mail** bag, container   74 **plantain** tree whose
leaves were used for healing   77 **spleen** mirth   79 **inconsiderate**
unthinking   84 **precedence** preceding statement   84 **tofore been
sain** been said before   93 **stayed . . . four** turned them into evens
by adding a fourth

Now will I begin your moral, and do you follow
95   with my l'envoy.
        The fox, the ape, and the humble-bee
        Were still at odds, being but three.

Armado. Until the goose came out of door,
        Staying the odds by adding four.

100 *Moth.* A good l'envoy, ending in the goose. Would
    you desire more?

Costard. The boy hath sold him a bargain,° a goose
    —that's flat.
    Sir, your pennyworth is good, and° your goose be
    fat.
    To sell a bargain well is as cunning as fast and
    loose.°
105   Let me see: a fat l'envoy—ay, that's a fat goose.

Armado. Come hither, come hither. How did this
    argument begin?

Moth. By saying that a costard was broken in a shin.
    Then called you for the l'envoy.

Costard. True, and I for a plantain; thus came your
    argument in;
    Then the boy's fat l'envoy, the goose that you
110   bought,
    And he ended the market.

Armado. But tell me, how was there a costard broken
    in a shin?

Moth. I will tell you sensibly.°

115 *Costard.* Thou hast no feeling of it, Moth. I will speak
    that l'envoy:
    I, Costard, running out, that was safely within,
    Fell over the threshold and broke my shin.

Armado. We will talk no more of this matter.

120 *Costard.* Till there be more matter° in the shin.

102 **sold him a bargain** made a fool of him 103 **and** if 104 **fast
and loose** cheating 114 **sensibly** with feeling 120 **matter** pus

Armado. Sirrah Costard, I will enfranchise° thee.

Costard. O, marry me to one Frances! I smell some
l'envoy, some goose, in this.

Armado. By my sweet soul, I mean setting thee at
liberty, enfreedoming thy person. Thou wert im-   125
mured, restrained, captivated, bound.

Costard. True, true, and now you will be my purga-
tion and let me loose.

Armado. I give thee thy liberty, set thee from dur-
ance, and in lieu thereof, impose on thee nothing   130
but this. [*Gives a letter.*] Bear this significant° to
the country maid Jaquenetta. [*Gives a coin.*] There
is remuneration; for the best ward° of mine honor
is rewarding my dependents. Moth, follow.

Moth. Like the sequel, I. Signior Costard, adieu.   135
                      Exit [*Armado, followed by Moth*].

Costard. My sweet ounce of man's flesh, my incony°
Jew!—Now will I look to his remuneration. Remuneration? O that's the Latin word for three farthings. Three farthings—remuneration. "What's the
price of this inkle?"° "One penny." "No, I'll give   140
you a remuneration." Why, it carries it! Remuneration! Why, it is a fairer name than French
crown.° I will never buy and sell out of this word.

                      Enter Berowne.

Berowne. O my good knave Costard, exceedingly well
met.   145

Costard. Pray you, sir, how much carnation° ribbon
may a man buy for a remuneration?

Berowne. O, what is a remuneration?

---

121 **enfranchise** set free   131 **significant** letter   133 **ward** protection
136 **incony** darling   140 **inkle** band of linen   142–43 **French crown**
(in two senses: a coin, and the baldness caused by syphilis, the so-
called "French disease")   146 **carnation** flesh-colored

Costard. Marry, sir, halfpenny farthing.

150 *Berowne.* O, why then, three-farthing-worth of silk.

Costard. I thank your worship. God be wi' you!

Berowne. O stay, slave, I must employ thee.
As thou wilt win my favor, good my knave,
Do one thing for me that I shall entreat.

155 *Costard.* When would you have it done, sir?

Berowne. O, this afternoon.

Costard. Well, I will do it, sir. Fare you well.

Berowne. O, thou knowest not what it is.

Costard. I shall know, sir, when I have done it.

160 *Berowne.* Why, villain, thou must know first.

Costard. I will come to your worship tomorrow morning.

Berowne. It must be done this afternoon. Hark, slave,
it is but this:
165 The princess comes to hunt here in the park,
And in her train there is a gentle lady;
When tongues speak sweetly, then they name her
name,
And Rosaline they call her. Ask for her,
And to her white hand see thou do commend
This sealed-up counsel. [*Gives him a letter and a*
170 *shilling.*] There's thy guerdon.° Go.

Costard. Gardon, O sweet gardon! Better than remuneration—a 'leven-pence farthing better. Most
sweet gardon! I will do it, sir, in print.° Gardon!
Remuneration!   *Exit.*

175 *Berowne.* O, and I, forsooth, in love!
I, that have been love's whip,
A very beadle° to a humorous sigh,

170 **guerdon** reward   173 **in print** most carefully   177 **beadle** parish constable

A critic, nay, a night-watch constable,
A domineering pedant o'er the boy,
Than whom no mortal so magnificent!   180
This wimpled,° whining, purblind,° wayward boy,
This senior-junior, giant-dwarf, Dan° Cupid,
Regent of love-rhymes, lord of folded arms,
Th' anointed sovereign of sighs and groans,
Liege° of all loiterers and malcontents,   185
Dread prince of plackets,° king of codpieces,°
Sole imperator and great general
Of trotting paritors°—O my little heart!—
And I to be a corporal of his field,°
And wear his colors like a tumbler's° hoop!   190
What? I love? I sue? I seek a wife?
A woman that is like a German clock,
Still a-repairing, ever out of frame,°
And never going aright, being a watch,
But being watched that it may still go right!   195
Nay, to be perjured, which is worst of all;
And, among three, to love the worst of all,
A whitely° wanton with a velvet brow,
With two pitch balls stuck in her face for eyes.
Ay, and, by heaven, one that will do the deed,°   200
Though Argus° were her eunuch and her guard!
And I to sigh for her, to watch for her,
To pray for her! Go to, it is a plague
That Cupid will impose for my neglect
Of his almighty dreadful little might.   205
Well, I will love, write, sigh, pray, sue, groan.
Some men must love my lady, and some Joan.

                                        [*Exit.*]

_____

181 **wimpled** covered with a muffler   181 **purblind** completely blind
182 **Dan** ("don," a derivation of *dominus*, lord)   185 **Liege** lord
186 **plackets** slits in petticoats (vulgar term for women)   186 **codpieces** cloth covering the opening in men's breeches   188 **paritors**
(officers of the Ecclesiastical Court who serve summonses for certain, often sexual, offenses)   189 **corporal of his field** aide to a
general   190 **tumbler's** acrobat's   193 **frame** order   198 **whitely**
pale   200 **do the deed** perform the act of coition   201 **Argus** (ancient mythological being with a hundred eyes)

[ACT 4

Scene 1. *The park.*]

*Enter the Princess, a Forester, her Ladies,
and her Lords.*

Princess. Was that the king, that spurred his horse so
    hard
  Against the steep uprising of the hill?

Forester. I know not, but I think it was not he.

Princess. Whoe'er 'a° was, 'a showed a mounting
    mind.°
5   Well, lords, today we shall have our dispatch;
  On Saturday we will return to France.
  Then, forester, my friend, where is the bush
  That we must stand and play the murderer in?

Forester. Hereby, upon the edge of yonder coppice,°
10   A stand where you may make the fairest shoot.

Princess. I thank my beauty, I am fair that shoot,
  And thereupon thou speak'st the fairest shoot.

Forester. Pardon me, madam, for I meant not so.

Princess. What, what? First praise me, and again say
    no?
15   O short-lived pride! Not fair? Alack for woe!

Forester. Yes, madam, fair.

4.1.4 **'a** he   4 **mounting mind** lofty spirit (with pun on "mountain")
9 **coppice** undergrowth of small trees

Princess.   Nay, never paint° me now!
Where fair is not, praise cannot mend the brow.°
Here, good my glass,° take this for telling true—
                                          [*giving him money*]
Fair payment for foul words is more than due.

Forester. Nothing but fair is that which you inherit.   20

Princess. See, see—my beauty will be saved by
    merit!°
O heresy in fair,° fit for these days!
A giving hand, though foul, shall have fair praise.
But come, the bow! Now mercy goes to kill,°
And shooting well is then accounted ill.   25
Thus will I save my credit in the shoot:
Not wounding, pity would not let me do 't;
If wounding, then it was to show my skill,
That more for praise than purpose meant to kill.
And out of question so it is sometimes,   30
Glory° grows guilty of detested crimes,
When, for fame's sake, for praise, an outward part,
We bend to that the working of the heart;
As I for praise alone now seek to spill
The poor deer's blood that my heart means no ill.   35

Boyet. Do not curst° wives hold that self-sovereignty
Only for praise sake, when they strive to be
Lords o'er their lords?

Princess. Only for praise, and praise we may afford
To any lady that subdues a lord.   40

                Enter [*Costard, the*] *Clown.*

Boyet. Here comes a member of the commonwealth.°

---

16 **paint** flatter   17 **mend the brow** make the brow more beautiful
18 **good my glass** my fine mirror   21 **saved by merit** saved by what
I truly deserve   22 **heresy in fair** heresy with respect to beauty
24 **mercy goes to kill** (the merciful huntsman goes forth to kill—
instead of leaving the prey wounded—but such killing is not well
regarded)   31 **Glory** i.e., ambition for glory   36 **curst** peevish
41 **member of the commonwealth** i.e., one of our group

Costard. God dig-you-den° all! Pray you, which is the head lady?

Princess. Thou shalt know her, fellow, by the rest
45   that have no heads.

Costard. Which is the greatest lady, the highest?

Princess. The thickest and the tallest.

Costard. The thickest and the tallest—it is so. Truth is truth.
     And° your waist, mistress, were as slender as my
50   wit,
     One o' these maids' girdles for your waist should be fit.
     Are not you the chief woman? You are the thickest here.

Princess. What's your will, sir? What's your will?

Costard. I have a letter from Monsieur Berowne to one Lady Rosaline.

Princess. O thy letter, thy letter! He's a good friend
55   of mine.
     Stand aside, good bearer. Boyet, you can carve°—
     Break up this capon.°

Boyet.   I am bound to serve.
     This letter is mistook; it importeth° none here.
     It is writ to Jaquenetta.

Princess.   We will read it, I swear.
     Break the neck° of the wax, and every one give
60   ear.

Boyet. (*Reads.*) "By heaven, that thou art fair is most infallible; true that thou art beauteous; truth itself that thou art lovely. More fairer than fair, beautiful than beauteous, truer than truth itself,

42 **God dig-you-den** God give you good evening   50 **And** if   56 **carve** (with pun on the sense "flirt")   57 **Break up this capon** (1) carve this chicken (2) open this love-letter   58 **importeth** concerns   60 **Break the neck** (still referring to the capon)

have commiseration on thy heroical vassal. The 65
magnanimous and most illustrate° king Cophetua
set eye upon the pernicious and indubitate° beggar
Zenelophon,° and he it was that might rightly say
veni, vidi, vici; which to annothanize° in the vulgar
(O base and obscure vulgar!) *videlicet,°* he came, 70
saw, and overcame. He came, one; saw, two;
overcame, three. Who came? The king. Why did
he come? To see. Why did he see? To overcome.
To whom came he? To the beggar. What saw he?
The beggar. Who overcame he? The beggar. The 75
conclusion is victory. On whose side? The king's.
The captive is enriched. On whose side? The beggar's. The catastrophe is a nuptial. On whose side?
The king's. No—on both in one, or one in both.
I am the king, for so stands the comparison, thou 80
the beggar, for so witnesseth thy lowliness. Shall
I command thy love? I may. Shall I enforce thy
love? I could. Shall I entreat thy love? I will. What
shalt thou exchange for rags? Robes. For tittles?°
Titles. For thyself? Me. Thus, expecting thy reply, 85
I profane my lips on thy foot, my eyes on thy pic-
ture, and my heart on thy every part.
    Thine in the dearest design of industry,°
                Don Adriano de Armado.
Thus dost thou hear the Nemean lion° roar 90
   'Gainst thee, thou lamb, that standest as his prey.
Submissive fall his princely feet before,
   And he from forage° will incline to play.
But if thou strive, poor soul, what art thou then?
Food for his rage, repasture° for his den." 95

Princess. What plume of feathers is he that indited°
    this letter?

---

66 **illustrate** illustrious   67 **indubitate** undoubted   68 **Zenelophon**
(character in the ballad of King Cophetua and the Beggar)   69 **an-
nothanize** anatomize (or a mock-Latin word to mean "annotate")
70 **videlicet** namely (Latin)   84 **tittles** small jottings in ink   88 **in-
dustry** faithful service   90 **Nemean lion** (lion killed by Hercules)
93 **from forage** turning away from feeding   95 **repasture** food
96 **indited** wrote

What vane?° What weathercock?° Did you ever
hear better?

Boyet. I am much deceived but I remember the style.

Princess. Else your memory is bad, going o'er it ere-
while.

Boyet. This Armado is a Spaniard that keeps here in
100 court;
A phantasime,° a Monarcho,° and one that makes
sport
To the prince and his book-mates.

Princess.   Thou fellow, a word.
Who gave thee this letter?

Costard.   I told you—my lord.

Princess. To whom shouldst thou give it?

Costard.   From my lord to my lady.

105 *Princess.* From which lord to which lady?

Costard. From my lord Berowne, a good master of
mine,
To a lady of France that he called Rosaline.

Princess. Thou hast mistaken° his letter. Come, lords,
away.
Here, sweet, put up this; 'twill be thine another day.
    [*Exeunt Princess and Train. Boyet remains.*]

Boyet. Who is the suitor?° Who is the suitor?

110 *Rosaline.*   Shall I teach you to know?

Boyet. Ay, my continent° of beauty.

Rosaline.   Why, she that bears the bow.
Finely put off!°

---

97 **vane** weather-vane 97 **weathercock** ostentatious thing 101
phantasime person of wild imaginings 101 **Monarcho** (nickname of
a crazy Italian at the court of Elizabeth) 108 **mistaken** taken to
the wrong person 110 **suitor** (pronounced "shooter") 111 **continent** container 112 **put off** repulsed

Boyet. My lady goes to kill horns, but, if thou marry,
 Hang me by the neck if horns that year miscarry.°
 Finely put on!°   *115*

Rosaline. Well then, I am the shooter.

Boyet.   And who is your deer?

Rosaline. If we choose by the horns, yourself. Come
 not near.
 Finely put on indeed!

Maria. You still wrangle with her, Boyet, and she
 strikes at the brow.°

Boyet. But she herself is hit lower. Have I hit her
 now?   *120*

Rosaline. Shall I come upon thee with an old saying
 that was a man when King Pepin of France was a
 little boy, as touching the hit it?°

Boyet. So I may answer thee with one as old, that was
 a woman when Queen Guinever of Britain was a *125*
 little wench, as touching the hit it.

Rosaline. "Thou canst not hit it, hit it, hit it,
  Thou canst not hit it, my good man.

Boyet.   "And° I cannot, cannot, cannot,
  And I cannot, another can."   *130*
      Exit [Rosaline with Katharine].

Costard. By my troth, most pleasant, how both did
 fit it!

Maria. A mark marvelous well shot, for they both did
 hit it.

Boyet. A mark! O, mark but that mark!° A mark,
 says my lady!

---

114 **if horns that year miscarry** i.e., if someone is not made a
cuckold 115 **put on** lay on, as a blow 119 **strikes at the brow**
takes careful aim (with an allusion to the cuckold's horns) 123 **hit
it** name of a dance tune (leading to pun on the sense of *hit* = to
copulate) 129 **And** if 133 **mark** (1) target (2) pudend

Let the mark have a prick° in 't, to mete° at if it
may be.

Maria. Wide o' the bow hand!° I' faith, your hand
135   is out.

Costard. Indeed 'a must shoot nearer, or he'll ne'er
hit the clout.°

Boyet. And if my hand be out, then belike your hand
is in.

Costard. Then will she get the upshoot° by cleaving
the pin.°

Maria. Come, come, you talk greasily;° your lips grow
foul.

Costard. She's too hard for you at pricks, sir. Chal-
140   lenge her to bowl.

Boyet. I fear too much rubbing.° Good night, my
good owl.

[Exeunt Boyet and Maria.]

Costard. By my soul, a swain,° a most simple clown!
Lord, lord, how the ladies and I have put him
down!
O' my troth,° most sweet jests, most incony° vul-
gar wit.
When it comes so smoothly off, so obscenely as it
145   were, so fit!
Armado to th' one side—O, a most dainty man!
To see him walk before a lady, and to bear her fan!
To see him kiss his hand, and how most sweetly
'a will swear!

---

134 **prick** mark within the target (with additional bawdy suggestion)
134 **mete** aim   135 **Wide o' the bow hand** far from the target on
the bow-hand side   136 **clout** nail in the center of the target
138 **upshoot** best shot   138 **cleaving the pin** (1) striking the center
of the target (2) causing emission in the male   139 **greasily** in-
decently   141 **rubbing** (bowling balls striking each other; with
sexual innuendo)   142 **swain** herdsman   144 **O' my troth** by my
faith   144 **incony** fine

And his page o' t' other side, that handful of wit,
Ah, heavens, it is a most pathetical nit!°   150

Shout within.

Sola,° sola!   [*Exit.*]

[Scene 2. *The park.*]

Enter Dull, Holofernes the Pedant, and Nathaniel.

Nathaniel. Very reverend sport, truly, and done in
the testimony° of a good conscience.

Holofernes. The deer was, as you know, *sanguis,* in
blood; ripe as the pomewater,° who now hangeth
like a jewel in the ear of *coelo,* the sky, the welkin,   5
the heaven; and anon falleth like a crab° on the
face of *terra,* the soil, the land, the earth.

Nathaniel. Truly, Master Holofernes, the epithets are
sweetly varied, like a scholar at the least. But sir,
I assure ye it was a buck of the first head.°   10

Holofernes. Sir Nathaniel, *haud credo.*°

Dull. 'Twas not a *haud credo,* 'twas a pricket.°

Holofernes. Most barbarous intimation!° Yet a kind
of insinuation, as it were, *in via,* in way, of expli-
cation;° *facere,*° as it were, replication,° or rather,   15
ostentare, to show, as it were, his inclination—after
his undressed, unpolished, uneducated, unpruned,
untrained, or, rather, unlettered, or, ratherest, un-

---

150 **nit** small thing (louse)   151 **Sola** (a hunting cry)   4.2.2 **testi-
mony** approval   4 **pomewater** (variety of a sweet apple)   6 **crab**
crab apple   10 **buck of the first head** full-grown buck   11 **haud
credo** I do not believe it (Latin; in the next line, Dull apparently
takes the words as *old gray doe*)   12 **pricket** two-year-old red deer
13 **intimation** (a pedantic substitute for "insinuation")   14–15 **ex-
plication** explanation   15 **facere** to make   15 **replication** unfold-
ing, revelation

20 confirmed fashion—to insert again my *haud credo*
for a deer.

Dull. I said the deer was not a *haud credo,* 'twas a
pricket.

Holofernes. Twice sod° simplicity, *bis coctus!*°
O thou monster Ignorance, how deformed dost
thou look!

Nathaniel. Sir, he hath never fed of the dainties that
25 are bred in a book.
He hath not eat paper, as it were, he hath not
drunk ink. His intellect is not replenished. He is
only an animal, only sensible in the duller parts.
And such barren plants are set before us that we
thankful should be,
Which we of taste and feeling are, for those parts
30 that do fructify° in us more than he.
For as it would ill become me to be vain, indiscreet, or a fool,
So were there a patch° set on learning, to see him
in a school.
But, *omne bene,*° say I, being of an old father's
mind,
Many can brook° the weather that love not the
wind.

Dull. You two are book-men. Can you tell me by
35 your wit
What was a month old at Cain's birth that's not
five weeks old as yet?

Holofernes. Dictynna,° goodman Dull. Dictynna,
goodman Dull.

Dull. What is Dictynna?

Nathaniel. A title to Phoebe, to Luna, to the moon.

---

23 **Twice sod** soaked twice (again and again)   23 **bis coctus** cooked
twice   30 **fructify** bear fruit   32 **patch** fool   33 **omne bene** all is
well   34 **brook** endure   37 **Dictynna** Diana, the moon

Holofernes. The moon was a month old when Adam   *40*
    was no more,
    And raught° not to five weeks when he came to
    fivescore.
    Th' allusion holds in the exchange.°

Dull. 'Tis true indeed; the collusion° holds in the exchange.

Holofernes. God comfort thy capacity! I say th' allu-   *45*
sion holds in the exchange.

Dull. And I say the pollution holds in the exchange,
for the moon is never but a month old; and I say
beside that 'twas a pricket that the princess killed.

Holofernes. Sir Nathaniel, will you hear an extempo-   *50*
ral° epitaph on the death of the deer? And, to
humor the ignorant, I call the deer the princess
killed, a pricket.

Nathaniel. Perge,° good Master Holofernes, *perge,* so
it shall please you to abrogate scurrility.°   *55*

Holofernes. I will something affect the letter° for it
    argues facility.
    The preyful° princess pierced and pricked a pretty
    pleasing pricket;
    Some say a sore,° but not a sore till now made sore
    with shooting.
    The dogs did yell. Put L° to sore, then sorel° jumps
    from thicket;
    Or pricket, sore, or else sorel. The people fall a
    hooting.   *60*
    If sore be sore, then L to sore makes fifty sores—
    o' sorel.

---

41 **raught** attained   42 **Th' allusion . . . exchange** (the riddle serves
for Adam as well as for Cain)   43 **collusion** (a pedantic misunder-
standing)   50–51 **extemporal** on the spur of the moment   54 **Perge**
continue   55 **abrogate scurrility** put aside foul talk   56 **affect the
letter** alliterate   57 **preyful** killing much prey   58 **sore** four-year-
old buck   59 **L** (the Roman numeral fifty)   59 **sorel** young buck

Of one sore I an hundred make by adding but one
more L.

Nathaniel. A rare talent!°

Dull. If a talent be a claw, look how he claws° him
65   with a talent.

Holofernes. This is a gift that I have, simple, simple;
a foolish extravagant spirit, full of forms, figures,
shapes, objects, ideas, apprehensions, motions, rev-
olutions. These are begot in the ventricle° of mem-
70   ory, nourished in the womb of *pia mater,*° and delivered upon the mellowing of occasion.° But the
gift is good in those in whom it is acute, and I am
thankful for it.

Nathaniel. Sir, I praise the Lord for you, and so may
75   my parishioners, for their sons are well tutored by
you, and their daughters profit very greatly under
you. You are a good member of the commonwealth.

Holofernes. Mehercle,° if their sons be ingenious, they
shall want no instruction; if their daughters be ca-
80   pable, I will put it to them. But *vir sapit qui pauca
loquitur.*° A soul feminine saluteth us.

    Enter Jaquenetta and [Costard,] the Clown.

Jaquenetta. God give you good morrow, Master Parson.

Holofernes. Master Parson, *quasi*° pierce-one? And if
85   one should be pierced, which is the one?

Costard. Marry, Master Schoolmaster, he that is likest
to a hogshead.°

Holofernes. Of piercing a hogshead!° A good luster

---

63 **talent** talon   64 **claws** flatters   69 **ventricle** part of the brain
containing the memory   70 **pia mater** membrane enclosing the
brain   71 **mellowing of occasion** fit time   78 **Mehercle** By Hercules
80–81 **vir . . . loquitur** "the man is wise who speaks little"   84 **quasi**
as if   87 **hogshead** fathead   88 **piercing a hogshead** getting drunk

of conceit° in a turf° of earth, fire enough for a
flint, pearl enough for a swine. 'Tis pretty; it is well.   *90*

Jaquenetta. Good Master Parson, be so good as read
me this letter. It was given me by Costard, and
sent me from Don Armado. I beseech you read it.

*Holofernes. Fauste, precor, gelida quando pecus omne
sub umbra ruminat,*° and so forth. Ah, good old   *95*
Mantuan. I may speak of thee as the traveler doth
of Venice:
>   *Venetia, Venetia,*
>   *Chi non ti vede, non ti pretia.*°
Old Mantuan, old Mantuan! Who understandeth   *100*
thee not, loves thee not. *Ut, re, sol, la, mi, fa.* Under pardon, sir, what are the contents? Or, rather,
as Horace says in his—What, my soul, verses?

Nathaniel. Ay, sir, and very learned.

Holofernes. Let me hear a staff,° a stanze, a verse.   *105*
Lege, domine.°

[*Nathaniel reads.*] "If love make me forsworn, how
    shall I swear to love?
    Ah, never faith could hold if not to beauty
        vowed!
Though to myself forsworn, to thee I'll faithful
        prove;
    Those thoughts to me were oaks, to thee like
        osiers bowed.   *110*
Study his bias leaves° and makes his book thine
        eyes,
    Where all those pleasures live that art would
        comprehend.
If knowledge be the mark, to know thee shall suf-
        fice:

88–89 **luster of conceit** brilliant idea   89 **turf** clod   94–95 **Fauste
. . . ruminat** "I pray thee, Faustus, when all the cattle ruminate
beneath the cool shade" (a quotation from a Latin poem by Mantuan, an Italian Renaissance poet)   98–99 **Venetia . . . pretia** "Venice, Venice, only those who do not see thee do not value thee"
(Italian)   105 **staff** stanza   106 **Lege, domine** read, master   111
Study his bias leaves (the student leaves his favorite studies)

Well learnèd is that tongue that well can thee
    commend,
All ignorant that soul that sees thee without won-
115   der;
    Which is to me some praise, that I thy parts
        admire.
Thy eye Jove's lightning bears, thy voice his dread-
    ful thunder,
    Which, not to anger bent, is music and sweet fire.
Celestial as thou art, O pardon love this wrong,
That sings heaven's praise with such an earthly
120   tongue!"

Holofernes. You find not the apostrophus,° and so
miss the accent. Let me supervise the canzonet.°
Here are only numbers ratified;° but, for the ele-
gancy, facility, and golden cadence of poesy, *caret.*°
125 Ovidius Naso was the man; and why indeed
"Naso"° but for smelling out the odoriferous flowers of fancy, the jerks of invention?° *Imitari*° is
nothing. So doth the hound his master, the ape his
keeper, the tired horse his rider. But, damosella
130 virgin, was this directed to you?

Jaquenetta. Ay, sir, from one Monsieur Berowne, one
of the strange° queen's lords

Holofernes. I will overglance the superscript.° "To
the snow-white hand of the most beauteous Lady
135 Rosaline." I will look again on the intellect° of the
letter for the nomination° of the party writing to
the person written unto. "Your ladyship's, in all
desired employment, Berowne." Sir Nathaniel, this
Berowne is one of the votaries° with the king; and
140 here he hath framed° a letter to a sequent° of the

---

121 **apostrophus** (mark of punctuation taking the place of a vowel
122 **canzonet** song   123 **numbers ratified** rhythm regularized   124
caret it is deficient   126 **Naso** nose   127 **jerks of invention** clever
strokes of wit   127 **Imitari** to imitate   132 **strange** foreign   133
superscript address   135 **intellect** purport   136 **nomination** name
139 **votaries** persons who have taken a vow   140 **framed** devised
140 **sequent** follower

stranger queen's, which accidentally, or by the way
of progression,° hath miscarried. Trip and go,° my
sweet, deliver this paper into the royal hand of the
king; it may concern much. Stay not thy compli-
ment;° I forgive thy duty. Adieu.   *145*

Jaquenetta. Good Costard, go with me. Sir, God save
your life.

Costard. Have with thee, my girl.
                                    Exit [with Jaquenetta].

Nathaniel. Sir, you have done this in the fear of God
very religiously; and as a certain father saith—   *150*

Holofernes. Sir, tell not me of the father, I do fear
colorable colors.° But to return to the verses—did
they please you, Sir Nathaniel?

Nathaniel. Marvelous well for the pen.°

Holofernes. I do dine today at the father's of a certain   *155*
pupil of mine, where, if before repast it shall please
you to gratify the table with a grace, I will, on my
privilege I have with the parents of the foresaid
child or pupil, undertake your *ben venuto;*° where
I will prove those verses to be very unlearned,   *160*
neither savoring of poetry, wit, nor invention. I beseech your society.

Nathaniel. And thank you too, for society (saith the
text) is the happiness of life.

Holofernes. And, certes,° the text most infallibly con-   *165*
cludes it. *[To Dull]* Sir, I do invite you too; you
shall not say me nay. *Pauca verba.*° Away! The
gentles are at their game, and we will to our recreation.   *Exeunt.*

141–42 **by the way of progression** on its way   142 **Trip and go**
(phrase used of a morris dance)   144–45 **Stay not thy compliment**
do not wait on ceremony   152 **colorable colors** plausible excuses
154 **pen** penmanship, or style of writing   159 **ben venuto** welcome
(Italian)   165 **certes** certainly   167 **Pauca verba** few words

[Scene 3. *The park.*]

Enter Berowne with a paper in his hand, alone.

Berowne. The king he is hunting the deer; I am cours-
ing° myself. They have pitched a toil;° I am toiling
in a pitch—pitch that defiles. Defile—a foul word!
Well, set thee down, sorrow, for so they say the
5 fool said, and so say I, and I the fool. Well proved,
wit! By the Lord, this love is as mad as Ajax:°
it kills sheep; it kills me—I a sheep. Well proved
again o' my side! I will not love; if I do, hang me!
I' faith, I will not. O but her eye! By this light, but
10 for her eye, I would not love her—yes, for her two
eyes. Well, I do nothing in the world but lie, and
lie in my throat. By heaven, I do love, and it hath
taught me to rhyme, and to be melancholy; and here
is part of my rhyme, and here my melancholy. Well,
15 she hath one o' my sonnets already. The clown
bore it, the fool sent it, and the lady hath it—
sweet clown, sweeter fool, sweetest lady! By the
world, I would not care a pin if the other three
were in. Here comes one with a paper. God give
20 him grace to groan!   *He stands aside.*

The King ent'reth [with a paper].

King. Ay me!

Berowne. [*Aside*] Shot, by heaven! Proceed, sweet
Cupid. Thou hast thumped him with thy bird-bolt°
under the left pap.° In faith, secrets!

4.3.1–2 **coursing** chasing   2 **pitched a toil** set a snare   6 **Ajax**
(ancient Greek warrior who, going mad, killed sheep, believing
them his enemies)   23 **bird-bolt** arrow for shooting birds   24 **pap**
breast

King. [*Reads.*] "So sweet a kiss the golden sun gives
    not   25
  To those fresh morning drops upon the rose,
As thy eye-beams when their fresh rays have smote
  The night of dew that on my cheeks down flows.
Nor shines the silver moon one half so bright
  Through the transparent bosom of the deep   30
As doth thy face, through tears of mine, give light.
  Thou shin'st in every tear that I do weep;
No drop but as a coach doth carry thee.
  So ridest thou triumphing in my woe.
Do but behold the tears that swell in me,   35
  And they thy glory through my grief will show.
But do not love thyself—then thou will keep
My tears for glasses° and still make me weep.
O queen of queens, how far dost thou excel
No thought can think, nor tongue of mortal tell!"   40
How shall she know my griefs? I'll drop the paper.
Sweet leaves, shade folly. Who is he comes here?

Enter Longaville [*with a paper*]. *The King steps aside.*

What, Longaville, and reading! Listen, ear.

Berowne. Now, in thy likeness, one more fool appear!

Longaville. Ay me, I am forsworn.   45

Berowne. Why, he comes in like a perjure,° wearing
  papers.°

King. In love, I hope—sweet fellowship in shame!

Berowne. One drunkard loves another of the name.

Longaville. Am I the first that have been perjured so?   50

Berowne. I could put thee in comfort—not by two
    that I know.

---

38 **glasses** mirrors 46 **perjure** perjurer 46 **wearing papers** (a punishment for perjury, to wear a paper on the head as a public shame;
presumably Longaville has a sonnet in his hatband)

Thou makest the triumviry,° the corner-cap° of
    society,
The shape of Love's Tyburn,° that hangs up sim-
    plicity.

Longaville. I fear these stubborn lines lack power to
    move.
55 O sweet Maria, empress of my love!
These numbers will I tear, and write in prose.

Berowne. O, rhymes are guards° on wanton Cupid's
    hose;
Disfigure not his shop.°

Longaville.   This same shall go.

He reads the sonnet.

"Did not the heavenly rhetoric of thine eye,
60   'Gainst whom the world cannot hold argument,
Persuade my heart to this false perjury?
      Vows for thee broke deserve not punishment.
A woman I forswore, but I will prove,
      Thou being a goddess, I forswore not thee.
65 My vow was earthly, thou a heavenly love;
      Thy grace, being gained, cures all disgrace in me.
Vows are but breath, and breath a vapor is;
      Then thou, fair sun, which on my earth dost
        shine,
Exhal'st this vapor-vow; in thee it is.
70   If broken then, it is no fault of mine;
If by me broke, what fool is not so wise
To lose an oath to win a paradise?"

Berowne. This is the liver-vein,° which makes flesh a
    deity,
A green goose° a goddess. Pure, pure idolatry.

52 **triumviry** triumvirate 52 **corner-cap** cap with corners (worn
by divines, judges, and scholars) 53 **Tyburn** place of execution
(the triangular-shaped gallows bears a resemblance to a corner-cap)
57 **guards** ornaments 58 **shop** organ of generation, or codpiece
73 **liver-vein** vein coming from the liver (the place of the origin of
love) 74 **green goose** goose born the previous autumn (and so, a
young girl)

God amend us, God amend! We are much out o'
th' way.°   75

Enter Dumaine [with a paper].

Longaville. By whom shall I send this?—Company?
Stay.   [*Steps aside.*]

Berowne. All hid,° all hid—an old infant play.
Like a demi-god here sit I in the sky,
And wretched fools' secrets heedfully o'er-eye.
More sacks to the mill°—O heavens, I have my
wish!   80
Dumaine transformed! Four woodcocks° in a dish!

Dumaine. O most divine Kate!

Berowne. O most profane coxcomb!

Dumaine. By heaven, the wonder in a mortal eye!

Berowne. By earth, she is not, Corporal.° There you
lie!   85

Dumaine. Her amber hairs for foul hath amber
quoted.°

Berowne. An amber-colored raven was well noted.

Dumaine. As upright as the cedar.

Berowne.   Stoop,° I say—
Her shoulder is with child.°

Dumaine.   As fair as day.

Berowne. Ay, as some days; but then no sun must
shine.   90

Dumaine. O that I had my wish!

75 **out o' th' way** on the wrong track   77 **All hid** (formula from a
child's game)   80 **More sacks to the mill** more yet to do   81 **wood-
cocks** silly birds   85 **Corporal** officer (with a pun on the word for
bodily, human)   86 **Her amber . . . quoted** her amber-colored hair
made amber look ugly by contrast   88 **Stoop** stooped   89 **with
child** i.e., rounded

Longaville.   And I had mine!

King. And I mine too, good Lord!

Berowne. Amen, so I had mine! Is not that a good
     word?

Dumaine. I would forget her, but a fever she
95   Reigns in my blood, and will rememb'red be.

Berowne. A fever in your blood? Why, then incision
     Would let her out in saucers. Sweet misprision!°

Dumaine. Once more I'll read the ode that I have writ.

Berowne. Once more I'll mark how love can vary wit.

               Dumaine reads his sonnet.

100 *Dumaine.* "On a day—alack the day!—
               Love, whose month is ever May,
               Spied a blossom passing fair
               Playing in the wanton air.
               Through the velvet leaves the wind,
105   All unseen, can passage find;
               That the lover, sick to death,
               Wished himself the heaven's breath.
               Air, quoth he, thy cheeks may blow;
               Air, would I might triumph so!
110   But, alack, my hand is sworn
               Ne'er to pluck thee from thy thorn.
               Vow, alack, for youth unmeet,
               Youth so apt to pluck a sweet!
               Do not call it sin in me,
115   That I am forsworn for thee;
               Thou for whom Jove would swear
               Juno but an Ethiop° were,
               And deny himself for Jove,
               Turning mortal for thy love."
120   This will I send, and something else more plain,
         That shall express my true love's fasting pain.°

94 **misprision** mistake   117 **Ethiop** black person   121 **fasting pain**
pain caused by deprivation

O, would the king, Berowne, and Longaville
Were lovers too! Ill, to example ill,
Would from my forehead wipe a perjured note,°
For none offend where all alike do dote.   125

Longaville. [*Advancing*] Dumaine, thy love is far from
    charity,
That in love's grief desir'st society.
You may look pale, but I should blush, I know,
To be o'erheard and taken napping so.

King. [*Advancing*] Come, sir, you blush! As his your
    case is such;   130
You chide at him, offending twice as much.
You do not love Maria! Longaville
Did never sonnet for her sake compile,
Nor never lay his wreathèd arms athwart
His loving bosom to keep down his heart.   135
I have been closely shrouded in this bush,
And marked you both, and for you both did blush.
I heard your guilty rhymes, observed your fashion,
Saw sighs reek° from you, noted well your passion.
"Ay me!" says one; "O Jove!" the other cries.   140
One, her hairs were gold; crystal, the other's eyes.
[*To Longaville*] You would for paradise break faith
    and troth,
[*To Dumaine*] And Jove, for your love, would in-
    fringe an oath.
What will Berowne say when that he shall hear
Faith infringèd, which such zeal did swear?   145
How will he scorn, how will he spend his wit!
How will he triumph, leap and laugh at it!
For all the wealth that ever I did see,
I would not have him know so much by me.°

Berowne. [*Advancing*] Now step I forth to whip hy-
    pocrisy.   150
Ah, good my liege, I pray thee pardon me.
Good heart, what grace hast thou, thus to reprove

123–24 **Ill . . . note** wickedness, not liking to make itself an example,
would remove from me the papers I bear as the punishment for
perjury   139 **reek** exhale   149 **by me** concerning me

These worms for loving, that art most in love?
Your eyes do make no coaches;° in your tears
155 There is no certain princess that appears.
You'll not be perjured, 'tis a hateful thing.
Tush, none but minstrels like of sonneting!
But are you not ashamed? Nay, are you not,
All three of you, to be thus much o'ershot?°
160 You found his mote, the king your mote did see;
But I a beam° do find in each of three.
O what a scene of fool'ry have I seen,
Of sighs, of groans, of sorrow, and of teen!°
O me, with what strict patience have I sat,
165 To see a king transformèd to a gnat!
To see great Hercules whipping a gig,°
And profound Solomon to tune a jig,
And Nestor° play at push-pin° with the boys,
And critic Timon° laugh at idle toys!
170 Where lies thy grief? O, tell me, good Dumaine.
And, gentle Longaville, where lies thy pain?
And where my liege's? All about the breast.
A caudle,° ho!

King.   Too bitter is thy jest.
Are we betrayed thus to thy over-view?

175 *Berowne.* Not you by me, but I betrayed to you;
I that am honest, I that hold it sin
To break the vow I am engagèd in,
I am betrayed by keeping company
With men like you, men of inconstancy.
180 When shall you see me write a thing in rhyme?
Or groan for Joan? Or spend a minute's time
In pruning° me? When shall you hear that I
Will praise a hand, a foot, a face, an eye,
A gait, a state, a brow, a breast, a waist,
A leg, a limb—

154 **coaches** (for love to ride in—as in line 33)   159 **o'ershot** wide
of the mark   160–61 **mote . . . beam** (the contrast is between small
and large faults; see Matthew 7:3–5; Luke 6:41–42)   163 **teen** grief
166 **gig** top   168 **Nestor** ancient Greek sage   168 **push-pin** child's
game   169 **critic Timon** Greek misanthrope   173 **caudle** healing drink
for an invalid   182 **pruning** preening

King. 　　　　　　Soft!° Whither away so fast?　　　*185*
　A true° man or a thief, that gallops so?

Berowne. I post° from love. Good lover, let me go.

　　　Enter Jaquenetta and [Costard, the] Clown.

Jaquenetta. God bless the king!

King. 　　　　　　What present hast thou there?

Costard. Some certain treason.

King. 　　　　　　What makes° treason here?

Costard. Nay, it makes nothing, sir.

King. 　　　　　　If it mar nothing neither,　*190*
　The treason and you go in peace away together.

Jaquenetta. I beseech your Grace let this letter be read.
　Our parson misdoubts° it; 'twas treason, he said.

King. Berowne, read it over.
　　　　　　　He [Berowne] reads the letter.
　Where hadst thou it?　　　　　　　　　*195*

Jaquenetta. Of Costard.

King. Where hadst thou it?

Costard. Of Dun Adramadio, Dun Adramadio.
　　　　　　　　　[Berowne tears the letter.]

King. How now, what is in you? Why dost thou tear it?

Berowne. A toy, my liege, a toy. Your Grace needs
　not fear it.　　　　　　　　　　　　　*200*

Longaville. It did move him to passion, and therefore
　let's hear it.

Dumaine. [*Gathering up the pieces*] It is Berowne's
　writing, and here is his name.

---

185 **Soft** wait a minute (an exclamation)　186 **true** honest　187 **post**
ride in haste　189 **makes** does　193 **misdoubts** mistrusts

Berowne. [*To Costard*] Ah, you whoreson loggerhead,° you were born to do me shame!
  Guilty, my lord, guilty. I confess, I confess.

205 *King.* What?

Berowne. That you three fools lacked me fool to make
   up the mess.°
  He, he, and you—and you, my liege, and I,
  Are pick-purses in love, and we deserve to die.
  O dismiss this audience, and I shall tell you more.

Dumaine. Now the number is even.

210 *Berowne.*   True, true, we are four.
  Will these turtles° be gone?

King.   Hence, sirs, away!

Costard. Walk aside the true folk, and let the traitors
   stay.   [*Exeunt Costard and Jaquenetta.*]

Berowne. Sweet lords, sweet lovers, O let us embrace!
  As true we are as flesh and blood can be.
215 The sea will ebb and flow, heaven show his face;
  Young blood doth not obey an old decree.
  We cannot cross° the cause why we were born;
  Therefore of all hands must we be forsworn.

King. What, did these rent° lines show some love of
   thine?

Berowne. Did they? quoth you. Who sees the heavenly
220   Rosaline,
  That, like a rude and savage man of Inde
  At the first op'ning of the gorgeous East,
  Bows not his vassal head and, strooken blind,
  Kisses the base ground with obedient breast?
225 What peremptory° eagle-sighted eye
  Dares look upon the heaven of her brow
  That is not blinded by her majesty?

203 **whoreson loggerhead** rascally blockhead   206 **mess** party of
four at table   211 **turtles** turtledoves, lovers   217 **cross** thwart
219 **rent** damaged   225 **peremptory** resolute

King. What zeal, what fury, hath inspired thee now?
  My love, her mistress, is a gracious moon;
  She, an attending star, scarce seen a light.   230

Berowne. My eyes are then no eyes, nor I Berowne.
  O, but for my love, day would turn to night!
  Of all complexions the culled sovereignty°
  Do meet, as at a fair, in her fair cheek,
  Where several worthies° make one dignity,   235
  Where nothing wants° that want itself doth seek.
  Lend me the flourish° of all gentle tongues—
  Fie, painted rhetoric!° O, she needs it not!
  To things of sale° a seller's praise belongs:
  She passes praise; then praise too short doth blot.   240
  A withered hermit, five-score winters worn,
  Might shake off fifty, looking in her eye.
  Beauty doth varnish° age as if new-born,
  And gives the crutch the cradle's infancy.
  O, 'tis the sun that maketh all things shine.   245

King. By heaven, thy love is black as ebony!

Berowne. Is ebony like her? O wood divine!
  A wife of such wood were felicity.
  O, who can give an oath? Where is a book?
  That I may swear beauty doth beauty lack   250
  If that she learn not of her eye to look.
  No face is fair that is not full so black.

King. O paradox! Black is the badge of hell,
  The hue of dungeons, and the school of night;°
  And beauty's crest becomes the heavens well.°   255

Berowne. Devils soonest tempt, resembling spirits of
  light.

---

233 **culled sovereignty** chosen as the best   235 **worthies** good qualities 236 **wants** lacks 237 **flourish** adornment 238 **painted rhetoric** extravagant speech 239 **of sale** for sale 243 **varnish** lend
freshness 254 **school of night** (some editors emend "school" to
"suit" or to "shade," but perhaps the term means a place for learning dark things) 255 **beauty's . . . well** true beauty, which is bright,
is heavenly, but if blackness is taken as the sign of beauty, it would
be ironic to link beauty with heaven, which is the source of light

　　　　O, if in black my lady's brows be decked,
　　　　It mourns that painting and usurping° hair
　　　　Should ravish doters with a false aspect;°
260　　　And therefore is she born to make black fair.
　　　　Her favor° turns the fashion of the days,
　　　　For native blood° is counted painting now;
　　　　And therefore red that would avoid dispraise
　　　　Paints itself black to imitate her brow.

Dumaine. To look like her are chimney-sweepers
265　　　black.

Longaville. And since her time are colliers° counted
　　　　bright.

King. And Ethiops of their sweet complexion crack.°

Dumaine. Dark needs no candles now, for dark is
　　　　light.

Berowne. Your mistresses dare never come in rain,
270　　　For fear their colors should be washed away.

King. 'Twere good yours did; for, sir, to tell you plain,
　　　　I'll find a fairer face not washed today.

Berowne. I'll prove her fair or talk till doomsday here.

King. No devil will fright thee then so much as she.

275 *Dumaine.* I never knew man hold vile stuff so dear.

Longaville. Look, here's thy love; [*showing his shoe*]
　　　　my foot° and her face see.

Berowne. O, if the streets were pavèd with thine eyes,
　　　　Her feet were much too dainty for such tread.

Dumaine. O vile! Then, as she goes, what upward lies
280　　　The street should see as she walked overhead.

King. But what of this? Are we not all in love?

---

258 **usurping** false　259 **aspect** appearance　261 **favor** complexion
262 **native blood** naturally red complexion　266 **colliers** coal-men
267 **crack** boast　276 **my foot** (he is wearing black shoes)

Berowne. O, nothing so sure, and thereby all forsworn.

King. Then leave this chat, and, good Berowne, now
prove
Our loving lawful and our faith not torn.

Dumaine. Ay marry, there, some flattery for this evil! 285

Longaville. O, some authority how to proceed!
Some tricks, some quillets,° how to cheat the devil!

Dumaine. Some salve for perjury.

Berowne.   O, 'tis more than need!
Have at you, then, affection's men-at-arms!°
Consider what you first did swear unto.   290
To fast, to study, and to see no woman—
Flat treason 'gainst the kingly state of youth.
Say, can you fast? Your stomachs are too young,
And abstinence engenders maladies.
[And where that° you have vowed to study, lords,   295
In that each of you have forsworn his book,
Can you still dream and pore and thereon look?
For when would you, my lord, or you, or you,
Have found the ground of study's excellence
Without the beauty of a woman's face?   300
From women's eyes this doctrine I derive:
They are the ground, the books, the academes,°
From whence doth spring the true Promethean
fire.°
Why, universal plodding poisons° up
The nimble spirits in the arteries,   305
As motion and long-during° action tires
The sinewy vigor of the traveler.
Now for not looking on a woman's face,

---

287 **quillets** subtleties   289 **affection's men-at-arms** love's warriors
295 **where that** whereas (after writing lines 295–316, here bracketed,
Shakespeare apparently decided he could do better, and rewrote the
passage in the ensuing lines, but the printer mistakenly printed
both versions)   302 **academes** academies   303 **Promethean fire** fire
stolen from heaven by Prometheus   304 **poisons** (some editors
emend to *prisons*)   306 **long-during** long-lasting

You have in that forsworn the use of eyes,
310 And study too, the causer of your vow;
For where is any author in the world
Teaches such beauty as a woman's eye?
Learning is but an adjunct to ourself,
And where we are our learning likewise is.
315 Then when ourselves we see in ladies' eyes,
Do we not likewise see our learning there?]
O, we have made a vow to study, lords,
And in that vow we have forsworn our books;
For when would you, my liege, or you, or you,
320 In leaden contemplation have found out
Such fiery numbers° as the prompting eyes
Of beauty's tutors have enriched you with?
Other slow arts entirely keep the brain,
And therefore, finding barren practisers,
325 Scarce show a harvest of their heavy toil;
But love, first learnèd in a lady's eyes,
Lives not alone immurèd in the brain,
But with the motion of all elements,°
Courses as swift as thought in every power,
330 And gives to every power a double power
Above their functions and their offices.
It adds a precious seeing to the eye:
A lover's eyes will gaze an eagle blind.
A lover's ear will hear the lowest sound,
335 When the suspicious head of theft° is stopped.
Love's feeling is more soft and sensible
Than are the tender horns of cockled° snails.
Love's tongue proves dainty Bacchus gross in taste.
For valor, is not Love a Hercules,
340 Still climbing trees in the Hesperides?°
Subtle as Sphinx; as sweet and musical
As bright Apollo's lute, strung with his hair.
And when Love speaks, the voice of all the gods

321 **fiery numbers** passionate verses 328 **with the motion of all elements** i.e., with the force of all the components of the universe 335 **the suspicious head of theft** i.e., a thief's hearing, suspicious of every sound 337 **cockled** in shells 340 **Hesperides** (garden where Hercules picked the golden apples)

Make heaven drowsy with the harmony.
Never durst poet touch a pen to write   345
Until his ink were temp'red with Love's sighs.
O, then his lines would ravish savage ears
And plant in tyrants mild humility.
From women's eyes this doctrine I derive.
They sparkle still the right Promethean fire;   350
They are the books, the arts, the academes,
That show, contain, and nourish all the world;
Else none at all in aught proves excellent.
Then fools you were these women to forswear,
Or, keeping what is sworn, you will prove fools.   355
For wisdom's sake, a word that all men love,
Or for love's sake, a word that loves all men,
Or for men's sake, the authors of these women,
Or women's sake, by whom we men are men—
Let us once lose our oaths to find ourselves,   360
Or else we lose ourselves to keep our oaths.
It is religion to be thus forsworn,
For charity itself fulfils the law,°
And who can sever love from charity?

King. Saint Cupid then! And, soldiers, to the field!   365

Berowne. Advance your standards, and upon them,
    lords!
Pell-mell, down with them! But be first advised,
In conflict that you get the sun of them.°

Longaville. Now to plain-dealing. Lay these glozes°
    by.
Shall we resolve to woo these girls of France?   370

King. And win them too! Therefore let us devise
Some entertainment for them in their tents.

Berowne. First from the park let us conduct them
    thither;
Then homeward every man attach the hand

---

363 **charity . . . law** (Romans 13:8: "he that loveth another hath fulfilled the law")   368 **get the sun of them** approach when the sun
is in their eyes   369 **glozes** trivial comments

375   Of his fair mistress. In the afternoon
       We will with some strange pastime solace them,
       Such as the shortness of the time can shape;
       For revels, dances, masks, and merry hours
       Forerun fair Love, strewing her way with flowers.

380   *King.* Away, away! No time shall be omitted
       That will be time,° and may by us be fitted.

       Berowne. Allons!° Allons! Sowed cockle reaped no
          corn,°
       And justice always whirls in equal measure.
       Light wenches may prove plagues to men forsworn;
385   If so, our copper buys no better treasure.   [*Exeunt.*]

---

381 **be time** come to pass   382 **Allons** let's go (French)   382 **Sowed ...**
corn if weeds are sown, wheat is not reaped

[ACT 5

Scene 1. *The park.*]

*Enter [Holofernes,] the Pedant, [Nathaniel,] the
Curate, and Dull, [the Constable].*

Holofernes. Satis quid sufficit.°

Nathaniel. I praise God for you, sir. Your reasons°
at dinner have been sharp and sententious,° pleasant without scurrility, witty without affection,° au-
dacious without impudency, learned without   5
opinion,° and strange without heresy. I did converse this *quondam*° day with a companion of the
king's, who is intituled, nominated, or called, Don
Adriano de Armado.

Holofernes. *Novi hominem tanquam te.*° His humor   10
is lofty, his discourse peremptory,° his tongue
filed,° his eye ambitious, his gait majestical, and
his general behavior vain, ridiculous, and thrasonical.° He is too picked,° too spruce, too affected, too odd, as it were, too peregrinate,° as I   15
may call it.

5.1.1 **Satis quid sufficit** enough is as good as a feast   2 **reasons**
discourses   3 **sententious** full of meaning   4 **affection** affectation
6 **opinion** dogmatism   7 **quondam** former   10 **Novi hominem tanquam te** I know the man as well as I know you   11 **peremptory**
decisive   12 **filed** polished   13–14 **thrasonical** boastful   14 **picked** refined   15 **peregrinate** foreign in manner

Nathaniel. A most singular and choice epithet.
                    Draw out his table-book.°

Holofernes. He draweth out the thread of his ver-
        bosity finer than the staple° of his argument. I
20   abhor such fanatical phantasimes,° such insociable°
        and point-devise° companions; such rackers° of
        orthography as to speak "dout" fine when he
        should say "doubt," "det" when he should pro-
        nounce "debt"—d, e, b, t, not d, e, t. He clepeth°
25   a calf "cauf," half "hauf," neighbor *vocatur*°
        "nebor," neigh abbreviated "ne." This is abhomina-
        ble, which he would call "abominable." It insinu-
        ateth me of insanie.° *Ne intelligis, domine?*° To
        make frantic, lunatic.

30 *Nathaniel. Laus Deo bone intelligo.*°

Holofernes. Bone?° *Bone* for *bene!* Priscian° a little
        scratched;° 'twill serve.

        Enter [Armado, the] Braggart, [Moth, the] Boy,
                [and Costard, the Clown].

Nathaniel. Videsne quis venit?°

Holofernes. Video, et gaudeo.°

35 *Armado. [To Moth]* Chirrah!°

Holofernes. Quare° "chirrah," not "sirrah"?

Armado. Men of peace, well encount'red.

17s.d. **table-book** tablet (stage directions are often, as here, in the im-
perative) 19 **staple** fiber 20 **phantasimes** wild imaginers 20
insociable impossible to associate with 21 **point-devise** perfectly
correct 21 **rackers** torturers 24 **clepeth** calls 25 **vocatur** is called
27–28 **insinuateth me of insanie** suggests insanity to me 28 **Ne in-
telligis, domine** do you not understand, sir? 30 **Laus Deo bone
intelligo** praise be to God, I well understand 31 **Bone** (probably
a mixture of Latin *bene* and French *bon*) 31 **Priscian** Latin gram-
marian of sixth century A.D. 32 **scratched** damaged 33 **Videsne quis
venit?** do you see who is coming? 34 **Video, et gaudeo** I see, and
I rejoice 35 **Chirrah** (dialect form for "sirrah") 36 **Quare** why?

Holofernes. Most military sir, salutation.

Moth. [*Aside to Costard*] They have been at a great
feast of languages and stol'n the scraps.   40

Costard. O, they have lived long on the alms-basket°
of words. I marvel thy master hath not eaten thee
for a word; for thou art not so long by the head
as *honorificabilitudinitatibus.*° Thou art easier swallowed than a flapdragon.°   45

Moth. Peace! The peal° begins.

Armado. Monsieur, are you not lett'red?°

Moth. Yes, yes! He teaches boys the hornbook.°
What is a, b, spelled backward with the horn on
his head?   50

Holofernes. Ba, *pueritia,*° with a horn added.

Moth. Ba, most silly sheep with a horn. You hear his
learning.

Holofernes. Quis,° *quis,* thou consonant?

Moth. The last of the five vowels, if you repeat them;   55
or the fifth, if I.

Holofernes. I will repeat them: a, e, i—

Moth. The sheep. The other two concludes it—o, u.

Armado. Now, by the salt wave of the Mediterranean,
a sweet touch, a quick venew° of wit! Snip, snap,   60
quick and home! It rejoiceth my intellect. True wit!

Moth. Offered by a child to an old man—which is
wit-old.°

41 **alms-basket** (basket used at feasts to collect scraps from the table
for the poor) 44 **honorificabilitudinitatibus** (Latin tongue-twister,
thought to be the longest word known) 45 **flapdragon** (burning
raisin or plum floating in liquor, and so drunk) 46 **peal** (of bells)
47 **lett'red** man of letters 48 **hornbook** (parchment with alphabet
and numbers, covered with transparent horn, for teaching spelling
and counting) 51 **pueritia** childishness 54 **Quis** what? 60 **venew**
thrust 63 **wit-old** i.e., mentally feeble (with pun on *wittol* = cuckold)

Holofernes. What is the figure?° What is the figure?

65 *Moth.* Horns.

Holofernes. Thou disputes like an infant. Go whip thy gig.°

Moth. Lend me your horn to make one, and I will whip about your infamy *manu cita.°* A gig of a
70 cuckold's horn.

Costard. And° I had but one penny in the world, thou shouldst have it to buy gingerbread. Hold, there is the very remuneration I had of thy master, thou halfpenny purse of wit, thou pigeon-egg of
75 discretion. O, and the heavens were so pleased that thou wert but my bastard, what a joyful father wouldest thou make me! Go to, thou hast it *ad* dunghill,° at the fingers' ends, as they say.

Holofernes. O, I smell false Latin! "Dunghill" for
80 *unguem.*

Armado. Arts-man,° preambulate.° We will be singled from the barbarous. Do you not educate youth at the charge-house° on the top of the mountain?

Holofernes. Or *mons,* the hill.

85 *Armado.* At your sweet pleasure, for the mountain.

Holofernes. I do, *sans question.*

Armado. Sir, it is the king's most sweet pleasure and affection to congratulate the princess at her pavilion in the posteriors° of this day, which the rude mul-
90 titude call the afternoon.

Holofernes. The posterior of the day, most generous

---

64 **figure** figure of speech   67 **gig** top   69 **manu cita** with a swift hand   71 **And** if   77–78 **ad dunghill** (perhaps a schoolboy's corruption of the proverb "ad unguem," to the fingernail, meaning "precisely")   81 **Arts-man** learned man   81 **preambulate** walk forth   83 **charge-house** school (perhaps an allusion to a specific school on a hill, mentioned by Erasmus)   89 **posteriors** hind parts

sir, is liable, congruent, and measurable° for the
afternoon. The word is well culled, chose, sweet
and apt, I do assure you, sir, I do assure.

Armado. Sir, the king is a noble gentleman, and my   95
familiar,° I do assure ye, very good friend. For
what is inward° between us, let it pass. I do beseech thee, remember thy courtesy.° I beseech thee
apparel thy head. And among other importunate
and most serious designs, and of great import in-   100
deed, too—but let that pass; for I must tell thee,
it will please his Grace, by the world, sometime to
lean upon my poor shoulder, and with his royal
finger thus dally with my excrement,° with my
mustachio—but, sweet heart, let that pass. By the   105
world, I recount no fable! Some certain special
honors it pleaseth his greatness to impart to Armado, a soldier, a man of travel, that hath seen
the world—but let that pass. The very all of all
is (but, sweet heart, I do implore secrecy) that the   110
king would have me present the princess (sweet
chuck) with some delightful ostentation, or show,
or pageant, or antic,° or fire-work. Now, understanding that the curate and your sweet self are
good at such eruptions and sudden breaking out   115
of mirth, as it were, I have acquainted you withal,
to the end to crave your assistance.

Holofernes. Sir, you shall present before her the Nine
Worthies.° Sir Nathaniel, as concerning some entertainment of time, some show in the posterior of   120
this day, to be rend'red by our assistance, the king's
command, and this most gallant, illustrate, and

92 **liable, congruent, measurable** (all synonyms for "suitable") 96
familiar close friend 97 **inward** private 98 **remember thy courtesy**
(possibly: remove your hat when the king's name is mentioned)
104 **excrement** that which grows out (such as hair, nails, feathers)
113 **antic** fanciful pageant 118–19 **Nine Worthies** (traditionally,
Hector, Caesar, Joshua, David, Judas Maccabaeus, Alexander, King
Arthur, Charlemagne, Godfrey of Boulogne; here Hercules and
Pompey are included)

learned gentleman, before the princess—I say, none so fit as to present the Nine Worthies.

125 *Nathaniel.* Where will you find men worthy enough to present them?

Holofernes. Joshua, yourself; myself; and this gallant gentleman, Judas Maccabaeus; this swain, because of his great limb or joint, shall pass° Pompey the 130 Great; the page, Hercules—

Armado. Pardon, sir—error! He is not quantity enough for that Worthy's thumb; he is not so big as the end of his club.

Holofernes. Shall I have audience?° He shall present 135 Hercules in minority.° His enter and exit shall be strangling a snake; and I will have an apology° for that purpose.

Moth. An excellent device! So if any of the audience hiss, you may cry, "Well done, Hercules! Now 140 thou crushest the snake!" That is the way to make an offense gracious, though few have the grace to do it.

Armado. For the rest of the Worthies?

Holofernes. I will play three myself.

145 *Moth.* Thrice-worthy gentleman!

Armado. Shall I tell you a thing?

Holofernes. We attend.

Armado. We will have, if this fadge° not, an antic. I beseech you, follow.

150 *Holofernes.* Via,° goodman Dull! Thou hast spoken no word all this while.

Dull. Nor understood none neither, sir.

---

129 **pass** represent   134 **have audience** be heard   135 **minority** early youth   136 **apology** justification   148 **fadge** succeed   150 **Via** come on (Italian)

Holofernes. *Allons,* we will employ thee.

Dull. I'll make one in a dance, or so; or I will play
on the tabor° to the Worthies, and let them dance   155
the hay.°

Holofernes. Most dull, honest Dull! To our sport,
away!   *Exeunt.*

[Scene 2. *The park.*]

Enter the Ladies [the Princess, Katharine,
Rosaline, and Maria].

Princess. Sweet hearts, we shall be rich ere we depart
If fairings° come thus plentifully in.
A lady walled about with diamonds!
Look you what I have from the loving king.

Rosaline. Madam, came nothing else along with that?   5

Princess. Nothing but this? Yes, as much love in
rhyme
As would be crammed up in a sheet of paper,
Writ o' both sides the leaf, margent° and all,
That he was fain° to seal on Cupid's name.

Rosaline. That was the way to make his godhead
wax,°   10
For he hath been five thousand year a boy.

Katharine. Ay, and a shrowd° unhappy gallows° too.

Rosaline. You'll ne'er be friends with him: 'a killed
your sister.

155 **tabor** small drum   156 **hay** country dance   5.2.2 **fairings** presents   8 **margent** margin   9 **fain** eager   10 **wax** grow (and with a
pun on sealing-wax)   12 **shrowd** accursed   12 **gallows** one fit to be
hanged

Katharine. He made her melancholy, sad, and heavy;
15   And so she died. Had she been light, like you,
Of such a merry, nimble, stirring spirit,
She might ha' been a grandam ere she died.
And so may you, for a light heart lives long.

Rosaline. What's your dark meaning, mouse, of this
light word?

20 *Katharine.* A light condition in a beauty dark.

Rosaline. We need more light to find your meaning
out.

Katharine. You'll mar the light by taking it in snuff,°
Therefore, I'll darkly end the argument.

Rosaline. Look what° you do, you do it still i' th'
dark.

25 *Katharine.* So do not you, for you are a light wench.

Rosaline. Indeed I weigh° not you, and therefore
light.

Katharine. You weigh me not? O, that's you care not
for me!

Rosaline. Great reason, for past care is still past cure.

Princess. Well bandied° both! A set of wit well
played.
30   But Rosaline, you have a favor too—
Who sent it? And what is it?

Rosaline.   I would you knew.
And if my face were but as fair as yours,
My favor were as great. Be witness this.
Nay, I have verses too, I thank Berowne;
35   The numbers° true, and, were the numb'ring° too,
I were the fairest goddess on the ground.

---

22 **taking it in snuff** being annoyed 24 **Look what** whatever 26
weigh value at a certain rate 29 **bandied** hit back and forth (figure
from tennis) 35 **numbers** meter 35 **numb'ring** estimate

I am compared to twenty thousand fairs.°
O, he hath drawn my picture in his letter!

Princess. Anything like?

Rosaline. Much in the letters, nothing in the praise.   *40*

Princess. Beauteous as ink—a good conclusion.

Katharine. Fair as a text B in a copy-book.

Rosaline. 'Ware° pencils, ho! Let me not die your
    debtor,
  My red dominical,° my golden letter.
  O, that your face were not so full of O's!°   *45*

Princess. A pox of° that jest, and I beshrow all
    shrows!°
  But Katharine, what was sent to you from fair
    Dumaine?

Katharine. Madam, this glove.

Princess.   Did he not send you twain?

Katharine. Yes, madam; and moreover,
  Some thousand verses of a faithful lover.   *50*
  A huge translation of hypocrisy,
  Vilely compiled, profound simplicity.°

Maria. This, and these pearls, to me sent Longaville.
  The letter is too long by half a mile.

Princess. I think no less. Dost thou not wish in heart   *55*
  The chain were longer and the letter short?

Maria. Ay, or I would these hands might never part.

Princess. We are wise girls to mock our lovers so.

Rosaline. They are worse fools to purchase mocking
    so.

---

37 **fairs** beautiful women   43 **'Ware** beware   44 **red dominical** red
S (for Sunday, the Lord's Day)   45 **O's** smallpox scars   46 **A pox
of** may a plague strike   46 **beshrow all shrows** curse all shrews
52 **simplicity** simple-mindedness

60   That same Berowne I'll torture ere I go.
      O that I knew he were but in by th' week!°
      How I would make him fawn, and beg, and seek,
      And wait the season, and observe the times,
      And spend his prodigal wits in bootless rhymes,
65   And shape his service wholly to my hests,°
      And make him proud to make me proud that jests!
      So pertaunt-like° would I o'ersway his state°
      That he should be my fool, and I his fate.

      Princess. None are so surely caught, when they are
         catched,
70   As wit turned fool. Folly, in wisdom hatched,
      Hath wisdom's warrant and the help of school
      And wit's own grace to grace a learnèd fool.

      Rosaline. The blood of youth burns not with such
         excess
      As gravity's revolt to wantonness.

75   *Maria.* Folly in fools bears not so strong a note
      As fool'ry in the wise when wit doth dote;
      Since all the power thereof it doth apply
      To prove, by wit, worth in simplicity.

                    Enter Boyet.

      Princess. Here comes Boyet, and mirth is in his face.

      Boyet. O, I am stabbed with laughter! Where's her
80   Grace?

      Princess. Thy news, Boyet?

      Boyet.   Prepare, madam, prepare!
      Arm, wenches, arm! Encounters mounted are
      Against your peace. Love doth approach disguised,
      Armèd in arguments; you'll be surprised.
85   Muster your wits; stand in your own defense,
      Or hide your heads like cowards and fly hence.

      61 **in by th' week** trapped 65 **hests** commands 67 **pertaunt-like**
      (like a winning hand [*Pair-taunt*] in a certain card game) 67 **o'er-
      sway his state** overrule his power

Princess. Saint Denis° to Saint Cupid! What are they
   That charge their break against us? Say, scout, say.

Boyet. Under the cool shade of a sycamore
   I thought to close mine eyes some half an hour,   90
   When, lo, to interrupt my purposed rest,
   Toward that shade I might behold addresst°
   The king and his companions! Warily
   I stole into a neighbor thicket by,
   And overheard what you shall overhear—   95
   That, by and by, disguised they will be here.
   Their herald is a pretty knavish page
   That well by heart hath conned his embassage.°
   Action and accent did they teach him there:
   "Thus must thou speak, and thus thy body bear."   100
   And ever and anon they made a doubt°
   Presence majestical would put him out;
   "For," quoth the king, "an angel shalt thou see,
   Yet fear not thou, but speak audaciously."
   The boy replied, "An angel is not evil;   105
   I should have feared her had she been a devil."
   With that all laughed and clapped him on the
      shoulder,
   Making the bold wag by their praises bolder.
   One rubbed his elbow thus, and fleered,° and swore
   A better speech was never spoke before.   110
   Another, with his finger and his thumb,
   Cried "*Via,* we will do 't, come what will come!"
   The third he capered and cried, "All goes well!"
   The fourth turned on the toe,° and down he fell.
   With that they all did tumble on the ground   115
   With such a zealous laughter, so profound,
   That in this spleen° ridiculous appears,
   To check their folly, passion's solemn tears.

Princess. But what, but what? Come they to visit us?

Boyet. They do, they do, and are apparelled thus—   120

87 **Saint Denis** patron saint of France   92 **addresst** approaching
98 **conned his embassage** learned his commission   101 **made a
doubt** expressed a fear   109 **fleered** grinned   114 **turned on the toe**
turned quickly to leave   117 **spleen** excess of mirth

Like Muscovites or Russians, as I guess.
Their purpose is to parley,° court and dance,
And every one his love-feat° will advance
Unto his several mistress, which they'll know
125   By favors several which they did bestow.

Princess. And will they so? The gallants shall be
        tasked;°
For, ladies, we will every one be masked,
And not a man of them shall have the grace,
Despite of suit,° to see a lady's face.
130   Hold, Rosaline, this favor thou shalt wear,
And then the king will court thee for his dear.
Hold, take thou this, my sweet, and give me thine;
So shall Berowne take me for Rosaline.
And change you favors too; so shall your loves
135   Woo contrary, deceived by these removes.°

Rosaline. Come on, then; wear the favors most in
        sight.°

Katharine. But in this changing what is your intent?

Princess. The effect of my intent is to cross° theirs.
They do it but in mockery merriment,
140   And mock for mock is only my intent.
Their several counsels they unbosom° shall
To loves mistook and so be mocked withal
Upon the next occasion that we meet,
With visages displayed, to talk and greet.

145 *Rosaline.* But shall we dance if they desire us to 't?

Princess. No, to the death° we will not move a foot,
Nor to their penned speech render we no grace,
But while 'tis spoke each turn away her face.

Boyet. Why, that contempt will kill the speaker's
        heart,
150   And, quite divorce his memory from his part.

122 **parley** hold a conference   123 **love-feat** exploit prompted by
love   126 **tasked** tested   129 **Despite of suit** in spite of his pleading
135 **removes** changes   136 **most in sight** conspicuously   138 **cross**
thwart   141 **unbosom** confide   146 **to the death** as long as we live

Princess. Therefore I do it, and I make no doubt
   The rest will e'er come in if he be out.
   There's no such sport as sport by sport o'erthrown,
   To make theirs ours, and ours none but our own.
   So shall we stay, mocking intended game,°   *155*
   And they, well mocked, depart away with shame.
                                    Sound trumpet.

Boyet. The trumpet sounds. Be masked—the maskers
   come.
                              [*The Ladies mask.*]

   *Enter Blackamoors with music; [Moth,] the Boy,
   with a speech, and [the King, Berowne, and] the
   rest of the Lords [in Russian dress and] disguised.*

Moth. "All hail, the richest beauties on the earth!"

Boyet. Beauties no richer than rich taffeta.

Moth. "A holy parcel of the fairest dames,   *160*
             The Ladies turn their backs to him.
   That ever turned their backs to mortal views!"

Berowne. "Their eyes," villain, "their eyes!"

Moth. "That ever turned their eyes to mortal views!
   Out—"

Boyet. True. "Out" indeed!   *165*

Moth. "Out of your favors, heavenly spirits, vouchsafe
   Not to behold"—

Berowne. "Once to behold," rogue!

Moth. "Once to behold with your sun-beamèd eyes,
   —with your sun-beamèd eyes"—   *170*

Boyet. They will not answer to that epithet.
   You were best call it "daughter-beamèd eyes."

Moth. They do not mark me, and that brings° me out.

155 **game** sport   173 **brings** puts

Berowne. Is this your perfectness? Be gone, you rogue!
                                     [*Exit Moth.*]

Rosaline. What would these strangers? Know their
175   minds, Boyet.
     If they do speak our language, 'tis our will
     That some plain man recount their purposes.
     Know what they would.

Boyet. What would you with the Princess?

180 *Berowne.* Nothing but peace and gentle visitation.

Rosaline. What would they, say they?

Boyet. Nothing but peace and gentle visitation.

Rosaline. Why, that they have, and bid them so be
     gone.

Boyet. She says you have it and you may be gone.

185 *King.* Say to her, we have measured many miles,
     To tread a measure with her on this grass.

Boyet. They say that they have measured many a mile,
     To tread a measure° with you on this grass.

Rosaline. It is not so. Ask them how many inches
190   Is in one mile. If they have measured many,
     The measure then of one is eas'ly told.

Boyet. If to come hither you have measured miles,
     And many miles, the princess bids you tell
     How many inches doth fill up one mile.

195 *Berowne.* Tell her we measure them by weary steps.

Boyet. She hears herself.

Rosaline.   How many weary steps,
     Of many weary miles you have o'ergone,
     Are numb'red in the travel of one mile?

Berowne. We number nothing that we spend for you.
200   Our duty is so rich, so infinite,

188 **measure** stately dance

That we may do it still without accompt.°
Vouchsafe to show the sunshine of your face,
That we like savages may worship it.

Rosaline. My face is but a moon, and clouded too.

King. Blessèd are clouds, to do as such clouds do.   *205*
    Vouchsafe, bright moon, and these thy stars, to
        shine
    (Those clouds removed) upon our watery eyne.°

Rosaline. O vain petitioner, beg a greater matter!
    Thou now requests but moonshine in the water.°

King. Then in our measure do but vouchsafe one
        change.°   *210*
    Thou bid'st me beg; this begging is not strange.°

Rosaline. Play, music then. Nay, you must do it soon.
                    [*The musicians play.*]
    Not yet? No dance! Thus change I like the moon.

King. Will you not dance? How come you thus es-
        trangèd?

Rosaline. You took the moon at full, but now she's
        changèd.   *215*

King. Yet still she is the moon, and I the man.
    The music plays; vouchsafe some motion to it.

Rosaline. Our ears vouchsafe it.

King.   But your legs should do it.

Rosaline. Since you are strangers and come here by
        chance,
    We'll not be nice.° Take hands. We will not dance.   *220*

King. Why take we hands then?

Rosaline.   Only to part friends.
    Curtsy, sweet hearts. And so the measure ends.

___

201 **accompt** reckoning   207 **eyne** eyes   209 **moonshine in the water**
a mere nothing   210 **change** round of dancing   211 **not strange** not
unsuitably foreign   220 **nice** fastidious

King. More measure of this measure! Be not nice.

Rosaline. We can afford no more at such a price.

225 *King.* Price you yourselves. What buys your company?

Rosaline. Your absence only.

King.   That can never be.

Rosaline. Then cannot we be bought; and so adieu—
    Twice to your visor,° and half once to you.

King. If you deny to dance, let's hold more chat.

Rosaline. In private then.

230 *King.*   I am best pleased with that.
                    [*They converse apart.*]

Berowne. White-handed mistress, one sweet word with
    thee.

Princess. Honey, and milk, and sugar—there is three.

Berowne. Nay then, two treys,° an if° you grow so
    nice,
    Metheglin,° wort,° and malmsey.° Well run, dice!
    There's half a dozen sweets.

235 *Princess.*   Seventh sweet, adieu.
    Since you can cog,° I'll play no more with you.

Berowne. One word in secret.

Princess.   Let it not be sweet.

Berowne. Thou grievest my gall.°

Princess.   Gall! Bitter.

Berowne.   Therefore meet.°
                    [*They converse apart.*]

228 **visor** mask   233 **treys** threes (at dice)   233 **an if** if   234 **Metheglin** drink mixed with honey   234 **wort** unfermented beer   234 **malmsey** a Mediterranean wine   236 **cog** cheat   238 **gall** sore spot 238 **meet** fitting

Dumaine. Will you vouchsafe with me to change° a
    word?

Maria. Name it.

Dumaine.   Fair lady—

Maria.   Say you so? Fair lord.   240
    Take that for your "fair lady."

Dumaine.   Please it you,
    As much in private, and I'll bid adieu.
                        [*They converse apart.*]

Katharine. What, was your vizard° made without a
    tongue?

Longaville. I know the reason, lady, why you ask.

Katharine. O for your reason! Quickly, sir, I long.   245

Longaville. You have a double tongue° within your
    mask
    And would afford my speechless vizard half.

Katharine. "Veal,"° quoth the Dutchman. Is not
    "veal" a calf?

Longaville. A calf, fair lady?

Katharine.   No, a fair lord calf.

Longaville. Let's part the word.

Katharine.   No, I'll not be your half.   250
    Take all and wean it, it may prove an ox.

Longaville. Look how you butt yourself in these sharp
    mocks.
    Will you give horns,° chaste lady? Do not so.

Katharine. Then die a calf before your horns do grow.

Longaville. One word in private with you ere I die.   255

---

239 **change** exchange   243 **vizard** mask   246 **double tongue** (an inner projection or tongue held in the mouth to keep the mask in place)
248 **Veal** (Dutch or German pronunciation of "well")   253 **give horns**
prove unfaithful

Katharine. Bleat softly then. The butcher hears you
         cry.   [*They converse apart.*]

Boyet. The tongues of mocking wenches are as keen
         As is the razor's edge invisible,
         Cutting a smaller hair than may be seen,
260   Above the sense° of sense; so sensible
         Seemeth their conference,° their conceits° have
            wings
         Fleeter than arrows, bullets, wind, thought, swifter
            things.

Rosaline. Not one word more, my maids, break off,
         break off.

Berowne. By heaven, all dry-beaten° with pure scoff!

265 *King.* Farewell, mad wenches. You have simple wits.
                 Exeunt [King, Lords, and Blackamoors].

Princess. Twenty adieus, my frozen Muscovits.
         Are these the breed of wits so wondered at?

Boyet. Tapers they are, with your sweet breaths
         puffed out.

Rosaline. Well-liking° wits they have; gross, gross,
         fat, fat.

270 *Princess.* O poverty in wit, kingly-poor flout!°
         Will they not, think you, hang themselves tonight?
         Or ever but in vizards show their faces?
         This pert Berowne was out of count'nance quite.

Rosaline. They were all in lamentable cases.°
275   The king was weeping-ripe° for a good word.

Princess. Berowne did swear himself out of all suit.°

Maria. Dumaine was at my service, and his sword.
         "No point,"° quoth I; my servant straight was mute.

260 **Above the sense** above the reach   261 **conference** conferring
261 **conceits** witticisms   264 **dry-beaten** beaten with blood being
drawn   269 **Well-liking** plump, sleek   270 **kingly-poor flout** a poor
jest for a king   274 **cases** (with pun on the sense "masks" or "costumes")   275 **weeping-ripe** about to weep   276 **out of all suit** beyond
all reasonableness   278 **No point** not at all

Katharine. Lord Longaville said I came o'er his heart;
  And trow° you what he called me?

Princess.   Qualm,° perhaps.   280

Katharine. Yes, in good faith.

Princess.   Go, sickness as thou art!

Rosaline. Well, better wits have worn plain statute-
  caps.°
  But will you hear? The king is my love sworn.

Princess. And quick Berowne hath plighted faith to
  me.

Katharine. And Longaville was for my service born.   285

Maria. Dumaine is mine as sure as bark on tree.

Boyet. Madam, and pretty mistresses, give ear.
  Immediately they will again be here
  In their own shapes, for it can never be
  They will digest this harsh indignity.   290

Princess. Will they return?

Boyet.   They will, they will, God knows,
  And leap for joy though they are lame with blows.
  Therefore change° favors, and when they repair,°
  Blow° like sweet roses in this summer air.

Princess. How blow? How blow? Speak to be understood.   295

Boyet. Fair ladies masked are roses in their bud;
  Dismasked, their damask° sweet commixture shown,
  Are angels vailing° clouds, or roses blown.

Princess. Avaunt, perplexity!° What shall we do
  If they return in their own shapes to woo?   300

---

280 **trow** know   280 **Qualm** sudden sickness   282 **statute-caps** caps
apprentices were required to wear   293 **change** exchange   293 **repair** come again   294 **Blow** blossom   297 **damask** red and white
(like the Damascus rose)   298 **vailing** letting fall   299 **Avaunt, perplexity** away, confusion

Rosaline. Good madam, if by me you'll be advised,
    Let's mock them still, as well known as disguised.
    Let us complain to them what fools were here,
    Disguised like Muscovites in shapeless gear;°
305   And wonder what they were, and to what end
    Their shallow shows and prologue vilely penned,
    And their rough carriage so ridiculous,
    Should be presented at our tent to us.

Boyet. Ladies, withdraw. The gallants are at hand.

310 *Princess.* Whip to our tents, as roes run o'er land.
                    Exeunt [Princess and Ladies].

    *Enter the King and the rest: [Berowne, Longaville,
        and Dumaine, all in their proper habits].*

King. Fair sir, God save you. Where's the princess?

Boyet. Gone to her tent. Please it your Majesty
    Command me any service to her thither?

King. That she vouchsafe me audience for one word.

315 *Boyet.* I will; and so will she, I know, my lord.   *Exit.*

Berowne. This fellow pecks up wit, as pigeons peas,
    And utters it again when God doth please.
    He is wit's pedlar, and retails his wares
    At wakes° and wassails,° meetings, markets, fairs;
320   And we that sell by gross, the Lord doth know,
    Have not the grace to grace it with such show.
    This gallant pins the wenches° on his sleeve.
    Had he been Adam, he had tempted Eve.
    'A can carve° too, and lisp. Why, this is he
325   That kissed his hand away in courtesy.
    This is the ape of form,° Monsieur the Nice,°
    That, when he plays at tables,° chides the dice
    In honorable terms. Nay, he can sing

304 **gear** outfit   319 **wakes** vigils and feastings   319 **wassails** revelry
322 **pins the wenches** wears maidens' favors   324 **carve** make gestures of courtship   326 **form** etiquette   326 **Nice** exquisite   327 **at
tables** backgammon

A mean° most, meanly; and in ushering
Mend° him who can. The ladies call him sweet.   *330*
The stairs, as he treads on them, kiss his feet.
This is the flow'r that smiles on every one,
To show his teeth as white as whalës-bone;
And consciences that will not die in debt
Pay him the due of "honey-tongued Boyet."   *335*

King. A blister on his sweet tongue, with my heart,
    That put Armado's page out of his part!

    Enter [the Princess and] the Ladies [with Boyet].

Berowne. See where it comes! Behavior, what wert
    thou
    Till this madman showed thee, and what art thou
    now?

King. All bail, sweet madam, and fair time of day.   *340*

Princess. "Fair" in "all hail"° is foul, as I conceive.

King. Construe my speeches better, if you may.

Princess. Then wish me better, I will give you leave.

King. We came to visit you, and purpose now
    To lead you to our court. Vouchsafe it then.   *345*

Princess. This field shall hold me, and so hold your
    vow.
    Nor God nor I delights in perjured men.

King. Rebuke me not for that which you provoke.
    The virtue° of your eye must break my oath.

Princess. You nickname° virtue. "Vice" you should
    have spoke;   *350*
    For virtue's office never breaks men's troth.
    Now, by my maiden honor, yet as pure
    As the unsullied lily, I protest,

---

329 **mean** intermediate part 330 **Mend** surpass 341 **hail** (with a
pun on hail meaning "sleet") 349 **virtue** power 350 **nickname**
name by mistake

A world of torments though I should endure,
355   I would not yield to be your house's guest,
So much I hate a breaking cause° to be
Of heavenly oaths, vowed with integrity.

King. O, you have lived in desolation here,
Unseen, unvisited, much to our shame.

360 *Princess.* Not so, my lord. It is not so, I swear.
We have had pastimes here and pleasant game.
A mess° of Russians left us but of late.

King. How, madam? Russians?

Princess.   Ay, in truth, my lord;
Trim gallants, full of courtship and of state.

365 *Rosaline.* Madam, speak true. It is not so, my lord.
My lady, to the manner of the days,°
In courtesy gives undeserving praise.
We four indeed confronted were with four
In Russian habit.° Here they stayed an hour
370   And talked apace; and in that hour, my lord,
They did not bless us with one happy° word.
I dare not call them fools, but this I think,
When they are thirsty, fools would fain have drink.

Berowne. This jest is dry to me. Gentle sweet,
375   Your wit makes wise things foolish. When we greet
With eyes best seeing heaven's fiery eye,°
By light we lose light. Your capacity
Is of that nature that to your huge store
Wise things seem foolish and rich things but poor.

Rosaline. This proves you wise and rich, for in my
380   eye—

Berowne. I am a fool, and full of poverty.

Rosaline. But that you take what doth to you belong,
It were a fault to snatch words from my tongue.

356 **breaking cause** cause for breaking off   362 **mess** group of four
366 **to the manner of the days** according to the fashion of the time
369 **habit** dress   371 **happy** appropriate   376 **heaven's fiery eye** the
sun

Berowne. O, I am yours, and all that I possess.

Rosaline. All the fool mine?

Berowne.　　　　　　　　I cannot give you less.　　　385

Rosaline. Which of the vizards was it that you wore?

Berowne. Where, when, what vizard? Why demand
　　you this?

Rosaline. There, then, that vizard, that superfluous
　　case°
　　That hid the worse, and showed the better face.

King. We were descried. They'll mock us now down-
　　right.　　　390

Dumaine. Let us confess, and turn it to a jest.

Princess. Amazed, my lord? Why looks your High-
　　ness sad?

Rosaline. Help? Hold his brows! He'll sound.° Why
　　look you pale?
　　Seasick, I think, coming from Muscovy.

Berowne. Thus pour the stars down plagues for per-
　　jury.　　　395
　　Can any face of brass° hold longer out?
　　Here stand I, lady, dart thy skill at me.
　　Bruise me with scorn, confound me with a flout,
　　Thrust thy sharp wit quite through my ignorance,
　　Cut me to pieces with thy keen conceit,°　　　400
　　And I will wish thee never more to dance,
　　Nor never more in Russian habit wait.
　　O, never will I trust to speeches penned,
　　Nor to the motion of a schoolboy's tongue,
　　Nor never come in vizard to my friend,　　　405
　　Nor woo in rhyme, like a blind harper's song!
　　Taffeta phrases,° silken terms precise,
　　Three-piled° hyperboles, spruce affectation,

388 **case** covering　393 **sound** swoon　396 **face of brass** brazen
manner　400 **conceit** imagination　407 **Taffeta phrases** fine speech
408 **Three-piled** (the finest-weight velvet)

Figures° pedantical—these summer flies
410 Have blown° me full of maggot ostentation.
I do forswear them; and I here protest
By this white glove (how white the hand, God
        knows!)
Henceforth my wooing mind shall be expressed
In russet° yeas and honest kersey° noes.
415 And to begin, wench—so God help me, law!—
My love to thee is sound, sans° crack or flaw.

Rosaline. Sans "sans," I pray you.

Berowne.   Yet I have a trick°
Of the old rage. Bear with me, I am sick.
I'll leave it by degrees. Soft, let us see—
420 Write "Lord have mercy on us"° on those three.
They are infected, in their hearts it lies;
They have the plague, and caught it of your eyes.
These lords are visited;° you are not free,°
For the Lord's tokens° on you do I see.

425 *Princess.* No, they are free that gave these tokens to us.

Berowne. Our states° are forfeit. Seek not to undo us.

Rosaline. It is not so, for how can this be true,
That you stand forfeit, being those that sue?

Berowne. Peace! for I will not have to do with you.

430 *Rosaline.* Nor shall not if I do as I intend.

Berowne. Speak for yourselves. My wit is at an end.

King. Teach us, sweet madam, for our rude transgres-
        sion
Some fair excuse.

Princess.   The fairest is confession.
Were not you here but even now disguised?

409 **Figures** figures of speech   410 **blown** filled   414 **russet** (characteristic red-brown color of peasants' clothes)   414 **kersey** plain
wool cloth   416 **sans** without   417 **trick** trace   420 **Lord have
mercy on us** (inscription posted on the doors of houses harboring the
plague)   423 **visited** attacked by plague   423 **free** free of infection
424 **the Lord's tokens** plague spots   426 **states** estates

King. Madam, I was.

Princess.   And were you well advised?   *435*

King. I was, fair madam.

Princess.   When you then were here,
   What did you whisper in your lady's ear?

King. That more than all the world I did respect. her.

Princess. When she shall challenge this, you will re-
   ject her.

King. Upon mine honor, no.

Princess.   Peace, peace, forbear!   *440*
   Your oath once broke, you force not° to forswear.

King. Despise me when I break this oath of mine.

Princess. I will, and therefore keep it. Rosaline,
   What did the Russian whisper in your ear?

Rosaline. Madame, he swore that he did hold me dear *445*
   As precious eyesight, and did value me
   Above this world; adding thereto, moreover,
   That he would wed me or else die my lover.

Princess. God give thee joy of him. The noble lord
   Most honorably doth uphold his word.   *450*

King. What mean you, madam? By my life, my troth,
   I never swore this lady such an oath.

Rosaline. By heaven you did! And to confirm it plain,
   You gave me this, but take it, sir, again.

King. My faith and this the princess I did give.   *455*
   I knew her by this jewel on her sleeve.

Princess. Pardon me, sir, this jewel did she wear,
   And Lord Berowne, I thank him, is my dear.
   What! Will you have me, or your pearl again?

Berowne. Neither of either, I remit both twain.   *460*
   I see the trick on 't. Here was a consent,

441 **force not** do not think it wrong

Knowing aforehand of our merriment,
To dash° it like a Christmas comedy.
Some carry-tale, some please-man,° some slight
    zany,°
Some mumble-news,° some trencher-knight,° some
465   Dick°
That smiles his cheek in years,° and knows the trick
To make my lady laugh when she's disposed,
Told our intents before; which once disclosed,
The ladies did change favors, and then we,
470 Following the signs, wooed but the sign of she.
Now, to our perjury to add more terror,
We are again forsworn, in will and error.
Much upon this 'tis.° [To Boyet] And might not you
Forestall our sport, to make us thus untrue?
475 Do not you know my lady's foot by th' squier,°
And laugh upon the apple of her eye?°
And stand between her back, sir, and the fire,
Holding a trencher,° jesting merrily?
You put our page out.° Go, you are allowed.°
480 Die when you will, a smock° shall be your shroud.
You leer upon me, do you? There's an eye
Wounds like a leaden sword.

Boyet.   **Full merrily**
Hath this brave manage,° this career,° been run.

Berowne. Lo, he is tilting straight.° Peace! I have
    done.

          Enter [Costard, the] Clown.

485 Welcome, pure wit! Thou part'st a fair fray.

463 **dash** ridicule 464 **please-man** toady 464 **zany** buffoon 465 **mumble-news** prattler 465 **trencher-knight** brave man at the table 465 **Dick** fellow 466 **smiles his cheek in years** laughs his face into wrinkles 473 **Much upon this 'tis** it is very much like this 475 **by th' squier** by the rule (that is, have her measure) 476 **laugh . . . eye** laugh, looking closely into her eyes 478 **trencher** wooden plate 479 **put our page out** take him out of his part 479 **allowed** permitted (licensed, like a court fool) 480 **smock** woman's garment 483 **manage** display of horsemanship 483 **career** charge 484 **tilting straight** already jousting

Costard. O Lord, sir, they would know
    Whether the three Worthies shall come in or no.

Berowne. What, are there but three?

Costard.   No, sir, but it is vara° fine,
    For every one pursents° three.

Berowne.   And three times thrice is nine.

Costard. Not so, sir, under correction, sir, I hope, it
    is not so.   *490*
    You cannot beg us,° sir, I can assure you, sir; we
    know what we know.
    I hope, sir, three times thrice, sir—

Berowne.   Is not nine?

Costard. Under correction, sir, we know whereuntil it
    doth amount.

Berowne. By Jove, I always took three threes for nine. *495*

Costard. O Lord, sir, it were pity you should get your
    living by reck'ning, sir.

Berowne. How much is it?

Costard. O Lord, sir, the parties themselves, the ac-
    tors, sir, will show whereuntil it doth amount. For *500*
    mine own part, I am, as they say, but to parfect°
    one man in one poor man—Pompion° the Great,
    sir.

Berowne. Art thou one of the Worthies?

Costard. It pleased them to think me worthy of Pom- *505*
    pey the Great. For mine own part, I know not the
    degree° of the Worthy, but I am to stand for him.

Berowne. Go, bid them prepare.

Costard. We will turn it finely off, sir; we will take
    some care.   *Exit.*

---

488 **vara** (northern pronunciation of "very") 489 **pursents** represents 491 **beg us** prove us fools 501 **parfect** play the part of
502 **Pompion** pumpkin (for Pompey) 507 **degree** rank

King. Berowne, they will shame us. Let them not ap-
510   proach.

Berowne. We are shame-proof, my lord; and 'tis some
        policy°
    To have one show worse than the king's and his
        company.

King. I say they shall not come.

Princess. Nay, my good lord, let me o'errule you now.
515   That sport best pleases that doth least know how,
    Where zeal strives to content, and the contents
    Dies in the zeal of that which it presents.°
    Their form confounded makes most form in mirth°
    When great things laboring perish in their birth.

520 *Berowne.* A right description of our sport, my lord.

                Enter [Armado, the] Braggart.

Armado. Anointed, I implore so much expense of thy
    royal sweet breath as will utter a brace° of words.
            [*Converses apart with the King, and delivers
                    a paper to him.*]

Princess. Doth this man serve God?

Berowne. Why ask you?

525 *Princess.* 'A speaks not like a man of God his making.

Armado. That is all one, my fair, sweet, honey mon-
    arch; for, I protest, the schoolmaster is exceeding
    fantastical; too-too vain, too-too vain; but we will
    put it, as they say, to *fortuna de la guerra.*° I wish
530 you the peace of mind, most royal couplement!°
                                        Exit.

King. Here is like to be a good presence of Worthies.

---

511 **policy** crafty device   516–17 **contents . . . presents** i.e., the
substance is destroyed by the excessive zeal in presenting it   518
Their form . . . mirth i.e., art that is confused is most laughable
entertainment   522 **brace** pair   529 **fortuna de la guerra** fortune
of war (Italian)   530 **couplement** pair

He presents Hector of Troy; the swain, Pompey the
Great; the parish curate, Alexander; Armado's page,
Hercules; the pedant, Judas Maccabaeus:
And if these four Worthies in their first show thrive,   *535*
These four will change habits° and present the
    other five.

Berowne. There is five in the first show.

King. You are deceivèd, 'tis not so.

Berowne. The pedant, the braggart, the hedge-priest,°
the fool, and the boy—   *540*
Abate throw at novum,° and the whole world again
Cannot pick out five such, take each one in his
    vein.°

King. The ship is under sail, and here she comes
amain.°

            Enter [Costard, for] Pompey.

Costard. "I Pompey am—"

Berowne.   You lie, you are not he!

Costard. "I Pompey am—"

Boyet.   With libbard's head° on knee.   *545*

Berowne. Well said, old mocker. I must needs be
    friends with thee.

Costard. "I Pompey am, Pompey surnamed the Big—"

Dumaine. The "Great."

Costard. It is "Great," sir—"Pompey surnamed the
    Great,
That oft in field, with targe° and shield, did make
    my foe to sweat,   *550*
And traveling along this coast I here am come by
    chance,

536 **habits** costumes   539 **hedge-priest** unlearned priest   541 **Abate
throw at novum** except for the throw at nine (in a game of dice)
542 **vein** characteristic way   543 **amain** swiftly   545 **libbard's head**
heraldic painting of leopard   550 **targe** shield

And lay my arms before the legs of this sweet lass
   of France."
If your ladyship would say, "Thanks, Pompey," I
had done.

555 *Princess.* Great thanks, great Pompey.

Costard. 'Tis not so much worth, but I hope I was
   perfect. I made a little fault in "Great."

Berowne. My hat to a halfpenny, Pompey proves the
   best Worthy.

   Enter [Nathaniel, the] Curate, for Alexander.

Nathaniel. "When in the world I lived, I was the
560   world's commander;
   By east, west, north, and south, I spread my con-
      quering might;
   My scutcheon° plain declares that I am Alis-
      ander—"

Boyet. Your nose says, no, you are not; for it stands
   too right.°

Berowne. Your nose smells "no" in this, most tender-
   smelling knight.

Princess. The conqueror is dismayed. Proceed, good
565   Alexander.

Nathaniel. "When in the world I lived, I was the
   world's commander—"

Boyet. Most true, 'tis right—you were so, Alisander.

Berowne. Pompey the Great—

Costard. Your servant, and Costard.

570 *Berowne.* Take away the conqueror, take away Alisander.

Costard. [*To Nathaniel*] O, sir, you have overthrown

562 **scutcheon** coat of arms   563 **right** straight (Alexander's nose
was a little awry)

Alisander the conqueror! You will be scraped out
of the painted cloth° for this. Your lion that holds
his pole-ax° sitting on a close-stool° will be given   575
to Ajax.° He will be the ninth Worthy. A conqueror, and afeard to speak? Run away for shame,
Alisander. [*Nathaniel stands aside.*] There, an 't°
shall please you, a foolish mild man; an honest
man, look you, and soon dashed. He is a marvelous   580
good neighbor, faith, and a very good bowler; but
for Alisander—alas! you see how 'tis—a little o'erparted.° But there are Worthies a-coming will speak
their mind in some other sort.

Princess. Stand aside, good Pompey.   585

                    [*Costard stands aside.*]

   *Enter [Holofernes, the] Pedant, for Judas, and
      [Moth,] the Boy, for Hercules.*

Holofernes. "Great Hercules is presented by this imp,°
   Whose   club   killed   Cerberus,   that   three-headed
      canus;°
   And when he was a babe, a child, a shrimp,
   Thus did he strangle serpents in his *manus.*°
   Quoniam° he seemeth in minority,°   590
   Ergo° I come with this apology."
   Keep some state° in thy exit, and vanish.

                    Exit Boy [to one side].

   "Judas I am—"

Dumaine. A Judas?

Holofernes. Not Iscariot, sir.   595
   "Judas I am, ycleped° Maccabaeus."°

Dumaine. Judas Maccabaeus clipt° is plain Judas.

---

574 **painted cloth** wall-hanging   575 **pole-ax** battle-ax (and penis)
575 **close-stool** commode   576 **Ajax** Greek warrior (with a pun on
"jakes," privy)   578 **an 't** if it   582–83 **o'erparted** having too difficult a part   586 **imp** child   587 **canus** (from Latin *canis*) dog
589 **manus** hand   590 **Quoniam** since   590 **in minority** under age
591 **Ergo** therefore   592 **state** dignity   596 **ycleped** called   596
Maccabaeus Hebrew warrior   597 **clipt** (1) cut (2) embraced

Berowne. A kissing traitor. How, art thou proved Judas?

600 *Holofernes.* "Judas I am—"

Dumaine. The more shame for you, Judas.

Holofernes. What mean you, sir?

Boyet. To make Judas hang himself.

Holofernes. Begin, sir; you are my elder.

605 *Berowne.* Well followed: Judas was hanged on an elder.°

Holofernes. I will not be put out of countenance.

Berowne. Because thou hast no face.

Holofernes. What is this?

610 *Boyet.* A cittern-head.°

Dumaine. The head of a bodkin.°

Berowne. A death's face in a ring.°

Longaville. The face of an old Roman coin, scarce seen.

615 *Boyet.* The pommel of Caesar's falchion.°

Dumaine. The carved-bone face on a flask.

Berowne. Saint George's half-cheek° in a brooch.

Dumaine. Ay, and in a brooch of lead.°

Berowne. Ay, and worn in the cap of a toothdrawer.
620 And now forward, for we have put thee in countenance.

Holofernes. You have put me out of countenance.°

---

606 **elder** a kind of tree 610 **cittern-head** head of a stringed musical instrument 611 **bodkin** long hairpin 612 **death's face in a ring** finger ring with the carving of a skull 615 **falchion** sword 617 **half-cheek** profile 618 **brooch of lead** ornament worn in cap as badge of dentist's trade 622 **out of countenance** disconcerted

Berowne. False. We have given thee faces.

Holofernes. But you have outfaced them all.

Berowne. And° thou wert a lion, we would do so.   625

Boyet. Therefore as he is an ass, let him go.
  And so adieu, sweet Jude. Nay, why dost thou stay?

Dumaine. For the latter end of his name.

Berowne. For the ass to the Jude? Give it him. Jud-as,
  away!

Holofernes. This is not generous, not gentle, not humble.   630

Boyet. A light for Monsieur Judas! It grows dark, he
  may stumble.   [*Holofernes stands aside.*]

Princess. Alas, poor Maccabaeus, how hath he been
  baited! °

    Enter [Armado, the] Braggart, [for Hector].

Berowne. Hide thy head, Achilles! Here comes Hec-
  tor° in arms.

Dumaine. Though my mocks come home by me, I 635
  will now be merry.

King. Hector was but a Troyan in respect of this.

Boyet. But is this Hector?

King. I think Hector was not so clean-timbered.°

Longaville. His leg is too big for Hector's.   640

Dumaine. More calf, certain.

Boyet. No; he is best indued in the small.°

Berowne. This cannot be Hector.

Dumaine. He's a god or a painter; for he makes faces.

---

625 **And** if 632 **baited** tormented 633–34 **Achilles . . . Hector**
(the Greek and Trojan champions) 639 **clean-timbered** clean-
limbed 642 **small** lower part of the leg

Armado. "The armipotent° Mars, of lances the al-
645   mighty,
    Gave Hector a gift—"

Dumaine. A gilt nutmeg.°

Berowne. A lemon.

Longaville. Stuck with cloves.

650 *Dumaine.* No, cloven.

Armado. Peace!
    "The armipotent Mars, of lances the almighty,
    Gave Hector a gift, the heir of Ilion;
    A man so breathed° that certain he would fight, yea
655   From morn till night, out of his pavilion.°
    I am that flower—"

Dumaine.   That mint.

Longaville.   That columbine.

Armado. Sweet Lord Longaville, rein thy tongue.

Longaville. I must rather give it the rein, for it runs
    against Hector.

660 *Dumaine.* Ay, and Hector's a greyhound.

Armado. The sweet war-man is dead and rotten.
    Sweet chucks, beat not the bones of the buried.
    When he breathed, he was a man. But I will for-
    ward with my device. [*To the Princess*] Sweet roy-
665   alty, bestow on me the sense of hearing.
           Berowne steps forth [*to whisper to Costard*].

Princess. Speak, brave Hector; we are much delighted.

Armado. I do adore thy sweet Grace's slipper.

Boyet. [*Aside to Dumaine*] Loves her by the foot.

Dumaine. [*Aside to Boyet*] He may not by the yard.°

---

645 **armipotent** powerful in arms   647 **gilt nutmeg** (with special
icing)   654 **breathed** well-exercised   655 **pavilion** tent for a champion at a tournament   669 **yard** (slang word for male organ)

Armado. "This Hector far surmounted Hannibal—" 670
    The party is gone.°

Costard. Fellow Hector, she is gone.° She is two
    months on her way.

Armado. What meanest thou?

Costard. Faith, unless you play the honest Troyan, 675
    the poor wench is cast away. She's quick;° the child
    brags in her belly already. 'Tis yours.

Armado. Dost thou infamonize° me among poten-
    tates? Thou shalt die.

Costard. Then shall Hector be whipped for Jaquenetta 680
    that is quick by him, and hanged for Pompey that
    is dead by him.

Dumaine. Most rare Pompey!

Boyet. Renowned Pompey!

Berowne. Greater than great. Great, great, great Pom- 685
    pey! Pompey the Huge!

Dumaine. Hector trembles.

Berowne. Pompey is moved. More Ates,° more Ates!
    Stir them on, stir them on!

Dumaine. Hector will challenge him.   690

Berowne. Ay, if 'a have no more man's blood in his
    belly than will sup a flea.

Armado. By the North Pole, I do challenge thee.

Costard. I will not fight with a pole, like a northern
    man. I'll slash; I'll do it by the sword. I bepray 695
    you, let me borrow my arms again.

Dumaine. Room for the incensed Worthies!

Costard. I'll do it in my shirt.

---

671 **The party is gone** (referring to Hector)   672 **she is gone** she is
pregnant   676 **quick** pregnant   678 **infamonize** defame   688 **Ates**
goddess of mischief

Dumaine. Most resolute Pompey!

700 *Moth.* Master, let me take you a buttonhole lower.°
Do you not see, Pompey is uncasing° for the combat? What mean you? You will lose your reputation.

Armado. Gentlemen and soldiers, pardon me. I will
705 not combat in my shirt.

Dumaine. You may not deny it. Pompey hath made
the challenge.

Armado. Sweet bloods, I both may and will.

Berowne. What reason have you for 't?

710 *Armado.* The naked truth of it is, I have no shirt. I
go woolward° for penance.

Boyet. True, and it was enjoined° him in Rome for
want of linen; since when, I'll be sworn he wore
none but a dishclout of Jaquenetta's, and that 'a
715 wears next his heart for a favor.

Enter a Messenger, Monsieur Marcade.

Marcade. God save you, madam.

Princess. Welcome, Marcade,
But that thou interrupt'st our merriment.

Marcade. I am sorry, madam, for the news I bring
720 Is heavy in my tongue. The king your father—

Princess. Dead, for my life!

Marcade. Even so. My tale is told.

Berowne. Worthies, away! The scene begins to cloud.

Armado. For mine own part, I breathe free breath.

---

700 **take you a buttonhole lower** take you down a peg   701 **uncasing**
removing his coat   711 **go woolward** wearing wool next to the skin
712 **enjoined** commanded

I have seen the day of wrong through the little hole 725
of discretion, and I will right myself like a soldier.
Exeunt Worthies.

King. How fares your Majesty?

Princess. Boyet, prepare. I will away tonight.

King. Madam, not so. I do beseech you, stay.

Princess. Prepare, I say. I thank you, gracious lords, 730
For all your fair endeavors, and entreat
Out of a new-sad soul that you vouchsafe
In your rich wisdom to excuse, or hide
The liberal opposition of our spirits,
If over-boldly we have borne ourselves 735
In the converse of breath.° Your gentleness
Was guilty of it. Farewell, worthy lord.
A heavy heart bears not a humble° tongue.
Excuse me so, coming too short of thanks
For my great suit so easily obtained. 740

King. The extreme parts of time extremely forms
All causes to the purpose of his speed,°
And often at his very loose° decides
That which long process could not arbitrate.
And though the mourning brow of progeny° 745
Forbid the smiling courtesy of love
The holy suit which fain it would convince,°
Yet, since love's argument was first on foot,
Let not the cloud of sorrow justle it
From what it purposed; since to wail friends lost 750
Is not by much so wholesome-profitable
As to rejoice at friends but newly found.

Princess. I understand you not. My griefs are double.

Berowne. Honest plain words best pierce the ear of
    grief;
And by these badges° understand the king. 755

736 **converse of breath** conversation 738 **humble** i.e., civil, tactful
741–42 **The extreme . . . speed** time, as it runs out, directs everything
towards its conclusion 743 **at his very loose** in the act of letting go
745 **progeny** descendants 747 **convince** prove 755 **badges** tokens

For your fair sakes have we neglected time,
Played foul play with our oaths. Your beauty,
    ladies,
Hath much deformed us, fashioning our humors
Even to the opposèd end of our intents;
760 And what in us hath seemed ridiculous—
As love is full of unbefitting strains,
All wanton as a child, skipping and vain,
Formed by the eye and therefore, like the eye,
Full of straying shapes, of habits and of forms,
765 Varying in subjects as the eye doth roll
To every varied object in his glance;
Which parti-coated° presence of loose love
Put on by us, if, in your heavenly eyes,
Have misbecomed our oaths and gravities,
770 Those heavenly eyes that look into these faults
Suggested° us to make. Therefore, ladies,
Our love being yours, the error that love makes
Is likewise yours. We to ourselves prove false,
By being once false forever to be true
775 To those that make us both—fair ladies, you.
And even that falsehood, in itself a sin,
Thus purifies itself and turns to grace.

Princess. We have received your letters, full of love;
Your favors, the ambassadors of love;
780 And in our maiden council rated° them
At courtship, pleasant jest, and courtesy,
As bombast° and as lining to the time.
But more devout than this in our respects
Have we not been, and therefore met your loves
785 In their own fashion, like a merriment.

Dumaine. Our letters, madam, showed much more
    than jest.

Longaville. So did our looks.

Rosaline.   We did not quote° them so.

___

767 **parti-coated** fool's motley   771 **Suggested** tempted   780 **rated** valued   782 **bombast** padding   787 **quote** regard

King. Now, at the latest minute of the hour
    Grant us your loves.

Princess.   A time, methinks, too short
    To make a world-without-end bargain in.   790
    No, no, my lord, your Grace is perjured much,
    Full of dear guiltiness; and therefore this—
    If for my love (as there is no such cause)
    You will do aught, this shall you do for me:
    Your oath I will not trust, but go with speed   795
    To some forlorn and naked hermitage,
    Remote from all the pleasures of the world;
    There stay until the twelve celestial signs°
    Have brought about the annual reckoning.
    If this austere insociable life   800
    Change not your offer made in heat of blood—
    If frosts and fasts, hard lodging and thin weeds,°
    Nip not the gaudy blossoms of your love,
    But that it bear this trial, and last love—
    Then, at the expiration of the year,   805
    Come challenge me, challenge me by these deserts,
    And, by this virgin palm now kissing thine,
    I will be thine; and till that instant, shut
    My woeful self up in a mourning house,
    Raining the tears of lamentation   810
    For the remembrance of my father's death.
    If this thou do deny, let our hands part,
    Neither entitled in the other's heart.

King. If this, or more than this, I would deny,
    To flatter up° these powers of mine with rest,   815
    The sudden hand of death close up mine eye!
    Hence hermit then—my heart is in thy breast.

[*Berowne.* And what to me, my love? and what to me?

Rosaline. You must be purgèd, too, your sins are
    rank,
    You are attaint° with faults and perjury;   820

---

798 twelve celestial signs (of the Zodiac)   **802 weeds** garments   **815 flatter up** pamper   **820 attaint** charged

Therefore, if you my favor mean to get,
A twelvemonth shall you spend, and never rest,
But seek the weary beds of people sick.]°

Dumaine. But what to me, my love? But what to me?
825 A wife?

Katharine.   A beard, fair health, and honesty;
With three-fold love I wish you all these three.

Dumaine. O, shall I say "I thank you, gentle wife"?

Katharine. Not so, my lord. A twelvemonth and a day
I'll mark no words that smooth-faced wooers say.
830 Come when the king doth to my lady come;
Then, if I have much love, I'll give you some.

Dumaine. I'll serve thee true and faithfully till then.

Katharine. Yet swear not, lest ye be forsworn again.

Longaville. What says Maria?

Maria.   At the twelvemonth's end
835 I'll change my black gown for a faithful friend.

Longaville. I'll stay with patience, but the time is long.

Maria. The liker° you! Few taller are so young.

Berowne. Studies my lady? Mistress, look on me.
Behold the window of my heart, mine eye,
840 What humble suit attends thy answer there.
Impose some service on me for thy love.

Rosaline. Oft have I heard of you, my Lord Berowne,
Before I saw you, and the world's large tongue
Proclaims you for a man replete with mocks,
845 Full of comparisons and wounding flouts,°
Which you on all estates° will execute
That lie within the mercy of your wit.

818–23 (lines 838–72 duplicate this passage in an expanded form;
probably Shakespeare failed to indicate clearly that these six lines
had been superseded)   837 **liker** more like   845 **wounding flouts**
painful jokes   846 **all estates** men of all kinds

To weed this wormwood° from your fructful° brain,
And therewithal to win me, if you please,
Without the which I am not to be won,   *850*
You shall this twelvemonth term from day to day
Visit the speechless sick, and still° converse
With groaning wretches; and your task shall be
With all the fierce endeavor of your wit
To enforce the painèd impotent to smile.   *855*

Berowne. To move wild laughter in the throat of
     death?
  It cannot be; it is impossible;
  Mirth cannot move a soul in agony.

Rosaline. Why, that's the way to choke a gibing spirit,
  Whose influence is begot of that loose grace   *860*
  Which shallow laughing hearers give to fools.
  A jest's prosperity lies in the ear
  Of him that hears it, never in the tongue
  Of him that makes it. Then, if sickly ears,
  Deafed with the clamors of their own dear groans,   *865*
  Will hear your idle scorns, continue then,
  And I will have you and that fault withal;
  But if they will not, throw away that spirit,
  And I shall find you empty of that fault,
  Right joyful of your reformation.   *870*

Berowne. A twelvemonth? Well, befall what will be-
     fall,
  I'll jest a twelvemonth in an hospital.

Princess. [*To the King*] Ay, sweet my lord, and so I
     take my leave.

King. No, madam, we will bring you on your way.

Berowne. Our wooing doth not end like an old play;   *875*
  Jack hath not Jill. These ladies' courtesy
  Might well have made our sport a comedy.

---

848 **wormwood** bitterness   848 **fructful** fruitful   852 **still** always

King. Come, sir, it wants a twelvemonth and a day,
     And then 'twill end.

Berowne.   That's too long for a play.

          Enter [Armado, the] Braggart.

880 *Armado.* Sweet Majesty, vouchsafe me—

Princess. Was not that Hector?

Dumaine. The worthy knight of Troy.

Armado. I will kiss thy royal finger, and take leave.
     I am a votary;° I have vowed to Jaquenetta to hold
885 the plough for her sweet love three year. But, most
     esteemed greatness, will you hear the dialogue that
     the two learned men have compiled in praise of the
     owl and the cuckoo? It should have followed in
     the end of our show.

890 *King.* Call them forth quickly; we will do so.

Armado. Holla! Approach.

          Enter all.

This side is *Hiems,* Winter; this *Ver,* the Spring;
the one maintained by the owl, th' other by the
cuckoo. *Ver,* begin.

          The Song.

895 [*Spring.*]   When daisies pied° and violets blue
               And lady-smocks° all silver-white
          And cuckoo-buds° of yellow hue
               Do paint the meadows with delight,

---

884 **votary** sworn follower   895 **pied** parti-colored   896 **lady-smocks**
water-cresses, or cuckoo flowers   897 **cuckoo-buds** crowfoot, or
buttercup

The cuckoo then, on every tree,
Mocks married men; for thus sings he,   *900*
          "Cuckoo!
Cuckoo, cuckoo!" O word of fear,
Unpleasing to a married ear!
When shepherds pipe on oaten straws,
    And merry larks are ploughmen's clocks, *905*
When turtles tread,° and rooks, and daws,
    And maidens bleach their summer smocks,
The cuckoo then, on every tree,
Mocks married men; for thus sings he,
          "Cuckoo!   *910*
Cuckoo, cuckoo!" O word of fear,
Unpleasing to a married ear!

Winter. When icicles hang by the wall,
    And Dick the shepherd blows his nail,°
And Tom bears logs into the hall,   *915*
    And milk comes frozen home in pail,
When blood is nipped, and ways be foul,
Then nightly sings the staring owl,
          "Tu-whit,
Tu-who!" a merry note,   *920*
While greasy Joan doth keel° the pot.

When all aloud the wind doth blow,
    And coughing drowns the parson's saw,°
And birds sit brooding in the snow,
    And Marian's nose looks red and raw,   *925*
When roasted crabs° hiss in the bowl,
Then nightly sings the staring owl,
          "Tu-whit,

906 **turtles tread** turtledoves mate   914 **blows his nail** blows on his
fingernails to warm them (and so, waiting patiently)   921 **keel** cool,
by stirring or skimming   923 **saw** wise saying   926 **crabs** crab
apples

                Tu-who!" a merry note,
930   While greasy Joan doth keel the pot.

[*Armado.*] The words of Mercury are harsh after the
songs of Apollo.° [You that way, we this way.
                              Exeunt omnes.]

FINIS

931–32 **The words . . . Apollo** i.e., let us end with the songs, because
clever words of the god Mercury would come harshly after the songs of
Apollo, the god of poetry

Textual Note

This edition is based upon the quarto of 1598, which, it is generally agreed, was printed from a manuscript in Shakespeare's own hand. The title page reads: "A / Pleasant / Conceited Comedie / Called, / Loues labors lost. / As it was presented before her Highnes / this last Christmas. / Newly corrected and augmented / By W. Shakespere. / Imprinted at London by W. W. / for Cutbert Burby. / 1598."

Although here there may be a reference to a previous printing, there is no trace of an earlier edition. "Newly corrected and augmented" probably refers to revisions in the manuscript, some of which, as it happens, may be detected in examining the printed text. (See footnotes at 4.3.295 and 5.2.818–23.)

The printing of the 1623 Folio is based upon the quarto. It corrects some errors of the quarto and adds a number of its own. It provides act divisions (mistakenly heading the fifth act "Actus Quartus"), but the scene divisions as well as the list of the names of the persons in the play are the contributions of later editors.

Apart from a considerable number of misreadings the most noteworthy confusions in the quarto are in the speech headings. It is not merely that occasionally *Nathaniel* stands for *Holofernes,* that the *King* is sometimes *Navarre* and sometimes *Ferdinand* in the early part of the second act, and that in the same part of the play Rosaline and Katharine are confused. In the next act the character previously identified as Armado becomes "Braggart," Moth, the Page, becomes "Boy," Holofernes becomes "Pedant," Costard becomes "Clown." Later Sir Nathaniel becomes "Curate" and "Constable" becomes "Dull." The use of the generic names to take the place of the individual ones may be evidence of Shakespeare's revisions. In the present edition the speech headings have been made consistent, but the later substitutions are made evident by the supplementary stage directions indicating the entrances of the various characters.

The revision of the manuscript has left a couple of other obvious confusions. Berowne's speech in Act 4, Scene 3 contains lines that belong to an earlier version, and some of these should have been canceled. If lines 295–316 were omitted, the speech would continue connectedly and without obvious repetitions. It also seems that the exchange between Berowne and Rosaline in Act 5, Scene 2, lines 818–23, was meant to be struck out. In the present edition these passages are retained, but enclosed in square brackets.

The text of this edition is based upon the Heber-Daniel copy of the quarto in the British Museum; the spelling and punctuation have been modernized, obvious misspellings and wrong speech headings corrected, and the quotations from foreign languages regularized. Other departures from the quarto text are listed below: the adopted reading is given first, in italics, followed immediately by the quarto reading in roman letters.

1.1.24 *three* thee 31 *pomp* pome 62 *feast* fast 104 *an* any 114 *swore* sworne 127–31 [Q gives to Longaville] 127 *gentility* gentletie 130 *public* publibue 131 *possibly* possible 218 *welkin's vicegerent* welkis Vizgerent 240 *preposterous* propostrous 276 *worst* wost 289 *King* Ber. 308–09 *prosperity* prosperie

1.2.14 *epitheton* apethaton 100 *blushing* blush-in 143 *Dull* Clo.

2.1.32 *Importunes* Importuous 34 *visaged* visage 44 *parts* peerelsse 88 *unpeopled* vnpeeled 115–26 [the lines here given to Rosaline are in Q given to Katharine] 130 *half of an* halfe of, of an 140 *friendship* faiendship 142 *demand* pemaund 144 *On* One 179 *mine own* my none 195 *Katharine* Rosalin 210 *Rosaline* Katherin 221 [Q gives to *La.*] 222–23 [Q gives to *Lad.*] 224 [Q gives to *La.*] 236 *agate* Agot 246 *quote* coate 254 [Q gives to *Lad.*] 255 [Q gives to *Lad.* 2] 256 [Q gives to *Lad.* 3] 257 [Q gives to *Lad.*] 258 [Q gives to *Lad.*]

3.1.14 *throat as if* throate, if 16 *through the nose* through: nose 19 *thinbelly* thinbellies 25 *note me?—that* note men that 28 *penny* penne 67 *voluble* volable 74 *the mail* thee male 74 *plain* pline 136 *ounce* ouce 139 *remuneration* remuration 140 *One penny* i.d. 177 *beadle* Bedell 178 *critic* Crietick 182 *senior-junior* signior *Iunios* 186 *plackets* Placcats 188 *paritors* Parrators 192 *German clock* Iermane Cloake 198 *whitely* whitly 206 *sue* shue

4.1.6 *On* Ore 33 *heart* hart 71 *saw ... saw* See ... see 72 *overcame* couercame 76 *king's* King 110 *suitor ... suitor* shooter ... shooter

122 *Pepin* Pippen   125 *Guinever* Guinouer   132 *hit it* hit   134 *mete*
meate   136 *ne'er* neare   138 *pin* is in   140 *too* to   146 *to th'* one ath
toothen   149 *o' t' other* atother   150 *a most* most   150 s.d. *Shout* Shoot
151 *Exit* Exeunt

4.2.5 *coelo* Celo   8 *epithets* epythithes   30 *we of taste* we taste   31
indiscreet indistreell   37 *Dictynna . . . Dictynna* Dictisima . . . dictisima
38 *Dictynna* dictima   52 *ignorant, I call* ignorault cald   55 *scurrility*
squirilitie   57 *preyful* prayfull   61 *sores—o' sorel* sores o sorell   66–150
[all speech prefixes of Holofernes and Nathaniel are reversed in Q, except at
107]   70 *pia mater* primater   72 *those in whom* those whom   78 *ingenious* ingenous   80 *sapit* sapis   84 *pierce-one* Person   86 *likest* liklest
94–95 *Fauste . . . ruminat* Facile precor gellida, quando pecas omnia sub
vmbra ruminat   98–99 *Venetia . . . pretia* vemchie, vencha, que non te vnde,
que non te perreche   122 *canzonet* cangenet   136 *writing* written   138
Sir Nathaniel Ped. Sir Holofernes   159 *ben* bien

4.3.13,14 *melancholy* mallicholie   48 *King* Long.   52 *triumviry* tri-
umpherie   74 *idolatry* ydotarie   86 *quoted* coted   92 *And I mine* And
mine   98 *ode* Odo   107 *Wished* Wish   111 *thorn* throne   129 *o'erheard* ore-hard   154 *coaches* couches   160 *mote . . . mote* Moth . . . Moth
179 *men like you, men* men like men   181 *Joan* Ione   247 *wood* word
258 *painting and usurping* painting vsurping   259 *doters* dooters   312
woman's womas   315–16 [between these lines Q has: With our selues]
322 *beauty's* beautis   358 *authors* authhour   360 *Let us* Lets vs   382
Allons! Allons! Alone alone   384 *forsworn* forsorne

5.1.10 *hominem* hominum   28 *insanie* infamie   30 *bone* bene   31
Bone? Bone for bene! Priscian Bome boon for boon prescian   34 *gaudeo*
gaudio   36 *Quare* Quari   51 *pueritia* puericia   52 *silly* seely   59 *wave*
wane   59 *Mediterranean* meditaranium   60 *venew* vene we   69 *manu*
vnũ   78 *dunghill* dungil   79 *Dunghill* dunghel   99 *importunate* impor-
tunt   110 *secrecy* secretie   119 *Nathaniel* Holofernes   121 *rend'red*
rended   153 *Allons* Alone

5.2.13 *ne'er* neare   17 *ha' been a grandam* a bin Grandam   43 *'Ware
pencils, ho!* Ware pensalls, How?   53 *pearls* Pearle   65 *hests* deuice   74
wantonness wantons be   80 *stabbed* stable   89 *sycamore* Siccamone   93
Warily warely   95 *overheard* ouer hard   96 *they* thy   122 *parley, court*
parlee, to court   134 *too* two   148 *her* his   152 *e'er* ere   159 [Q gives
to Berowne]   163 *ever* euen   175 *strangers* stranges   217 [Q gives to
Rosaline]   225 *Price* Prise   243–56 [Q gives "Maria" for "Katharine"]
298 *vailing* varling   300 *woo* woo   310 *run* runs   324 *too* to   329 *ushering* hushering   342 *Construe* Consture   353 *unsullied* vnsallied   375
wit wits   408 *affectation* affection   461 *on't* ant   464 *zany* saine   483
manage nuage   501 *they* thy   515 *least* best   529 *de la guerra* delaguar
564 *this* his   584 [Q has "Exit Curat"]   598 *proved* proud   647 *gilt* gift
689 *Stir them on, stir* stir them, or stir   751 *wholesome* holdsome   779 *the
ambassadors* embassadours   783 *this in our* this our   787 *quote* cote
808 *instant* instance   813 *entitled* intiled   817 *hermit* herrite   819 *rank*
rackt   825 *A wife?* [included in following speech in Q]   829 *smooth-faced*
smothfast   896–97 [these lines transposed in Q]   917 *foul* full   931–32
The words . . . Apollo [printed in larger type in Q without any speech-heading;
F adds *You that way: we this way,* and heading *Brag.*]

A Note on the Sources of
Love's Labor's Lost

No source for the plot of *Love's Labor's Lost* is known to exist but it is often supposed that Shakespeare was building upon reports of historic events. The very names of Navarre and the lords,* the matter of property disputes involving the King of France, the existence of a learned academy favored by the French nobility, and accounts of political negotiations in which certain court ladies were involved, all these point to incidents in recent French history which were reported upon at the time. So far no record has been found of any single happening that is plainly the original of the episodes of the play. It is only in the sum of the reports of similar incidents that the idea that Shakespeare is building upon historical matters comes to seem truly likely.

The play, whether meant originally for performance at a great house, or at a children's theater, exploited these historical events presumably because they treated matters in which the audience was also interested. English court circles were also drawn to the idea of learned academies and were involved in disputes centering on Platonic theories of love. Upon reflection, the treatment of certain episodes in France would have served as comment upon the life of the court in England. Quite as naturally Shakespeare could work into the main story all sorts of allusions to the life of letters and introduce subsidiary plotting to expand upon the story of the aristocratic academicians. So the play directs particular satire against specific English fashions—euphuism, for instance—as well as the universal extravagances of humanists and pedants and actors. Here, too, the references seem again and again to point to particular persons and to specific incidents,

*The Marshal de Biron (Berowne) and Longueville were close associates of Henry, not Ferdinand, of Navarre. The Duc de Mayenne (Dumaine?) was once his enemy but later an ally. Boyet and Marcadé are the names of historical persons.

and scholars have therefore argued that Shakespeare took some of his contemporaries as models for the characters in his comic plot, and the characters that were in part borrowed from the *commedia dell'arte* from time to time present themselves in the guise of Thomas Nashe, Sir Walter Raleigh, John Florio, and perhaps others. To J. D. Wilson these matters become so important that he is convinced that the play "was written as a *topical* play." But G. L. Kittredge, and others after him, have thought it "merely whimsical" to identify Armado and Holofernes and the others in any such way.

On particular points it is seldom possible to resolve this dispute, most especially if the supposed allusions are studied primarily in the light of literary history. But the direction of much modern literary scholarship is to give precedence in the consideration of the elements of a work of art to a study of their relation to the work itself as an imaginative entity, and the effect of such an emphasis is to work in opposition to any theory that regards the work primarily as a historical record. In short, the impression of topical allusion is inescapable, but if one takes the play as substantially summed up by its title, the topicality seems to be absorbed in the imaginative and the fanciful, and in all the charm of the play's poetic and theatrical effects.

The historical documents that are most often cited in presenting analogues to certain incidents in the play are: *The Chronicles of Enguerrand de Monstrelet, 1440–1516;* Pierre de la Primaudaye, *The French Academie;* H. C. Davila, *The History of the Civil Wars of France; Gesta Grayorum: or The History of the High and Mighty Prince Henry, Prince of Purpoole . . . who Reigned and Died, A. D. 1594.* The relevant sections can be found in the first volume of Geoffrey Bullough's *Narrative and Dramatic Sources of Shakespeare.* There are of course no documents that in any substantial way support the ascriptions of topicality.

Commentaries

WALTER PATER

From Appreciations

Love's Labors Lost is one of the earliest of Shakespeare's dramas, and has many of the peculiarities of his poems, which are also the work of his earlier life. The opening speech of the king on the immortality of fame—on the triumph of fame over death—and the nobler parts of Biron, display something of the monumental style of Shakespeare's sonnets, and are not without their conceits of thought and expression. This connection of *Love's Labors Lost* with Shakespeare's poems is further enforced by the actual insertion in it of three sonnets and a faultless song; which, in accordance with his practice in other plays, are inwoven into the argument of the piece and, like the golden ornaments of a fair woman, give it a peculiar air of distinction. There is merriment in it also, with choice illustrations of both wit and humor; a laughter, often exquisite, ringing, if faintly, yet as genuine laughter still, though sometimes sinking into mere burlesque, which has not lasted quite so well. And Shakespeare brings a serious effect out of the trifling of his characters. A dainty lovemaking is interchanged

From *Appreciations* by Walter Pater. London and New York: The Macmillan Company, 1889. The essay was first published in *Macmillan's Magazine,* December 1885.

with the more cumbrous play: below the many artifices of
Biron's amorous speeches we may trace sometimes the
"unutterable longing"; and the lines in which Katherine
describes the blighting through love of her younger sister are
one of the most touching things in older literature.* Again,
how many echoes seem awakened by those strange words,
actually said in jest!—"The sweet war-man (Hector of Troy)
is dead and rotten; sweet chucks, beat not the bones of
the buried: when he breathed, he was a man!"—words
which may remind us of Shakespeare's own epitaph. In the
last scene, an ingenious turn is given to the action, so that
the piece does not conclude after the manner of other
comedies.—

> Our wooing doth not end like an old play;
> Jack hath not Jill:

and Shakespeare strikes a passionate note across it at last,
in the entrance of the messenger, who announces to the
princess that the king her father is suddenly dead.

The merely dramatic interest of the piece is slight enough;
only just sufficient, indeed, to form the vehicle of its wit and
poetry. The scene—a park of the King of Navarre—is unal-
tered throughout; and the unity of the play is not so much the
unity of a drama as that of a series of pictorial groups, in
which the same figures reappear, in different combinations
but on the same background. It is as if Shakespeare had
intended to bind together, by some inventive conceit, the
devices of an ancient tapestry, and give voices to its figures.
On one side, a fair palace; on the other, the tents of the
Princess of France, who has come on an embassy from her
father to the King of Navarre; in the midst, a wide space of
smooth grass. The same personages are combined over and
over again into a series of gallant scenes: the princess, the
three masked ladies, the quaint, pedantic king—one of those
amiable kings men have never loved enough, whose serious
occupation with the things of the mind seems, by contrast
with the more usual forms of kingship, like frivolity or play.
Some of the figures are grotesque merely, and all the male

*5.2

ones at least, a little fantastic. Certain objects reappearing from scene to scene—love letters crammed with verses to the margin, and lovers' toys—hint obscurely at some story of intrigue. Between these groups, on a smaller scale, come the slighter and more homely episodes, with Sir Nathaniel the curate, the country-maid Jaquenetta, Moth or Mote the elfin-page, with Hiems and Ver, who recite "the dialogue that the two learned men have compiled in praise of the owl and the cuckoo." The ladies are lodged in tents, because the king, like the princess of the modern poet's fancy, has taken a vow

> To make his court a little Academe,

and for three years' space no woman may come within a mile of it; and the play shows how this artificial attempt was broken through. For the king and his three fellow scholars are of course soon forsworn, and turn to writing sonnets, each to his chosen lady. These fellow scholars of the king— "quaint votaries of science" at first, afterwards "affection's men-at-arms"—three youthful knights, gallant, amorous, chivalrous, but also a little affected, sporting always a curious foppery of language, are, throughout, the leading figures in the foreground; one of them, in particular, being more carefully depicted than the others, and in himself very noticeable—a portrait with somewhat puzzling manner and expression, which at once catches the eye irresistibly and keeps it fixed.

Play is often that about which people are most serious; and the humorist may observe how, under all love of playthings, there is almost always hidden an appreciation of something really engaging and delightful. This is true always of the toys of children: it is often true of the playthings of grown-up people, their vanities, their fopperies even, their lighter loves; the cynic would add their pursuit of fame. Certainly, this is true without exception of the playthings of a past age, which to those who succeed it are always full of a pensive interest—old manners, old dresses, old houses. For what is called fashion in these matters occupies, in each age, much of the care of many of the most discerning people, furnishing them with a kind of mirror of their real inward refinements and their capacity for selection. Such modes or fashions are, at their best, an example of the artistic predominance of form over matter—of the manner of the doing of it over the thing done—and have a beauty of their own. It is so with that old euphuism of the Elizabethan age—that pride of dainty language and curious expression, which it is very easy to ridicule, which often made itself ridiculous, but which had below it a real sense of fitness and nicety; and which, as we see in this very play, and still more clearly in the sonnets, had some fascination for the young Shakespeare himself. It is this foppery of delicate language, this fashionable plaything of his time, with which Shakespeare is occupied in *Love's Labors Lost*. He shows us the manner in all its stages, passing from the grotesque and vulgar pedantry of Holofernes, through the extravagant but polished caricature of Armado, to become the peculiar characteristic of a real though still quaint poetry in Biron himself, who is still chargeable even at his best with just a little affectation. As Shakespeare laughs broadly at it in Holofernes or Armado, so he is the analyst of its curious charm in Biron; and this analysis involves a delicate raillery by Shakespeare himself at his own chosen manner.

This "foppery" of Shakespeare's day had, then, its really delightful side, a quality in no sense "affected," by which it satisfies a real instinct in our minds—the fancy so many of us have for an exquisite and curious skill in the use of words. Biron is the perfect flower of this manner:

A man of fire-new words, fashion's own knight:

—as he describes Armado, in terms which are really applicable to himself. In him this manner blends with a true gallantry of nature and an affectionate complaisance and grace. He has at times some of its extravagance or caricature also, but the shades of expression by which he passes from this to the "golden cadence" of Shakespeare's own most characteristic verse are so fine that it is sometimes difficult to trace them. What is a vulgarity in Holofernes, and a caricature in Armado, refines itself with him into the expression of a nature truly and inwardly bent upon a form of delicate perfection, and is accompanied by a real insight into the laws which determine what is exquisite in language and their root in the nature of things. He can appreciate quite the opposite style—

> In russet yeas, and honest kersey noes;

he knows the first law of pathos, that

> Honest plain words best suit the ear of grief.

He delights in his own rapidity of intuition; and, in harmony with the half-sensuous philosophy of the sonnets, exalts, a little scornfully, in many memorable expressions, the judgment of the senses, above all slower, more toilsome means of knowledge, scorning some who fail to see things only because they are so clear:

> So ere you find where light in darkness lies,
> Your light grows dark by losing of your eyes:—

as with some German commentators on Shakespeare. Appealing always to actual sensation from men's affected theories, he might seem to despise learning, as, indeed, he has taken up his deep studies partly in sport, and demands always the profit of learning in renewed enjoyment. Yet he surprises us from time to time by intuitions which could come only from a deep experience and power of observation; and men listen to him, old and young, in spite of themselves. He is quickly impressible to the slightest clouding of the spirits in social intercourse, and has moments of extreme seriousness: his trial-task may well be, as Rosaline puts it—

> To enforce the pained impotent to smile.

But still, through all, he is true to his chosen manner: that gloss of dainty language is a second nature with him; even at his best he is not without a certain artifice; the trick of playing on words never deserts him; and Shakespeare, in whose own genius there is an element of this very quality, shows us in this graceful, and, as it seems, studied, portrait, his enjoyment of it.

As happens with every true dramatist, Shakespeare is for the most part hidden behind the persons of his creation. Yet there are certain of his characters in which we feel that there is something of self-portraiture. And it is not so much in his grander, more subtle and ingenious creations that we feel this—in *Hamlet* and *King Lear*—as in those slighter and more spontaneously developed figures, who, while far from playing principal parts, are yet distinguished by a peculiar happiness and delicate ease in the drawing of them—figures which possess, above all, that winning attractiveness which there is no man but would willingly exercise, and which resemble those works of art which, though not meant to be very great or imposing, are yet wrought of the choicest material. Mercutio, in *Romeo and Juliet,* belongs to this group of Shakespeare's characters—versatile, mercurial people, such as make good actors, and in whom the

Nimble spirits of the arteries,

the finer but still merely animal elements of great wit, predominate. A careful delineation of minor, yet expressive traits seems to mark them out as the characters of his predilection; and it is hard not to identify him with these more than with others. Biron, in *Love's Labors Lost,* is perhaps the most striking member of this group. In this character, which is never quite in touch, never quite on a perfect level of understanding, with the other persons of the play, we see, perhaps, a reflex of Shakespeare himself, when he has just become able to stand aside from and estimate the first period of his poetry.

NORTHROP FRYE

The Argument of Comedy

The Greeks produced two kinds of comedy, Old Comedy, represented by the eleven extant plays of Aristophanes, and New Comedy, of which the best known exponent is Menander. About two dozen New Comedies survive in the work of Plautus and Terence. Old Comedy, however, was out of date before Aristophanes himself was dead; and today, when we speak of comedy, we normally think of something that derives from the Menandrine tradition.

New Comedy unfolds from what may be described as a comic Oedipus situation. Its main theme is the successful effort of a young man to outwit an opponent and possess the girl of his choice. The opponent is usually the father (*senex*), and the psychological descent of the heroine from the mother is also sometimes hinted at. The father frequently wants the same girl, and is cheated out of her by the son, the mother thus becoming the son's ally. The girl is usually a slave or courtesan, and the plot turns on a *cognitio* or discovery of birth which makes her marriageable. Thus it turns out that she is not under an insuperable taboo after all but is an accessible object of desire, so that the plot follows the regular wish-fulfillment pattern. Often the central Oedipus situation is thinly concealed by surrogates or doubles of the main characters, as when the heroine is discovered to be the hero's sister, and has to be married off to his best friend. In Congreve's *Love for Love,* to take a modern instance well

From *English Institute Essays, 1948,* edited by D. A. Robertson. New York: Columbia University Press, 1949. Copyright 1949 by Columbia University Press. Reprinted by permission of the publisher.

within the Menandrine tradition, there are two Oedipus themes in counterpoint: the hero cheats his father out of the heroine, and his best friend violates the wife of an impotent old man who is the heroine's guardian. Whether this analysis is sound or not, New Comedy is certainly concerned with the maneuvering of a young man toward a young woman, and marriage is the tonic chord on which it ends. The normal comic resolution is the surrender of the *senex* to the hero, never the reverse. Shakespeare tried to reverse the pattern in *All's Well That Ends Well,* where the king of France forces Bertram to marry Helena, and the critics have not yet stopped making faces over it.

New Comedy has the blessing of Aristotle, who greatly preferred it to its predecessor, and it exhibits the general pattern of Aristotelian causation. It has a material cause in the young man's sexual desire, and a formal cause in the social order represented by the *senex,* with which the hero comes to terms when he gratifies his desire. It has an efficient cause in the character who brings about the final situation. In classical times this character is a tricky slave; Renaissance dramatists often use some adaptation of the medieval "vice"; modern writers generally like to pretend that nature, or at least the natural course of events, is the efficient cause. The final cause is the audience, which is expected by its applause to take part in the comic resolution. All this takes place on a single order of existence. The action of New Comedy tends to become probable rather than fantastic, and it moves toward realism and away from myth and romance. The one romantic (originally mythical) feature in it, the fact that the hero or heroine turns out to be freeborn or someone's heir, is precisely the feature that trained New Comedy audiences tire of most quickly.

The conventions of New Comedy are the conventions of Jonson and Molière, and a fortiori of the English Restoration and the French rococo. When Ibsen started giving ironic twists to the same formulas, his startled hearers took them for portents of a social revolution. Even the old chestnut about the heroine's being really the hero's sister turns up in *Ghosts* and *Little Eyolf.* The average movie of today is a rigidly conventionalized New Comedy proceeding toward an act which, like death in Greek tragedy, takes place off-stage, and is symbolized by the final embrace.

In all good New Comedy there is a social as well as an individual theme which must be sought in the general atmosphere of reconciliation that makes the final marriage possible. As the hero gets closer to the heroine and opposition is overcome, all the right-thinking people come over to his side. Thus a new social unit is formed on the stage, and the moment that this social unit crystallizes is the moment of the comic resolution. In the last scene, when the dramatist usually tries to get all his characters on the stage at once, the audience witnesses the birth of a renewed sense of social integration. In comedy as in life the regular expression of this is a festival, whether a marriage, a dance, or a feast. Old Comedy has, besides a marriage, a *komos,* the processional dance from which comedy derives its name; and the masque, which is a by-form of comedy, also ends in a dance.

This new social integration may be called, first, a kind of moral norm and, second, the pattern of a free society. We can see this more clearly if we look at the sort of characters who impede the progress of the comedy toward the hero's victory. These are always people who are in some kind of mental bondage, who are helplessly driven by ruling passions, neurotic compulsions, social rituals, and selfishness. The miser, the hypochondriac, the hypocrite, the pedant, the snob: these are humors, people who do not fully know what they are doing, who are slaves to a predictable self-imposed pattern of behavior. What we call the moral norm is, then, not morality but deliverance from moral bondage. Comedy is designed not to condemn evil, but to ridicule a lack of self-knowledge. It finds the virtues of Malvolio and Angelo as comic as the vices of Shylock.

The essential comic resolution, therefore, is an individual release which is also a social reconciliation. The normal individual is freed from the bonds of a humorous society, and a normal society is freed from the bonds imposed on it by humorous individuals. The Oedipus pattern we noted in New Comedy belongs to the individual side of this, and the sense of the ridiculousness of the humor to the social side. But all real comedy is based on the principle that these two forms of release are ultimately the same: this principle may be seen at its most concentrated in *The Tempest.* The rule holds whether the resolution is expressed in social terms, as in *The Merchant of Venice,* or in individual terms, as in Ibsen's *An Enemy of the People.*

The freer the society, the greater the variety of individuals it can tolerate, and the natural tendency of comedy is to include as many as possible in its final festival. The motto of comedy is Terence's "Nothing human is alien to me." This may be one reason for the traditional comic importance of the parasite, who has no business to be at the festival but is nevertheless there. The spirit of reconciliation which pervades the comedies of Shakespeare is not to be ascribed to a personal attitude of his own, about which we know nothing whatever, but to his impersonal concentration on the laws of comic form.

Hence the moral quality of the society presented is not the point of the comic resolution. In Jonson's *Volpone* the final assertion of the moral norm takes the form of a social revenge on Volpone, and the play ends with a great bustle of sentences to penal servitude and the galleys. One feels perhaps that the audience's sense of the moral norm does not need so much hard labor. In *The Alchemist,* when Lovewit returns to his house, the virtuous characters have proved so weak and the rascals so ingenious that the action dissolves in laughter. Whichever is morally the better ending, that of *The Alchemist* is more concentrated comedy. *Volpone* is starting to move toward tragedy, toward the vision of a greatness which develops *hybris* and catastrophe.

The same principle is even clearer in Aristophanes. Aristophanes is the most personal of writers: his opinions on every subject are written all over his plays, and we have no doubt of his moral attitude. We know that he wanted peace with Sparta and that he hated Cleon, and when his comedy depicts the attaining of peace and the defeat of Cleon we know that he approved and wanted his audience to approve. But in *Ecclesiazusae* a band of women in disguise railroad a communistic scheme through the Assembly, which is a horrid parody of Plato's *Republic,* and proceed to inaugurate Plato's sexual communism with some astonishing improvements. Presumably Aristophanes did not applaud this, yet the comedy follows the same pattern and the same resolution. In *The Birds* the Peisthetairos who defies Zeus and blocks out Olympus with his Cloud-Cuckoo-Land is accorded the same triumph that is given to the Trygaeus of the *Peace* who flies to heaven and brings a golden age back to Athens.

Comedy, then, may show virtue her own feature and scorn her own image—for Hamlet's famous definition of drama was originally a definition of comedy. It may emphasize the birth of an ideal society as you like it, or the tawdriness of the sham society which is the way of the world. There is an important parallel here with tragedy. Tragedy, we are told, is expected to raise but not ultimately to accept the emotions of pity and terror. These I take to be the sense of moral good and evil, respectively, which we attach to the tragic hero. He may be as good as Caesar, and so appeal to our pity, or as bad as Macbeth, and so appeal to terror, but the particular thing called tragedy that happens to him does not depend on his moral status. The tragic catharsis passes beyond moral judgment, and while it is quite possible to construct a moral tragedy, what tragedy gains in morality it loses in cathartic power. The same is true of the comic catharsis, which raises sympathy and ridicule on a moral basis, but passes beyond both.

Many things are involved in the tragic catharsis, but one of them is a mental or imaginative form of the sacrificial ritual out of which tragedy arose. This is the ritual of the struggle, death, and rebirth of a God-Man, which is linked to the yearly triumph of spring over winter. The tragic hero is not really killed, and the audience no longer eats his body and drinks his blood, but the corresponding thing in art still takes place. The audience enters into communion with the body of the hero, becoming thereby a single body itself. Comedy grows out of the same ritual, for in the ritual the tragic story has a comic sequel. Divine men do not die: they die and rise again. The ritual pattern behind the catharsis of comedy is the resurrection that follows the death, the epiphany or manifestation of the risen hero. This is clear enough in Aristophanes, where the hero is treated as a risen God-Man, led in triumph with the divine honors of the Olympic victor, rejuvenated, or hailed as a new Zeus. In New Comedy the new human body is, as we have seen, both a hero and a social group. Aristophanes is not only closer to the ritual pattern, but contemporary with Plato; and his comedy, unlike Menander's, is Platonic and dialectic: it seeks not the entelechy of the soul but the Form of the Good, and finds it in the resurrection of the soul from the world of the cave to the sunlight. The audience gains a vision of that resurrection whether the conclusion is joyful or ironic, just as in tragedy it gains a vision of a heroic death whether the hero is morally innocent or guilty.

Two things follow from this: first, that tragedy is really implicit or uncompleted comedy; second, that comedy contains a potential tragedy within itself. With regard to the latter, Aristophanes is full of traces of the original death of the hero which preceded his resurrection in the ritual. Even in New Comedy the dramatist usually tries to bring his action as close to a tragic overthrow of the hero as he can get it, and reverses this movement as suddenly as possible. In Plautus the tricky slave is often forgiven or even freed after having been threatened with all the brutalities that a very brutal dramatist can think of, including crucifixion. Thus the resolution of New Comedy seems to be a realistic foreshortening of a death-and-resurrection pattern, in which the struggle and rebirth of a divine hero has shrunk into a marriage, the freeing of a slave, and the triumph of a young man over an older one.

As for the conception of tragedy as implicit comedy, we may notice how often tragedy closes on the major chord of comedy: the Aeschylean trilogy, for instance, proceeds to what is really a comic resolution, and so do many tragedies of Euripides. From the point of view of Christianity, too, tragedy is an episode in that larger scheme of redemption and resurrection to which Dante gave the name of *commedia*. This conception of *commedia* enters drama with the miracle-play cycles, where such tragedies as the Fall and the Crucifixion are episodes of a dramatic scheme in which the divine comedy has the last word. The sense of tragedy as a prelude to comedy is hardly separable from anything explicitly Christian. The serenity of the final double chorus in the St. Matthew Passion would hardly be attainable if composer and audience did not know that there was more to the story. Nor would the death of Samson lead to "calm of mind all passion spent" if Samson were not a prototype of the rising Christ.

New Comedy is thus contained, so to speak, within the symbolic structure of Old Comedy, which in its turn is contained within the Christian conception of *commedia*. This sounds like a logically exhaustive classification, but we have still not caught Shakespeare in it.

It is only in Jonson and the Restoration writers that English comedy can be called a form of New Comedy. The earlier tradition established by Peele and developed by Lyly, Greene, and the masque writers, which uses themes from romance and folklore and avoids the comedy of manners, is the one followed by Shakespeare. These themes are largely medieval in origin, and derive, not from the mysteries or the moralities or the interludes, but from a fourth dramatic tradition. This is the drama of folk ritual, of the St. George play and the mummers' play, of the feast of the ass and the Boy Bishop, and of all the dramatic activity that punctuated the Christian calendar with the rituals of an immemorial paganism. We may call this the drama of the green world, and its theme is once again the triumph of life over the waste land, the death and revival of the year impersonated by figures still human, and once divine as well.

When Shakespeare began to study Plautus and Terence, his dramatic instinct, stimulated by his predecessors, divined that there was a profounder pattern in the argument of comedy than appears in either of them. At once—for the process is beginning in *The Comedy of Errors*—he started groping toward that profounder pattern, the ritual of death and revival that also underlies Aristophanes, of which an exact equivalent lay ready to hand in the drama of the green world. This parallelism largely accounts for the resemblances to Greek ritual which Colin Still has pointed out in *The Tempest*.

The Two Gentlemen of Verona is an orthodox New Comedy except for one thing. The hero Valentine becomes captain of a band of outlaws in a forest, and all the other characters are gathered into this forest and become converted. Thus the action of the comedy begins in a world represented as a normal world, moves into the green world, goes into a metamorphosis there in which the comic resolution is achieved, and returns to the normal world. The forest in this play is the embryonic form of the fairy world of *A Midsummer Night's Dream,* the Forest of Arden in *As You Like It,* Windsor Forest in *The Merry Wives of Windsor,* and the pastoral world of the mythical sea-coasted Bohemia in *The Winter's Tale.* In all these comedies there is the same rhythmic movement from normal world to green world and back again. Nor is this second world confined to the forest comedies. In *The Merchant of Venice* the two worlds are a little harder to see, yet Venice is clearly not the same world as that of Portia's mysterious house in Belmont, where there are caskets teaching that gold and silver are corruptible goods, and from whence proceed the wonderful cosmological harmonies of the fifth act. In *The Tempest* the entire action takes place in the second world, and the same may be said of *Twelfth Night,* which, as its title implies, presents a carnival society, not so much a green world as an evergreen one. The second world is absent from the so-called problem comedies, which is one of the things that makes them problem comedies.

The green world charges the comedies with a symbolism in which the comic resolution contains a suggestion of the old ritual pattern of the victory of summer over winter. This is explicit in *Love's Labor's Lost.* In this very masque-like play, the comic contest takes the form of the medieval debate of winter and spring. In *The Merry Wives of Windsor* there is an elaborate ritual of the defeat of winter, known to folklorists as "carrying out Death," of which Falstaff is the victim; and Falstaff must have felt that, after being thrown into the water, dressed up as a witch and beaten out of a house with curses, and finally supplied with a beast's head and singed with candles while he said, "Divide me like a brib'd buck, each a haunch," he had done about all that could reasonably be asked of any fertility spirit.

The association of this symbolism with the death and revival of human beings is more elusive, but still perceptible. The fact that the heroine often brings about the comic resolution by disguising herself as a boy is familiar enough. In the Hero of *Much Ado About Nothing* and the Helena of

All's Well That Ends Well, this theme of the withdrawal and return of the heroine comes as close to a death and revival as Elizabethan conventions will allow. The Thaisa of *Pericles* and the Fidele of *Cymbeline* are beginning to crack the conventions, and with the disappearance and revival of Hermione in *The Winter's Tale,* who actually returns once as a ghost in a dream, the original nature-myth of Demeter and Proserpine is openly established. The fact that the dying and reviving character is usually female strengthens the feeling that there is something maternal about the green world, in which the new order of the comic resolution is nourished and brought to birth. However, a similar theme which is very like the rejuvenation of the *senex* so frequent in Aristophanes occurs in the folklore motif of the healing of the impotent king on which *All's Well That Ends Well* is based, and this theme is probably involved in the symbolism of Prospero.

The conception of a second world bursts the boundaries of Menandrine comedy, yet it is clear that the world of Puck is no world of eternal forms or divine revelation. Shakespeare's comedy is not Aristotelian and realistic like Menander's, nor Platonic and dialectic like Aristophanes', nor Thomist and sacramental like Dante's, but a fourth kind. It is an Elizabethan kind, and is not confined either to Shakespeare or to the drama. Spenser's epic is a wonderful contrapuntal intermingling of two orders of existence, one the red and white world of English history, the other the green world of the Faerie Queene. The latter is a world of crusading virtues proceeding from the Faerie Queene's court and designed to return to that court when the destiny of the other world is fulfilled. The fact that the Faerie Queene's knights are sent out during the twelve days of the Christmas festival suggests our next point.

Shakespeare too has his green world of comedy and his red and white world of history. The story of the latter is at one point interrupted by an invasion from the comic world, when Falstaff *senex et parasitus* throws his gigantic shadow over Prince Henry, assuming on one occasion the role of his father. Clearly, if the Prince is ever to conquer France he must reassert the moral norm. The moral norm is duly

reasserted, but the rejection of Falstaff is not a comic resolution. In comedy the moral norm is not morality but deliverance, and we certainly do not feel delivered from Falstaff
as we feel delivered from Shylock with his absurd and
vicious bond. The moral norm does not carry with it the
vision of a free society: Falstaff will always keep a bit of that
in his tavern.

Falstaff is a mock king, a lord of misrule, and his tavern is
a Saturnalia. Yet we are reminded of the original meaning of
the Saturnalia, as a rite intended to recall the golden age of
Saturn. Falstaff's world is not a golden world, but as long as
we remember it we cannot forget that the world of *Henry V*
is an iron one. We are reminded too of another traditional
denizen of the green world, Robin Hood, the outlaw who
manages to suggest a better kind of society than those who
make him an outlaw can produce. The outlaws in *The Two
Gentlemen of Verona* compare themselves, in spite of the
Italian setting, to Robin Hood, and in *As You Like It* Charles
the wrestler says of Duke Senior's followers: "There they
live like the old Robin Hood of England: they say many
young gentlemen flock to him every day, and fleet the time
carelessly, as they did in the golden world."

In the histories, therefore, the comic Saturnalia is a tem-
porary reversal of normal standards, comic "relief" as it is
called, which subsides and allows the history to continue. In
the comedies, the green world suggests an original golden
age which the normal world has usurped and which makes
us wonder if it is not the normal world that is the real Saturnalia. In *Cymbeline* the green world finally triumphs over a
historical theme, the reason being perhaps that in that play
the incarnation of Christ, which is contemporary with Cymbeline, takes place offstage, and accounts for the halcyon
peace with which the play concludes. From then on in
Shakespeare's plays, the green world has it all its own way,
and both in *Cymbeline* and in *Henry VIII* there may be suggestions that Shakespeare, like Spenser, is moving toward a
synthesis of the two worlds, a wedding of Prince Arthur and
the Faerie Queene.

This world of fairies, dreams, disembodied souls, and
pastoral lovers may not be a "real" world, but, if not, there is
something equally illusory in the stumbling and blinded fol-

lies of the "normal" world, of Theseus' Athens with its idiotic marriage law, of Duke Frederick and his melancholy tyranny, of Leontes and his mad jealousy, of the Court Party with their plots and intrigues. The famous speech of Prospero about the dream nature of reality applies equally to Milan and the enchanted island. We spend our lives partly in a waking world we call normal and partly in a dream world which we create out of our own desires. Shakespeare endows both worlds with equal imaginative power, brings them opposite one another, and makes each world seem unreal when seen by the light of the other. He uses freely both the heroic triumph of New Comedy and the ritual resurrection of its predecessor, but his distinctive comic resolution is different from either: it is a detachment of the spirit born of this reciprocal reflection of two illusory realities. We need not ask whether this brings us into a higher order of existence or not, for the question of existence is not relevant to poetry.

We have spoken of New Comedy as Aristotelian, Old Comedy as Platonic and Dante's *commedia* as Thomist, but it is difficult to suggest a philosophical spokesman for the form of Shakespeare's comedy. For Shakespeare, the subject matter of poetry is not life, or nature, or reality, or revelation, or anything else that the philosopher builds on, but poetry itself, a verbal universe. That is one reason why he is both the most elusive and the most substantial of poets.

RICHARD DAVID

From Shakespeare's Comedies
and the Modern Stage

[A study of production problems with particular reference to *Love's Labor's Lost* at the New Theatre (1949–50) . . .]

Dr. Johnson was the last critic who dared to say that Shakespeare's most characteristic and most inspired work lay in his comedies. The Romantics, putting an exaggerated value on tragedy as in some way nearer to the heart of the matter, degraded the comedies to the status of potboilers; and even today we have hardly escaped from the Romantics' spell. We have one expounder of the comedies for every ten on the tragedies; and for a Granville-Barker to stoop to *A Midsummer Night's Dream,* or an Edith Evans to Rosalind, is exceptional.

We may not agree with Johnson that the comedies deserve more effort than the tragedies, but clearly they require more if they are to make a comparable impression on a modern audience. Tragedy is large in gesture and effect, and even when its overtones are lost and the subsidiary strokes bungled, its main import can hardly be missed. Comedy depends much more on detail, on delicate adjustments of balance and of contrast; it seeks to reproduce the climate rather than the actual predicaments of real life and its method is rather allusiveness than direct presentation. Comedy has more and finer points of attachment to the world in which it is composed than has tragedy. For this reason, comedy dates the more rapidly and the more thoroughly, and after a lapse of

From *Shakespeare Survey 4* (1951), edited by Allardyce Nicoll, 129–35. Reprinted by permission of Richard David and the Cambridge University Press.

years a tragedy based even on so fantastic a convention as Fletcher's is easier to grasp than a comedy of Jonson or Middleton, for all its firm grounding in human nature. Tragedy can be understood in the original, as it were, even by those unacquainted with the tongue; whereas comedy, to be appreciated by a modern audience, must undergo some degree of translation into modern terms.

The difficulties that face the would-be translator are broadly of two kinds. Some old comedies have remained crystal clear in intention, though the details of the action and of the language through which that intention is conveyed are now largely incomprehensible without a gloss; in others, language and action are perfectly plain and yet the point of the whole has become obscure or capable of various interpretations. These peculiar difficulties are well exemplified in two distinguished recent productions, the *Love's Labor's Lost* directed by Hugh Hunt for the Old Vic Company in the winter of 1949–50, and Peter Brook's *Measure for Measure*, with which the Stratford Memorial Theatre opened its 1950 season. Whatever may be the topical implications of *Love's Labor's Lost* its main point is plain—the gentle ragging of youthful priggishness and affectation, as measured against natural good sense and natural good feeling—and it is a point that time has not dulled. Dons and donnishness are today even more popular as butts than they were in the 1590s, and the vivacity controlled by a good heart that Shakespeare praises is a virtue that does not grow stale. On the other hand, the almost Joycean reduplication of puns and the obscure allusions of the play are a byword. *Measure for Measure* is by comparison straightforwardness itself as far as the text goes; but the arguments as to whether the piece is comedy or problem-play, Isabella heroine or caricature, are unending.

Even though the intention of *Love's Labor's Lost* may be plain enough, some skill is required in the presentation to convey it to a modern audience. The point or moral of the play (as of so many comedies) is a code of manners, a demonstration of what rational behavior should be by a comparison with irrational behavior. Nathaniel is unwittingly providing an ironic commentary on himself and his peers when he says of Dull:

. . . such barren plants are set before us that we thankful
    should be,
Which we of taste and feeling are, for those parts that do
    fructify in us more than he.

(4.2.29–30)

The standards set are those of taste and feeling, aristocratic
standards, and the ladies must live up to them—the lords,
too, once they have come to their senses. Moreover, the
audience must be conscious throughout that the action is
enclosed in a coherent and self-contained world defined by
these standards.

The coherence of the play was admirably preserved in the
Old Vic production. The sets perfectly suggested the self-
contained world of Navarre's park, shut away among steep
hillslopes down which the hanging woods cascaded, exclud-
ing the everyday world and blanketing every sound that
might penetrate from it. Among the trees showed the turrets
of castles and hunting lodges, each retreat and secret corner
of the domain isolated from the others by the waters of a
spreading lake that was at the same time the means of com-
munication between them. One may criticize the elaboration
and heaviness of this set. It was no doubt suggested by the
backgrounds to Elizabethan miniatures, the more extended
works of Hillyard or of Oliver; but enlarged to backcloth
scale the effect was baroque rather than renaissance, more
Jacobean than Elizabethan. It accorded well with the autumnal ending of the play, but hardly with the green goose
season of its opening. The devotees are solemn enough, but
their solemnity must be seen to be against nature; the landscape (if we must have one) should be a laughing landscape
that mocks their sober suits and matches the frills and freshness of the ladies through whose eyes we judge them. And
yet the sense of a private and self-sufficient world, so suc-
cessfully achieved in this production, owed much to the
swathing and insistent scenery.

The structure of the play is uncomplicated. The first three
acts present the situation and the opposing parties in bold
and simple colors. Act 4 is a helter-skelter with everyone at
cross purposes, diversified by the to and fro of the hunt and
the entrances of the comics. The long last scene builds up

slowly but steadily, becoming more and more fantastic and
ebullient until the appearance of Marcade bursts the bubble
in an instant; this is one of the greatest *coups de théâtre* in
Shakespeare, and it brings, after the whirlwind of fooling
that has preceded it, the still small voice of sincerity and
actuality before the play dissolves in thin air and birdsong.
Hugh Hunt divided the whole naturally enough into three
movements, each set in a different part of the labyrinthine
park. In the first the nobles of Navarre made their pact to
forego female company, and rated Costard the clown for his
transgression of it; at the same spot Armado wandered
ashore, from a boat paddled by Moth, to meet the disquiet-
ing vision of Jaquenetta; here too the ladies of the French
embassy, advancing through the forest glades, were inter-
cepted by Navarre and his courtiers. The focus of the second
movement was a rustic cottage, again by the waterside,
which provided shelter for Armado's lovesick meditations,
and a prison for Costard; after the hunt arranged for the
entertainment of the French ladies had swept by, it served as
a convenient hiding place from which the eavesdropping
lords could overhear each other's confession of forbidden
love, and a rendezvous for Armado and the other devisers of
his pageant. The last movement (that is, the last scene of the
play) opened with the ladies idling outside their pavilion; to
them the masques of the Russians and of the Nine Worthies;
and over the lake at their back, when the merriment was at
its height, loomed the barge that brings the funereal Marcade
with his news of the French King's death to cloud the scene.
The management of this effect was overwhelmingly successful, as was the quiet recapitulation of the lovers' problems that follows, and the final fading of the play in trills and
falling darkness. This by itself was full justification for both
setting and production.

Such elaborate dressing and marshaling of the action,
though foreign to Shakespeare's theater, is legitimate as the
just translation of his intention into modern terms. The original audience of a coterie play or a play of manners (and
Love's Labor's Lost is in some sense this) is specially conditioned, by the community of interests it shares with the
author, to appreciate the mood of his work and accept his
illusion. A modern audience, unused even to the unifying

and sharpening effect of verse, may well be encouraged to draw the same sense of characteristic atmosphere from scenery and direction. In some of his efforts to this end Hunt nevertheless went outside his brief.

The play must open with a tableau of the lords signing their solemn declaration. It is tidy and elegant to balance this, at the point where the ladies are to take over the lead, with a similar tableau of the feminine party, and the last movement in the Old Vic production accordingly opened with a "still" of the ladies outside their pavilion. Shakespeare, however, has made no allowance for this, nor has he provided accompanying action. What are the ladies to do? They shall sing a song in chorus. This is "pretty and apt," but something irrelevant has been added to Shakespeare.

There were other instances of this striving to impose an extra formality on an already formal play. The second movement was rounded off—after Armado and Holofernes had completed their plans for the pageant—with a burlesque dance in which *all* the comics joined. Now it may be appropriate, as Granville-Barker has suggested, that Dull should here dance a few steps of his hay to show what he thinks is a suitable entertainment for the gentlefolk; but for Armado or Holofernes, who has just expressed his disgust at Dull's low suggestion, to take part in it is to deny their nature, and at this point of the play they must still be true to themselves. At the end, when comedy slips imperceptibly into vaudeville, let them dance their jig if you will. A more blatant, though less serious, reversal of Shakespeare's intention for the sake of spectacle occurred in the last movement, when the Russian maskers are begging the ladies for a dance. "Play, music then," says the mock princess. "Nay, you must do it soon. Not yet? No dance! Thus change I like the moon" (4.2.212–13). In the Old Vic production a formal dance did in fact follow the words "Play, music then," and continued some time before Rosaline, resuming her broken speech, brought the measure to an end. Yet it is clear that the lords, though constantly tantalized into thinking that the ladies may dance with them, are as constantly put off. Ten lines later the King is still begging the "princess" to begin.

Such dislocations, the first of dramatic propriety, the second of literal meaning, could hardly be justified even if the added dances succeeded perfectly in reinforcing the tone or continuity of the action. Here they had the opposite effect. The movements were perfunctory, the music feeble and banal to a degree. Yet even perfectly designed music and choreography would here have been an intrusion, a formal element introduced just where the text avoids it. Shakespeare has given plenty of opportunities in this play for formality, and we have now to see the opposite error, of trying to break down a given artificiality and make the scenes of spectacle "come to life." The tableaux, or scenes of ceremony, demand some supporting cast, and no doubt Shakespeare gave his king and princess as large a train of attendants as his company could muster. The sole function of these extras, however, is to add weight and volume to the dignity of their masters, and any attempt to give depth to the scene by making individuals of them is totally un-Shakespearian. A tendency to "work up" the crowd is one of the most dangerous features of modern productions of Shakespeare. In *Love's Labor's Lost,* it is true, there was nothing to equal the horrors of Komisarjevsky's *King Lear,* in which the hundred knights, vociferously echoing their master's "Return with her?" effectively broke not only the rhythm but the mounting tension of one of Shakespeare's greatest dramatic crescendos. The interpolations which the ladies were allowed to make in Boyet's reading of Armado's love letter were exactly similar but in this context harmless; while the caperings and posturings and beard-waggings of the burlesque philosophers in Navarre's train, which were employed to "lighten" the King's first speech and his reception of the ladies' embassy, were not so much destroying Shakespeare's intention, as grossly overplaying it. The solemn performance of Navarre and his peers has indeed its anti-masque; but that is later provided by Armado, Holofernes and Nathaniel and no duplication of it is needed. It was again an overzealous striving for vigor and variety that made a pantomime of the hunting scene.

Finally, a rather different form of overemphasis. At the beginning of the last scene the ladies' lighthearted chatter about Cupid suddenly steadies as Rosaline says to Katharine:

You'll ne'er be friends with him: 'a killed your sister.

(5.2.13)

Katharine's reply introduces the first note of seriousness into the play:

> He made her melancholy, sad, and heavy;
> And so she died. Had she been light, like you,
> Of such a merry, nimble, stirring spirit,
> She might ha' been a grandam ere she died.

(14–17)

Hunt properly seized on this as a forecast of the serious mood of the end of the play. For a moment the sun is hidden by a forerunner of those clouds that are later to overcast the scene, and we get a premonition of love's labor *lost*. This is admirable; but the mood was unduly prolonged in the repartee that follows between the two girls, which was worked up into a real quarrel, so that the Princess' "I beshrew all shrows" had to be delivered *tutta forza* in order to quell it. This gave a change of tempo and color, and showed us a new side of Rosaline's character, a hard shrewish side; but at this stage of the play neither the action nor the character has been sufficiently developed to bear this elaboration, and the only result was to turn the audience against so viperish a heroine.

This prolonged analysis of faults has been undertaken to show how the producer with the very best intentions—of giving continuity or variety to his play—may achieve the exact opposite. In general, however, the total mood of the play—buoyant, lyrical, penetrating, extravagant—had been so firmly and truly established by both producer and actors that it could not be shattered by incidental "wrong notes." As Elizabethans and as courtiers the ladies were perhaps more convincing than the men, who had a touch of the hobbledehoy about them; but that did little harm in a play wherein the ladies must show a superiority of wit and grace throughout, for all that their task is the harder, since there is less of substance in their badinage and only an exactly calculated bravura of speech and movement can carry it off. The greater delicacy of the ladies' playing was, however,

counterbalanced by Michael Redgrave's performance as
Berowne. He succeeded not only in conveying the wit, the
wisdom and the vitality of the man, but in making him completely sympathetic to the audience. The great set speech of
Act 3, Scene 1—"[A]nd I, forsooth, in love" (175–207), in
which he takes the audience into his confidence, was a *tour
de force*. The speech is by no means easy, for many of its
terms and turns of expression are obsolete today; but by
treating it simply and directly, by trusting himself to the
words (and his confidence clearly grew with practice), he
made its point clear and its effect captivating.

The comic performances in no way betrayed the standard
set by those of the straight parts, although (as, alas, so often
happens) their unnecessary business seemed to increase and
to get more out of hand as the run of the play proceeded.
George Benson gave us the perfect Costard; would that all
players of Shakespearian clowns were as direct and bold and
true to the text as this. On the other hand, the Holofernes
and the Nathaniel were rather translations into modern
equivalents—a Will Hay or a Groucho Marx with his stooge.
This is legitimate; the Crazy Gang or the Itma comics are
today the closest in line of descent to the figures of the Commedia dell'arte from whom the fantastics of *Love's Labor's
Lost* derive. The only characters that were totally off key
were Armado and Moth, presented as a seedy Don Quixote
and a ragged urchin. Now it is of the essence of both figures
that they are of the Court (Dull and Costard are quite enough
to represent the bumpkins). Armado is as much an exquisite
as Osric. It is part of the joke that his finery is only on the sur-
face (he cannot afford a shirt) but his every effort goes into
maintaining the *appearance* of finery, and finery it is. Moth
is the cheeky page boy, a "cit" if ever there was one, and
a diminutive echo of his master's finicking fashion. The
humor of their interchanges, already precarious after the
lapse of three and a half centuries, fades utterly if they are
presented not as the lightning duels of court rapiers but as
the rustic's solemn game of quarterstaff.

This brings us to the consideration of the topical jokes and
private humors that make up so large a part of the dialogue,
particularly between the farcical characters, and present the
second and more troublesome problem to any would-be

translator for the modern stage. There would seem to be four ways of dealing with this largely deadwood: (1) to cut the passage altogether; (2) to accompany it with some entirely extraneous piece of business, in the hope that this will distract attention from the words, which are "thrown away" as best may be; (3) to have the words spoken against music which will render them inaudible; (4) to try the passage straight and hope that *someone* will see, or pretend to see, the joke—at least the purists will be satisfied. The purists of course will object strongly to the first solution, but I do not see how with some passages it can be avoided if the performance of the play is to be living entertainment and not merely a (possibly edifying) ritual. Solutions two and three are clearly abominable, and though one would like always to see the direct method given a trial there are some things it cannot save. The trouble is that producers will differ in their judgment of what can be saved and what must be cut, and most of them are likely to err on the side of pessimism.

The Old Vic production used all four methods. Of the seven cruces that have notoriously baffled or divided commentators only two, the "envoy" of the fox, the ape and the humble-bee, and the play of Holofernes and Moth on "piercing a hogshead," were cut (and rightly cut) *in toto*. The "tender juvenal," the "school of night," and the "chargehouse on the mountain" were all given their chance, perhaps in the belief that their ill fame was too great for them to be ignored. Armado's odd salutation—"Chirrah"—was also left in, together with the reference to an eel that so strangely annoys him on his first appearance. This proved a dangerous course, however, at least in the case of the eel, for with the disappearance of the real occasion of the joke it was necessary to drop Armado's inexplicable irritation at it ("Thou heat'st my blood") and invent a new cue for it. Moth therefore made his entrance carrying a real eel, which he might be supposed recently to have fished out of the encircling lake; and I suspect this detail conditioned the producer's whole view of Moth's (and, with him, Armado's) appearance and status, which I have already tried to show were misconceived.

Some other jokes, of which the point is known but cannot be explained without a considerable gloss, were also wisely cut: Moth's play with the four complexions, his skirmish with Holofernes over sheep and vowels, and most of the "greasy" talk between Boyet and Maria at the end of the hunting scene. There was little excuse, however, for devoting to the same extinction such simple puns as those on style, stile and climbing in the merriness, or the frequent and pertinent comments on the fantastics' inability to count; and it was surely strange, if these were to go, that such obvious interpolations as the duplicated versions of the lovers' first dialogues, and Costard's comments on a vanished entry for Armado and Moth in the hunting scene, should have been spared to puzzle us.

Of the second method of dealing with an obscure passage, the introduction of distracting business, there were three prominent examples, two of them particularly unhappy. It was perhaps allowable that Dull, in the midst of Nathaniel's wordy tirade on his insensitivity, should be discovered to be carrying, apparently without being aware of it or discommoded by it, an arrow from the hunt still firmly embedded in his posterior. This is at least a fair gloss on Nathaniel's "only sensible in the duller parts"; but the disproportionate laughter it aroused in the audience shattered the continuity of the scene and the delicate balance between its actors. The other two instances of this technique were unhappy because the jokes so painstakingly masked remain perfectly valid ones today and if allowed to make their own effect would have raised greater and more relevant amusement than their substitutes. When Jaquenetta brings Berowne's letter to Nathaniel to interpret, Holofernes is consumed with curiosity to see it but feels it would be beneath his dignity to look over the Curate's shoulder. He therefore pretends to be very much absorbed in his own thoughts, on a plane far above mere mundane affairs. He murmurs (incorrectly) a verse from Mantuan, hums the notes of the scale (again wrongly) all the time striving, under cover of this pretended abstraction, to get a glimpse of the letter. In the Old Vic production all this was thrown away to the accompaniment of a stupid piece of byplay in which Nathaniel tried surreptitiously to put his arm round the trusting Jaquenetta and found himself embracing Costard instead. This is entirely out of character for the Curate, while the Pedant's itch to meddle, sacrificed for it, is a typical and essential trait. Again, when the comics return from the dinner to which Holofernes has invited Nathaniel to witness his eloquence, the Curate is more than ever impressed by his host's superior learning. When Holofernes utters a particularly choice word Nathaniel, according to a direction in the original First Quarto text, draws out his notebook and with admiring comments records the *trouvaille*. In place of this characteristic and revealing action, Hunt made his players enter as if tipsy, and for the unction and the notebook of the toady substituted slurred syllables and some sorry business with a bottle. This is presumption.

To resort to the third way out, on the other hand, is the rankest cowardice, and it speaks well for the Old Vic production that this all too popular device was only used once, for the admittedly involved and paradoxical lines in which Boyet describes to the ladies how, Navarre having fallen in love at first sight, all his faculties are concentrated in his longing gaze. This speech was half chanted to a musical accompaniment to which Boyet's audience swayed in time. The effect was odious, but it was certainly impossible that many words should be caught, much less interpreted. It was perhaps surprising that the producer should have funked this passage when such teasers as "Light seeking light doth light of light beguile," and many of the "sets of wit," were left to take care of themselves, and did so very nicely.

ROBERT SHORE

Love's Labour's Lost in 2003

Written under the influence of Philip Sidney's *Astrophil and Stella,* probably at about the same time as the Sonnets, Shakespeare's earliest stage comedy is at once besotted with the "sweet smoke of rhetoric" and deeply suspicious of it. It is entirely in keeping with the play's divided nature that Trevor Nunn should have adopted an adversarial stance and framed the lovers' dreamy idyll with a severe reality test. To do this, he takes the highfalutin' courtiers at their word and literalizes one of their most often repeated metaphors—that of battle.

Before the King of Navarre, in the play's opening speech, has the chance to open his mouth and address his companions as "brave conquerors" engaged in a "war against your own affections / And the huge army of the world's desires" (1.1.9–10), the young nobles' internal conflict is externalized in a dumbshow prologue that transports us forward in time to the battlefields of Flanders in the First World War. A huge tree extends naked branches across a windswept plain; gunfire rakes the stage and soldiers, among them Captain Berowne, are thrown to the ground by an earth-shaking explosion. The pyrotechnics ended, time is reversed, nature comes back into flower, and long, diaphanous veils descend from the heavens as the sun returns to bathe the stage in gentle dappled light. After a pause, Berowne emerges from the foliage like a ghostly revenant to join his companions in establishing their "little academe". By adding this brutal

Reprinted by permission from the *Times Literary Supplement*, March 14, 2003.

preface, Nunn preempts the play's celebrated *coup de théâtre* in which the seemingly inevitable pairing off of the lovers is thwarted, and reverses the logic of Armado's announcement "The words of Mercury are harsh after the songs of Apollo" (5.2.931–32). This is *Love's Labour's Lost* recast as elegy, as if the unworldly nobles' light trials and endlessly spinning word games can be appreciated in our more cynical times only if presented as a youthful reminiscence, an essentially nostalgic pleasure.

It is not the first time that "the faery breath of Edwardian idyll" has been made to blow through the play. In Ian Judge's production for the RSC, the First World War cast a shadow forward across the projected happy coupling of the men of Navarre and women of France. But it is perhaps the first time, following Kenneth Branagh's film version, that *Love's Labour's Lost* has been staged essentially as a musical. Many of the cast of Nunn's current production of *Anything Goes* reappear here.

Navarre, Longaville and Dumaine are inclined not so much to declaim their love verses as actually to sing them. Steven Edis's pastoral music, reminiscent of Vaughan Williams, saturates the evening, picturesque crowds of rural children trail the principals across the juicily Astroturfed stage (at the interval a stagehand emerges to smooth artificial divots), and the climactic song of the owl and the cuckoo turns into a full production number sung by a chorus of villagers. There's enough purely choreographic pleasure here to justify a transfer to the West End.

This is not necessarily a bad thing. Of all Shakespeare's comedies, the humour of *Love's Labour's Lost,* with its adoring satire of the contemporary Petrarchanizing vein, is perhaps the most alien to modern sensibilities; the formality of its wit can seem merely laborious and its heavily rhymed verse simply artificial. Nunn's carefully detailed and highly musical production surmounts both difficulties. It is genuinely funny, thanks in part to some excellent comic performances: Robin Soans is hilarious as the pedantic schoolmaster Holofernes, and his scenes with Dull (Duncan Smith) and Sir Nathaniel (Paul Grunert) evoke the spirit of that key Edwardian text, *The Wind in the Willows.* The staging of the Nine Worthies sequence, debunking the heroic comparisons endemic to Elizabethan versifying, is particularly satisfying, if perhaps a little too melancholically Chekhovian in inspiration. For a moment, it might almost be an Elizabethan *Seagull.* Treating the play like a musical pays unexpected dividends with the rhyming problem too. When Berowne balks at the severity of his academic oath of abstinence, Longaville teases him: "You swore to that, Berowne, and to the rest". Here, Joseph Fiennes's "merry madcap lord" delivers the rejoinder "By yea and nay, sir, then I swore in jest" (1.1.53–54) with a delicious sing-song ease, clinching the rhyme as if it were part of a self-consciously strained couplet in a Gershwin show-tune.

Nunn's final production as artistic director of the National Theatre is unlikely to silence the critics who have accused him of conservatism in his programming and of too great a penchant for musicals. But though the staging has faults—the rather forced framing device, the anachronistic tone—this is a bravura demonstration of extraordinary theatrical skill.

Love's Labor's Lost on Stage and Screen

Love's Labor's Lost was written about 1595, but the first printing, in quarto, is dated 1598: "A Pleasant Conceited Comedie Called, Loues labors lost. As it was presented before her Highnes this last Christmas. Newly corrected and augmented By *W. Shakespere*."

A certain irony attaches to the next production of the play, which was offered as part of the Christmas festivities of 1604. The Earl of Southampton, having been imprisoned for his part in the plot of Essex against Queen Elizabeth, in celebrating his release by King James entertained the King and Queen at his house with a production of the play. There was an agreeable humor in choosing a play in which the chief male persons, men of royal and noble rank, propose to abandon life in the great world in order to pursue a celibate existence in an academy, a theme not wholly incongruous under the circumstances. The humor would have been apparent to the King, and what is topical in the play—in particular references to relations between England and France—also would have suggested matters of interest to the King.

The second quarto (1631) tells that the play was publicly acted at the Black-Friars and the Globe, but no record of these productions is known to survive. There is no mention of a performance of the play in Henslowe's and Pepys's diaries, and Genest, who surveyed all productions of Shakespeare's plays from 1642 till 1830, found no notice of *Love's Labor's Lost* in all that time.

Explanations for the neglect of the work center upon the

opinion that the wordplay was so pervasive and complex that it was not stageworthy. There was also the frequent judgment that the supposed topicality was obscure and distracting. The critical reservations expressed by Hazlitt and Coleridge may also have been influential.

Madame Vestris, however, a gifted and popular actress, saw in the play the opportunity to make the most of the women's parts and put it on in the new Olympic Theatre in London in 1839. Although it was praised, it held the stage for only a few days, despite what was said to have been a talented cast.

The next notices available are of productions at Sadler's Wells in 1857 and, surprisingly, at the Arch Street Theater in Philadelphia in 1858. And it was in the United States, at Augustin Daly's theater in New York—in 1873 and again in 1891—that the marvelous quality of the work was evidently understood and appreciated. The liberties Daly took with the text were considerable, yet one may judge from the prefatory remarks attached to the prompter's copy that they were as thoughtfully conceived as they were successful. For example: "The pageant is transposed to the end of the comedy, which closes with one of the sweetest of all the Shakespeare melodies and leaves its spectators with a mental vision of all the lovely spring flowers that grow on Avon's banks." *The New York Herald*'s critic was most enthusiastic:

> The skill with which the sense of atmosphere and expanse was given to the forest scenes was delightful. The tableau of winter showed an ice-hung scene, in the midst of which a snow-clad figure sang the strongly picturesque lines beginning 'When icicles hang'. Spring was indicated by a Watteau tableau of great brilliancy. Cunning shepherds and shepherdesses sat on mossy elevations, fountains gurgled, arbors twined, gloomily green vistas opened, dazzling flowers and foliage spread seeming fragrance and rich growth, and over all fell a shower of changing light. The acting was respectable throughout, with special excellence in the case of Miss Dyas, whose refinement, intelligence and vivacity exhausted all the significance contained in the role of the Princess. . . . The costumes were brilliant beyond all precedent and description. From beginning to

end, the comedy was placed upon the stage in the most generous and splendid style.

With such a success one might have believed the play would be entering upon a new life in the theater, but there was to be, in fact, another long dry spell before *Love's Labor's Lost* was to establish its appeal securely, and we may only conclude that the times were not yet ripe for it despite this remarkable example.

There is no record of another production before the one at the Old Vic in 1906 and another at Stratford in 1907. There were three productions at the Old Vic in the next thirty years, but Tyrone Guthrie's in 1936 was accounted a failure even with Edith Evans as Rosaline and Michael Redgrave as the King of Navarre. There were a few successes at the Open Air Theatre in Regent's Park. It was only in 1946 that Peter Brook's "landmark" production demonstrated such attractive qualities in the work that it is credited with leading the way for the more than ninety productions in the English-speaking world in the next three decades.

Brook had seen a production in French at the Odéon in Paris in 1945 in which the pictorial potentialities of the play were effectively developed. J. Dapoigny had devised settings and provided costumes with the paintings of Watteau in mind: "The style of Watteau's dresses with its broad undecorated expanses of billowing satin seemed the ideal visual correlative of the essential sweet-sad mood of the play." (It is a curious coincidence that Daly's production had brought Watteau to the mind of the New York critic.)

Still, more than a pictorial emphasis was involved, however, in the stimulus Brook took from this production. The theories and practices of Artaud and Genet were also involved in the French adaptation, and Brook was evidently inspired by the rejection of naturalism and in particular by the refusal to be bound by the constraints imposed when adhering to normal time patterns. To begin with, this meant to Brook that a Shakespeare play should not be offered as a period piece; it should be wholly free of antiquarian appeal. He has made the point this way, in *The Empty Space:* "I dressed the character called the Constable Dull as a Victorian policeman because his name conjured up the typical figure of the London bobby. For other reasons the rest of the characters were dressed in Watteau-eighteenth-century clothes, but no one was conscious of an anachronism." He put the case in this way: the aim of drama is toward "immediacy." "A representation is the occasion when something is represented that once was, now is. For representation is not an imitation or a description of a past event, a representation denies time. It abolishes the difference between yesterday and today."

The success of Brook's production of *Love's Labor's Lost* was thus in part the success of the new drama, leading the way to other productions of the play that were to be equally free of the constraints of naturalistic imitation and as open to transformation. The example was evidently so attractive that in the years following it was a rare undertaking, such as the reputedly exquisite staging of Hugh Hunt's in 1949 at the New Theatre, that aimed to capture the atmosphere of an Elizabethan production, although here, too, the pictorial emphasis Brook had made so much of was key to the success of this production, Hunt following Nicholas Hillyard rather than Watteau. He also stressed the lyrical potentialities of the work, even in the humorous exchanges, and with such emphasis on choreography as to recall the manner of masques. Hunt was profoundly obligated to the doctrine Granville-Barker enunciated in his essay on *Love's Labor's Lost:*

> The actor, in fine, must think of the dialogue in terms of music; of the tune and rhythm of it as at one with the sense— sometimes outbidding the sense—in telling him what to do and how to do it, in telling him, indeed, what to *be.*

A City Center production in New York in 1953 gave the play a quasi-Oscar Wilde tone but with very turn-of-the-century furnishings—the ladies made their entrance in an ancient roadster, there was a gramophone with a great horn, a crooked croquet game—pleasing some critics but not Wolcott Gibbs and Brooks Atkinson. Brook's principles had gone astray, as they were to in several of the new ventures. What might have sustained the satirical intent of the play sometimes ended in travesty, as one may judge in Bernard

Beckerman's account of the 1968 production in Stratford, Connecticut:

> The academy was the retreat of a guru. Berowne, Longaville, and Dumaine were fashionable young men come to share the retreat with the Maharishi King of Navarre. Probably stimulated by the adventures of the Beatles in yoga-land, Dumaine turned out to be a rock-singer. Holofernes, in what I assume to be a parody of Mahatma Gandhi, wore silver-rimmed spectacles and a diaper-like sheet. And the ladies of France were cycle-riding, fast-moving members of the jet-set, chaperoned by a swishing Boyet chattering in a deep South drawl.

The BBC telecast in 1985 developed a similar kind of transformation, but on this occasion the television frame itself set limits on what can be done pictorially with what was originally a stage play. As the producer saw it, this limitation precluded any disposition to offer settings in the open country or in a park. The beautiful pastoral setting was obliterated, the Academy and the pavilion became, the reviewer said, "a cold-lit library, across whose chilly spaces—littered with frigid statuary and leathern tomes—tread bewigged would-be *philosophes*."

John Barton directed the Royal Shakespeare Company in a production of *Love's Labor's Lost* at Stratford-upon-Avon in 1965 and again in 1978. The later version especially gave the play an autumnal tone—in fact, it began with Costard, Jaquenetta, and a Forester sweeping away fallen leaves. During a rehearsal Barton told the cast, "Think Chekhov, not Elizabethan," by which he meant not that the play was set in the nineteenth century—the costumes were more or less Elizabethan—but that the play in his view was a serious (rather than frivolously witty) exploration of a single situation in a closed environment. The young men at the start are immature, pretentious, and cruel; pride goes before a fall. The play, as he saw it, was filled with poignant moments, and thus the serious note at the end was implicit in the beginning, and the punishment of the young men was serious and necessary.

Recently the wheel seems to have come full circle in the

1984 production of the Royal Shakespeare Company, or so it seemed to Giles Gordon:

> To me, *Love's Labor's Lost* is one of the supreme glories of dramatic art, the equal of that most essential of operas, Mozart's *Cosí fan Tutte*. The wit, brio and erudition of the verbal music are marvelous to experience. The stage is washed in white leaves which, from the first entrance of the princess of France and her court, suggests spring until the end, the arrival of the Messenger of Death, when Autumn gives way to Winter and icicles hang by the wall, and Dick the shepherd blows his nail.

Pace Brook, the sequential is once again at the heart of the play, although it is only fair to observe that the costumes were nineteenth century and the setting Chekhovian.

Quite as significant as the experimenting that followed Brook's example was the increasing recognition of the excellence of the play, as theater and as poetry. It was put into the hands of the best actors and actresses—Olivier, Derek Jacobi, Joan Plowright, Ian Richardson, Paul Scofield, to single out but a few. Again and again the word "exquisite" is applied to the conceits and humor that engage the characters, to the sequences that call for dancelike movements—not only in the masque but from the very beginning, as in the San Diego production of 1962, described by Eleanor Prosser:

> The brilliant choreography of Shirlee Dodge combined with creative direction to make this the artistic triumph of the season. The high style of dance was established in the opening scenes. To the accompaniment of music from the balcony, servants scurried from the center curtains in balanced patterns, setting up an abacus, a telescope, and a globe. The dance movement and the pretty artificiality of the props (a powder-blue telescope?) against a background of crystalline trees set the stage for Navarre's foolish game.

And at the end the musical impetus was irresistible:

> Accompanied solely by Don Armado on the tabor and two lonely recorders, the cast sang of the owl and the cuckoo while

the lovers moved through a series of measured dances. Bernard Windt had written new music for the song, two haunting melodies in a minor key, sung first in unison, then antiphonally by the divided cast banked on each side of the stage, and then together in a round. As the singers and the song faded through the side doors and the light gradually dimmed, one by one each couple parted in the center, still in dance, until finally only Rosaline and Berowne were left—each pausing at the side door for a final look and a gentle salute of promise and yet regret, before leaving the stage to hushed darkness and the night.

And finally, as so much talent and intelligence were lavished upon a play that had been so long neglected, so the humor and the wordplay that had once been supposed to be a drawback came to be understood as wonderfully effective dramatically. No one has pointed this out better than Richard David, unless it be the actors themselves, such as Paul Scofield and Tony Church:

David Jones, it seemed to me in the 1973 production of the Royal Shakespeare Company, had seized the essential fact that Shakespeare's comic effects are almost always very strongly visual; get these visual effects right, and the words will fall into place of themselves. Take one of the simplest, Armado and Moth: the basic jest is the mere juxtaposition of the lofty, slow-moving, and solemn Spaniard with his diminutive quicksilver page. The verbal altercations between Armado and Moth are little more than elaborations of the fundamental contrast between dignity and impudence. Or take the scene where Jacquenetta asks the Parson to interpret Berowne's letter which was mistakenly delivered to her instead of to Rosaline. The schoolmaster, convinced that he is the only man present who is competent to deal with the written word, itches to be involved but has to pretend to be thinking of higher things while he edges himself into the act. His impatience, his various mumming routines to cover his real intentions, and his efforts to look over the Parson's shoulder, are *visual* comedy. . . . The essentials of these and other comic scenes were given so clear a visual projection that they were able to carry any amount of verbal superstructure.

In short, the recent history of the play upon the stage justifies the judgment made upon it as beautifully and wonderfully conceived. But it has been a rocky road, and in some aspects still is. In 1733 when Theobald completed his edition of the play he wrote in exasperation: "I have now done with this Play, which in the Main may be call'd a very bad One: and I have found it so very troublesome in the Corruptions, that, I think, I may conclude with the old religious Editors, *Deo gratias*!" As for some of the modern versions, the reception has been less than complimentary, as W. L. Godshalk summarizes: "The more recent productions of *Love's Labor's Lost,* especially those of the 1960s and 1970s, are marked by a general distrust of the play on its merits, for what it attempts to say and its ability to do so." Godshalk gives examples, and then says:

> Such corruptions of the text seem to imply that the productions become, in the words of Vincent Canby, " 'such a flat denial of the original that it becomes an elaborate apology for anyone's being caught alive doing the play'." Brooks Atkinson was no more forgiving: "After a glimpse of *Love's Labor's Lost,* which opened at the City Center last evening, it is easy to see why this Shakespearean comedy had not been played since 1891."

All the same it is certain that the play now has a secure place in the repertory. Colleges and universities as well as the professional theaters are putting it on, many of the productions truly imaginative. It is increasingly understood that this comic treatment of some cultivated youngbloods, as Granville-Barker spoke of them, is as rich in intellectuality as in antics, and that the gloriously beautiful song at the end has been prepared for by a sustained articulation of ideas.

Postscript

As John Arthos suggests in the preceding pages, Peter Brook in 1946 emphatically rejected the idea of producing *Love's Labor's Lost* as an Elizabethan period piece, and Brook's lead was consistently followed throughout the remainder of the twentieth century and the early years of the twenty-first. Several directors have set the play in the late nineteenth century or early twentieth, thereby suggesting that it has a life beyond the contemporary society for which it was written, and yet by placing it in the past the directors have been able to give it a visual appeal, a stylishness, an interesting distance that a contemporary setting would not provide. But the most important production of the past fifty years has been Kenneth Branagh's musical film version (2000), evocative of the 1930s, which we will discuss in a moment.

The near total neglect of the play between the early seventeenth century and the middle of the nineteenth has been more than compensated in the last seventy-five years. Inevitably directors and critics tell us that the play is highly relevant, that even in *Love's Labor's Lost* Shakespeare is our contemporary, but the fact remains that vast stretches of dialogue—filled with wordplay that doubtless afforded delight to his contemporaries—are unintelligible to us unless they are footnoted. In the 1930s Granville-Barker wrote, "Here is a fashionable play; now by three hundred years, out of date," and to correct his statement we need merely change "three hundred" to "four hundred." Shakespeare's chief concern seems to be language rather than narrative; the plot—especially compared with the plots of such other early comedies as *The Comedy of Errors, The Taming of the Shrew,* and *A Midsummer Night's Dream*—is simple. True, language is not mere air when artists use it, it is action (Elizabeth Bowen aptly remarked, "Dialogue is what characters *do* to each other"). The fact remains, however, that especially in this play Shakespeare no less than his characters seems to delight in "Taffeta phrases, silken terms precise, / Three-piled hyperboles, spruce affectation, / Figures pedantical" (5.2.407–09), and much of this exuberant wordplay (cf. Berowne's "Light seeking light doth light of light beguile" [1.1.77]) is lost on today's audiences. It was otherwise in Shakespeare's own day, when his contemporary, Francis Meres—the first writer to mention *Love's Labor's Lost*—in 1598 praised "mellifluous and honey-tongued Shakespeare" for being among those writers who contributed to the English language "rare ornaments and resplendent habiliments." According to Meres, "The Muses would speak with Shakespeare's fine filed phrase if they would speak English." We need not take this chauvinistic puffery too seriously, but it does touch on the carefully wrought, refined and polished language ("fine filed phrase") that characterizes the play. The original audience doubtless responded to this language in a way that we cannot. We are, alas, like the ignorant Constable Dull, whom Sir Nathaniel loftily dismisses with this observation: "He hath not eat paper, as it were, he hath not drunk ink" (4.2.26–27). What then is a director to do with a public that (like Dull and unlike a dramatist and an audience infatuated with language) has not eaten paper and drunk ink?

One solution, widely adopted, is to cut the play heavily. Even John Barton cut some four hundred lines from his 1978 Royal Shakespeare Company production. Another solution, usually adopted along with the first, is to present the play in a novel way. Thus, in 1997 in New York the Women's Shakespeare Company presented a heavily cut version acted entirely by women, and in 2003 the Thirteenth Night Theatre Company (also in New York) reversed the gender of each role—Berowne became Birona, Armado Armada, Jacquenetta Jacques, and so on; thus, the Queen and her three attendants forswore men for three years. Both endeavors were serious, and the acting was earnest, but the experiments proved that good intentions and high spirits are not enough; actors need considerable talent if their lines (even when shorn of obscurities) are to delight an audience.

In 1990 Terry Hands directed the Royal Shakespeare Company's production, set in the late nineteenth century, with Simon Russell Beale as Navarre and Ralph Fiennes as Berowne. Three years later Ian Judge directed the play, again for the Royal Shakespeare Company, this time advancing the setting by a decade or two, into the Edwardian period, and establishing the locale as Oxbridge. Music was prominent, the young men's poems becoming songs. At the end, the sound of gunfire suggested that 1914 was not far away and that these college youths might not survive the next year. The autumnal quality that Peter Brook in 1946 and John Barton in 1978 had emphasized was thus given a darker tone and a more specific historical context.

Ian Judge's use of music anticipates in a small way Kenneth Branagh's film (2000), subtitled "A Romantic Musical Comedy," in which Branagh plays Berowne. The resemblance between *Love's Labor's Lost* and a revue, where no one expects a continuous plot and developing characters, has long been noticed; as early as 1937 H. B. Charlton wrote, "*Love's Labour's Lost* is more like a modern revue, or a musical comedy without music, than a play," and in 1952 G. B. Harrison characterized the play as "a musical comedy, a revue"—overstatements but with a deposit of truth. Branagh, who had recently filmed a four-hour *Hamlet,* cut about two-thirds of the play, creating a production that runs only ninety-three minutes even with the addition of musical numbers that consume thirty minutes. Branagh's film— evoking the film musicals of the 1930s, '40s, and early '50s, with Fred Astaire, Ginger Rogers, and Gene Kelly—contains ten show tunes (including "Cheek to Cheek" and "The Way You Look Tonight") by such notables as Cole Porter, Irving Berlin, and Jerome Kern. The camera work, for instance overhead shots of performers in a pool, reminds the film buff of Busby Berkeley. Set in September 1939, the film includes fake film clips in which Branagh, as narrator, summarizes the plot and introduces contemporary events, and it closes with shots of the men returning safely from the war, rejoining the women in front of Buckingham Palace. The dark note of war is thus introduced but is ultimately dissipated.

Like Branagh, most of the performers in the film are *not* song-and-dance folk, and indeed only Nathan Lane, who plays Costard and who gives a spirited rendering of "There's No Business Like Show Business," is an experienced performer of musical comedy. The result is an amateurishness in the singing and dancing that bothers some viewers but that engages others, who see the film as comparable to a college production of a musical, in which the audience enjoys the high spirits and good intentions and overlooks the failings of friends.

—SYLVAN BARNET

Bibliographic Note: Many of the titles cited below in the Suggested References, Section 4 ("Shakespeare on Stage and Screen"), include brief discussions of productions, and the editions of *Love's Labor's Lost* cited at the beginning of Section 11 include surveys of the stage history of the play (see especially the Arden edition, by H. R. Woudhuysen [1998]). Miriam Gilbert's *Shakespeare in Performance: Love's Labour's Lost* (New York: Manchester University Press, 1993), an admirable short book, covers the play on the Elizabethan stage and selected later productions: Peter Brook's 1946 production at Stratford-upon-Avon; the BBC televised version of 1984; Michael Kahn's 1968 Stratford, Connecticut; John Barton's 1965 and 1978 Stratford-upon-Avon versions; and Simon Russell Beale's 1990 Stratford-upon-Avon version. For twenty-five discussions of the play on the stage, including Barbara Hodgdon's important essay on John Barton's 1978 production, see Felicia Hardison Londré, ed. *Love's Labour's Lost: Critical Essays* (New York: Garland, 1997).

Shakespeare Quarterly is a good source for reviews of productions—not only in the English-speaking world but also elsewhere—since the middle of the twentieth century. *Shakespeare Survey,* an annual, includes reviews of British productions of the same period. *Shakespeare Bulletin,* though less readily available in libraries, is also an excellent source. For extracts from reviews of the BBC television production (1984) see J. C. Bulman and H. R. Coursen, *Shakespeare on Television* (1988).

For anyone concerned with the history of the production of the play, Miriam Gilbert's book, already mentioned, is the first study to look at, and perhaps the second is Felicia Hardison Londré's collection, but valuable discussions of productions also appear in:

Berry, Ralph. *On Directing Shakespeare: Interviews with Contemporary Directors.* London: Hamish Hamilton, 1989.

Brook, Peter. *The Empty Space.* New York: Atheneum, 1968.

———. *The Shifting Point.* New York: Harper, 1987.

Granville-Barker, Harley. *Prefaces to Shakespeare,* II. Princeton, NJ: Princeton University Press, 1947.

Suggested References

The number of possible references is vast and grows alarmingly. (The *Shakespeare Quarterly* devotes one issue each year to a list of the previous year's work, and *Shakespeare Survey*—an annual publication—includes a substantial review of biographical, critical, and textual studies, as well as a survey of performances.) The vast bibliography is best approached through James Harner, *The World Shakespeare Bibliography on CD-Rom: 1900–Present.* The first release, in 1996, included more than 12,000 annotated items from 1990–93, plus references to several thousand book reviews, productions, films, and audio recordings. The plan is to update the publication annually, moving forward one year and backward three years. Thus, the second issue (1997), with 24,700 entries, and another 35,000 or so references to reviews, newspaper pieces, and so on, covered 1987–94.

For guidance to the immense amount that has been written, consult Larry S. Champion, *The Essential Shakespeare: An Annotated Bibliography of Major Modern Studies,* 2nd ed. (1993), which comments briefly on 1,800 publications.

Though no works are indispensable, those listed below have been found especially helpful. The arrangement is as follows:

1. Shakespeare's Times
2. Shakespeare's Life
3. Shakespeare's Theater
4. Shakespeare on Stage and Screen
5. Miscellaneous Reference Works
6. Shakespeare's Plays: General Studies
7. The Comedies
8. The Romances
9. The Tragedies
10. The Histories
11. *Love's Labor's Lost*

The titles in the first five sections are accompanied by brief explanatory annotations.

1. Shakespeare's Times

Andrews, John F., ed. *William Shakespeare: His World, His Work, His Influence,* 3 vols. (1985). Sixty articles, dealing not only with such subjects as "The State," "The Church," "Law," "Science, Magic, and Folklore," but also with the plays and poems themselves and Shakespeare's influence (e.g., translations, films, reputation).

Byrne, Muriel St. Clare. *Elizabethan Life in Town and Country* (8th ed., 1970). Chapters on manners, beliefs, education, etc., with illustrations.

Dollimore, John, and Alan Sinfield, eds. *Political Shakespeare: New Essays in Cultural Materialism* (1985). Essays on such topics as the subordination of women and colonialism, presented in connection with some of Shakespeare's plays.

Greenblatt, Stephen. *Representing the English Renaissance* (1988). New Historicist essays, especially on connections between political and aesthetic matters, statecraft and stagecraft.

Joseph, B. L. *Shakespeare's Eden: the Commonwealth of England 1558–1629* (1971). An account of the social, political, economic, and cultural life of England.

Kernan, Alvin. *Shakespeare, the King's Playwright: Theater in the Stuart Court 1603–1613* (1995). The social setting and the politics of the court of James I, in relation to *Hamlet, Measure for Measure, Macbeth, King Lear, Antony and Cleopatra, Coriolanus,* and *The Tempest.*

Montrose, Louis. *The Purpose of Playing: Shakespeare and the Cultural Politics of the Elizabethan Theatre* (1996). A poststructuralist view, discussing the professional theater "within the ideological and material frameworks of Elizabethan culture and society," with an extended analysis of *A Midsummer Night's Dream.*

Mullaney, Steven. *The Place of the Stage: License, Play, and Power in Renaissance England* (1988). New Historicist analysis, arguing that popular drama became a cultural institution "only by . . . taking up a place on the margins of society."

Schoenbaum, S. *Shakespeare: The Globe and the World*

(1979). A readable, abundantly illustrated introductory book on the world of the Elizabethans.

Shakespeare's England, 2 vols. (1916). A large collection of scholarly essays on a wide variety of topics, e.g., astrology, costume, gardening, horsemanship, with special attention to Shakespeare's references to these topics.

2. Shakespeare's Life

Andrews, John F., ed. *William Shakespeare: His World, His Work, His Influence,* 3 vols. (1985). See the description above.

Bentley, Gerald E. *Shakespeare: A Biographical Handbook* (1961). The facts about Shakespeare, with virtually no conjecture intermingled.

Chambers, E. K. *William Shakespeare: A Study of Facts and Problems,* 2 vols. (1930). The fullest collection of data.

Fraser, Russell. *Young Shakespeare* (1988). A highly readable account that simultaneously considers Shakespeare's life and Shakespeare's art.

———. *Shakespeare: The Later Years* (1992).

Schoenbaum, S. *Shakespeare's Lives* (1970). A review of the evidence and an examination of many biographies, including those of Baconians and other heretics.

———. *William Shakespeare: A Compact Documentary Life* (1977). An abbreviated version, in a smaller format, of the next title. The compact version reproduces some fifty documents in reduced form. A readable presentation of all that the documents tell us about Shakespeare.

———. *William Shakespeare: A Documentary Life* (1975). A large-format book setting forth the biography with facsimiles of more than two hundred documents, and with transcriptions and commentaries.

3. Shakespeare's Theater

Astington, John H., ed. *The Development of Shakespeare's Theater* (1992). Eight specialized essays on theatrical companies, playing spaces, and performance.

Beckerman, Bernard. *Shakespeare at the Globe, 1599–1609* (1962). On the playhouse and on Elizabethan dramaturgy, acting, and staging.

Bentley, Gerald E. *The Profession of Dramatist in Shakespeare's Time* (1971). An account of the dramatist's status in the Elizabethan period.

————. *The Profession of Player in Shakespeare's Time, 1590–1642* (1984). An account of the status of members of London companies (sharers, hired men, apprentices, managers) and a discussion of conditions when they toured.

Berry, Herbert. *Shakespeare's Playhouses* (1987). Usefully emphasizes how little we know about the construction of Elizabethan theaters.

Brown, John Russell. *Shakespeare's Plays in Performance* (1966). A speculative and practical analysis relevant to all of the plays, but with emphasis on *The Merchant of Venice*, *Richard II*, *Hamlet*, *Romeo and Juliet*, and *Twelfth Night*.

————. *William Shakespeare: Writing for Performance* (1996). A discussion aimed at helping readers to develop theatrically conscious habits of reading.

Chambers, E. K. *The Elizabethan Stage*, 4 vols. (1945). A major reference work on theaters, theatrical companies, and staging at court.

Cook, Ann Jennalie. *The Privileged Playgoers of Shakespeare's London, 1576–1642* (1981). Sees Shakespeare's audience as wealthier, more middle-class, and more intellectual than Harbage (below) does.

Dessen, Alan C. *Elizabethan Drama and the Viewer's Eye* (1977). On how certain scenes may have looked to spectators in an Elizabethan theater.

Gurr, Andrew. *Playgoing in Shakespeare's London* (1987). Something of a middle ground between Cook (above) and Harbage (below).

————. *The Shakespearean Stage, 1579–1642* (3rd ed., 1992). On the acting companies, the actors, the playhouses, the stages, and the audiences.

————, and Mariko Ichikawa. *Staging in Shakespeare's Theatres* (2000). Like Alan C. Dessen's book, cited above, a careful analysis of what the Elizabethans saw on the stage.

Harbage, Alfred. *Shakespeare's Audience* (1941). A study of the size and nature of the theatrical public, emphasizing the representativeness of its working class and middle-class audience.

Hodges, C. Walter. *The Globe Restored* (1968). A conjectural restoration, with lucid drawings.

Hosley, Richard. "The Playhouses," in *The Revels History of Drama in English*, vol. 3, general editors Clifford Leech and T. W. Craik (1975). An essay of a hundred pages on the physical aspects of the playhouses.

Howard, Jane E. "Crossdressing, the Theatre, and Gender Struggle in Early Modern England," *Shakespeare Quarterly* 39 (1988): 418–40. Judicious comments on the effects of boys playing female roles.

Orrell, John. *The Human Stage: English Theatre Design, 1567–1640* (1988). Argues that the public, private, and court playhouses are less indebted to popular structures (e.g., innyards and bear-baiting pits) than to banqueting halls and to Renaissance conceptions of Roman amphitheaters.

Slater, Ann Pasternak. *Shakespeare the Director* (1982). An analysis of theatrical effects (e.g., kissing, kneeling) in stage directions and dialogue.

Styan, J. L. *Shakespeare's Stagecraft* (1967). An introduction to Shakespeare's visual and aural stagecraft, with chapters on such topics as acting conventions, stage groupings, and speech.

Thompson, Peter. *Shakespeare's Professional Career* (1992). An examination of patronage and related theatrical conditions.

———. *Shakespeare's Theatre* (1983). A discussion of how plays were staged in Shakespeare's time.

4. Shakespeare on Stage and Screen

Bate, Jonathan, and Russell Jackson, eds. *Shakespeare: An Illustrated Stage History* (1996). Highly readable essays on stage productions from the Renaissance to the present.

Berry, Ralph. *Changing Styles in Shakespeare* (1981). Discusses productions of six plays (*Coriolanus, Hamlet, Henry V, Measure for Measure, The Tempest,* and *Twelfth Night*) on the English stage, chiefly 1950–1980.

————. *On Directing Shakespeare: Interviews with Contemporary Directors* (1989). An enlarged edition of a book first published in 1977, this version includes the seven interviews from the early 1970s and adds five interviews conducted in 1988.

Brockbank, Philip, ed. *Players of Shakespeare: Essays in Shakespearean Performance* (1985). Comments by twelve actors, reporting their experiences with roles. See also the entry for Russell Jackson (below).

Bulman, J. C., and H. R. Coursen, eds. *Shakespeare on Television* (1988). An anthology of general and theoretical essays, essays on individual productions, and shorter reviews, with a bibliography and a videography listing cassettes that may be rented.

Coursen, H. P. *Watching Shakespeare on Television* (1993). Analyses not only of TV versions but also of films and videotapes of stage presentations that are shown on television.

Davies, Anthony, and Stanley Wells, eds. *Shakespeare and the Moving Image: The Plays on Film and Television* (1994). General essays (e.g., on the comedies) as well as essays devoted entirely to *Hamlet*, *King Lear*, and *Macbeth*.

Dawson, Anthony B. *Watching Shakespeare: A Playgoer's Guide* (1988). About half of the plays are discussed, chiefly in terms of decisions that actors and directors make in putting the works onto the stage.

Dessen, Alan. *Elizabethan Stage Conventions and Modern Interpretations* (1984). On interpreting conventions such as the representation of light and darkness and stage violence (duels, battles).

Donaldson, Peter. *Shakespearean Films/Shakespearean Directors* (1990). Postmodernist analyses, drawing on Freudianism, Feminism, Deconstruction, and Queer Theory.

Jackson, Russell, and Robert Smallwood, eds. *Players of Shakespeare 2: Further Essays in Shakespearean Performance by Players with the Royal Shakespeare Company* (1988). Fourteen actors discuss their roles in productions between 1982 and 1987.

————. *Players of Shakespeare 3: Further Essays in Shakespearean Performance by Players with the Royal Shakespeare Company* (1993). Comments by thirteen performers.

Jorgens, Jack. *Shakespeare on Film* (1977). Fairly detailed studies of eighteen films, preceded by an introductory chapter addressing such issues as music, and whether to "open" the play by including scenes of landscape.

Kennedy, Dennis. *Looking at Shakespeare: A Visual History of Twentieth-Century Performance* (1993). Lucid descriptions (with 170 photographs) of European, British, and American performances.

Leiter, Samuel L. *Shakespeare Around the Globe: A Guide to Notable Postwar Revivals* (1986). For each play there are about two pages of introductory comments, then discussions (about five hundred words per production) of ten or so productions, and finally bibliographic references.

McMurty, Jo. *Shakespeare Films in the Classroom* (1994). Useful evaluations of the chief films most likely to be shown in undergraduate courses.

Rothwell, Kenneth, and Annabelle Henkin Melzer. *Shakespeare on Screen: An International Filmography and Videography* (1990). A reference guide to several hundred films and videos produced between 1899 and 1989, including spinoffs such as musicals and dance versions.

Smallwood, Robert. *Players of Shakespeare 4* (1998). Like the volumes by Brockbank and Jackson, listed above, contains remarks by contemporary performers.

Sprague, Arthur Colby. *Shakespeare and the Actors* (1944). Detailed discussions of stage business (gestures, etc.) over the years.

Willis, Susan. *The BBC Shakespeare Plays: Making the Televised Canon* (1991). A history of the series, with interviews and production diaries for some plays.

5. Miscellaneous Reference Works

Abbott, E. A. *A Shakespearean Grammar* (new edition, 1877). An examination of differences between Elizabethan and modern grammar.

Allen, Michael J. B., and Kenneth Muir, eds. *Shakespeare's Plays in Quarto* (1981). One volume containing facsimiles of the plays issued in small format before they were collected in the First Folio of 1623.

Blake, Norman. *Shakespeare's Language: An Introduction* (1983). On vocabulary, parts of speech, and word order.

Bullough, Geoffrey. *Narrative and Dramatic Sources of Shakespeare*, 8 vols. (1957–75). A collection of many of the books Shakespeare drew on, with judicious comments.

Campbell, Oscar James, and Edward G. Quinn, eds. *The Reader's Encyclopedia of Shakespeare* (1966). Old, and in some ways superseded by Michael Dobson's *Oxford Companion* (see below), but still highly valuable.

Cercignani, Fausto. *Shakespeare's Works and Elizabethan Pronunciation* (1981). Considered the best work on the topic, but remains controversial.

Champion, Larry S. *The Essential Shakespeare: An Annotated Bibliography of Major Modern Studies* (2nd ed., 1993). An invaluable guide to 1,800 writings about Shakespeare.

Dent, R. W. *Shakespeare's Proverbial Language: An Index* (1981). An index of proverbs, with an introduction concerning a form Shakespeare frequently drew on.

Dobson, Michael, ed. *The Oxford Companion to Shakespeare* (2001). Probably the single most useful reference work for information (arranged alphabetically) about Shakespeare and his works.

Greg, W. W. *The Shakespeare First Folio* (1955). A detailed yet readable history of the first collection (1623) of Shakespeare's plays.

Harner, James. *The World Shakespeare Bibliography*. See headnote to Suggested References.

Hosley, Richard. *Shakespeare's Holinshed* (1968). Valuable presentation of one of Shakespeare's major sources.

Kökeritz, Helge. *Shakespeare's Names* (1959). A guide to pronouncing some 1,800 names appearing in Shakespeare.

———. *Shakespeare's Pronunciation* (1953). Contains much information about puns and rhymes, but see Cercignani (above).

Muir, Kenneth. *The Sources of Shakespeare's Plays* (1978). An account of Shakespeare's use of his reading. It covers all the plays, in chronological order.

Miriam Joseph, Sister. *Shakespeare's Use of the Arts of Language* (1947). A study of Shakespeare's use of rhetorical devices, reprinted in part as *Rhetoric in Shakespeare's Time* (1962).

The Norton Facsimile: The First Folio of Shakespeare's Plays (1968). A handsome and accurate facsimile of the first collection (1623) of Shakespeare's plays, with a valuable introduction by Charlton Hinman.

Onions, C. T. *A Shakespeare Glossary*, rev. and enlarged by R. D. Eagleson (1986). Definitions of words (or senses of words) now obsolete.

Partridge, Eric. *Shakespeare's Bawdy*, rev. ed. (1955). Relatively brief dictionary of bawdy words; useful, but see Williams, below.

Shakespeare Quarterly. See headnote to Suggested References.

Shakespeare Survey. See headnote to Suggested References.

Spevack, Marvin. *The Harvard Concordance to Shakespeare* (1973). An index to Shakespeare's words.

Vickers, Brian. *Appropriating Shakespeare: Contemporary Critical Quarrels* (1993). A survey—chiefly hostile—of recent schools of criticism.

Wells, Stanley, ed. *Shakespeare: A Bibliographical Guide* (new edition, 1990). Nineteen chapters (some devoted to single plays, others devoted to groups of related plays) on recent scholarship on the life and all of the works.

Williams, Gordon. *A Dictionary of Sexual Language and Imagery in Shakespearean and Stuart Literature*, 3 vols. (1994). Extended discussions of words and passages; much fuller than Partridge, cited above.

6. Shakespeare's Plays: General Studies

Bamber, Linda. *Comic Women, Tragic Men: A Study of Gender and Genre in Shakespeare* (1982).

Barnet, Sylvan. *A Short Guide to Shakespeare* (1974).

Callaghan, Dympna, Lorraine Helms, and Jyotsna Singh. *The Weyward Sisters: Shakespeare and Feminist Politics* (1994).

Clemen, Wolfgang H. *The Development of Shakespeare's Imagery* (1951).

Cook, Ann Jennalie. *Making a Match: Courtship in Shakespeare and His Society* (1991).

Dollimore, Jonathan, and Alan Sinfield. *Political Shakespeare: New Essays in Cultural Materialism* (1985).

Dusinberre, Juliet. *Shakespeare and the Nature of Women* (1975).

Granville-Barker, Harley. *Prefaces to Shakespeare*, 2 vols. (1946–47; volume 1 contains essays on *Hamlet, King Lear, Merchant of Venice, Antony and Cleopatra*, and *Cymbeline*; volume 2 contains essays on *Othello, Coriolanus, Julius Caesar, Romeo and Juliet, Love's Labor's Lost*).

———. *More Prefaces to Shakespeare* (1974; essays on *Twelfth Night, A Midsummer Night's Dream, The Winter's Tale, Macbeth*).

Harbage, Alfred. *William Shakespeare: A Reader's Guide* (1963).

Howard, Jean E. *Shakespeare's Art of Orchestration: Stage Technique and Audience Response* (1984).

Jones, Emrys. *Scenic Form in Shakespeare* (1971).

Lenz, Carolyn Ruth Swift, Gayle Greene, and Carol Thomas Neely, eds. *The Woman's Part: Feminist Criticism of Shakespeare* (1980).

Novy, Marianne. *Love's Argument: Gender Relations in Shakespeare* (1984).

Rose, Mark. *Shakespearean Design* (1972).

Scragg, Leah. *Discovering Shakespeare's Meaning* (1994).

———. *Shakespeare's "Mouldy Tales": Recurrent Plot Motifs in Shakespearean Drama* (1992).

Traub, Valerie. *Desire and Anxiety: Circulations of Sexuality in Shakespearean Drama* (1992).

Traversi, D. A. *An Approach to Shakespeare,* 2 vols. (3rd rev. ed, 1968–69).

Vickers, Brian. *The Artistry of Shakespeare's Prose* (1968).

Wells, Stanley. *Shakespeare: A Dramatic Life* (1994).

Wright, George T. *Shakespeare's Metrical Art* (1988).

7. The Comedies

Barber, C. L. *Shakespeare's Festive Comedy* (1959; discusses *Love's Labor's Lost, A Midsummer Night's Dream, The Merchant of Venice, As You Like It, Twelfth Night*).

Barton, Anne. *The Names of Comedy* (1990).

Berry, Ralph. *Shakespeare's Comedy: Explorations in Form* (1972).

Bradbury, Malcolm, and David Palmer, eds. *Shakespearean Comedy* (1972).

Bryant, J. A., Jr. *Shakespeare and the Uses of Comedy* (1986).

Carroll, William. *The Metamorphoses of Shakespearean Comedy* (1985).

Champion, Larry S. *The Evolution of Shakespeare's Comedy* (1970).

Evans, Bertrand. *Shakespeare's Comedies* (1960).

Frye, Northrop. *Shakespearean Comedy and Romance* (1965).

Leggatt, Alexander. *Shakespeare's Comedy of Love* (1974).

Miola, Robert S. *Shakespeare and Classical Comedy: The Influence of Plautus and Terence* (1994).

Nevo, Ruth. *Comic Transformations in Shakespeare* (1980).

Ornstein, Robert. *Shakespeare's Comedies: From Roman Farce to Romantic Mystery* (1986).

Richman, David. *Laughter, Pain, and Wonder: Shakespeare's Comedies and the Audience in the Theater* (1990).

Salingar, Leo. *Shakespeare and the Traditions of Comedy* (1974).

Slights, Camille Wells. *Shakespeare's Comic Commonwealths* (1993).

Waller, Gary, ed. *Shakespeare's Comedies* (1991).

Westlund, Joseph. *Shakespeare's Reparative Comedies: A Psychoanalytic View of the Middle Plays* (1984).

Williamson, Marilyn. *The Patriarchy of Shakespeare's Comedies* (1986).

8. The Romances (*Pericles, Cymbeline, The Winter's Tale, The Tempest, The Two Noble Kinsmen*)

Adams, Robert M. *Shakespeare: The Four Romances* (1989).

Felperin, Howard. *Shakespearean Romance* (1972).

Frye, Northrop. *A Natural Perspective: The Development of Shakespearean Comedy and Romance* (1965).

Mowat, Barbara. *The Dramaturgy of Shakespeare's Romances* (1976).

Warren, Roger. *Staging Shakespeare's Late Plays* (1990).

Young, David. *The Heart's Forest: A Study of Shakespeare's Pastoral Plays* (1972).

9. The Tragedies

Bradley, A. C. *Shakespearean Tragedy* (1904).

Brooke, Nicholas. *Shakespeare's Early Tragedies* (1968).

Champion, Larry. *Shakespeare's Tragic Perspective* (1976).

Drakakis, John, ed. *Shakespearean Tragedy* (1992).

Evans, Bertrand. *Shakespeare's Tragic Practice* (1979).

Everett, Barbara. *Young Hamlet: Essays on Shakespeare's Tragedies* (1989).

Foakes, R. A. *Hamlet versus Lear: Cultural Politics and Shakespeare's Art* (1993).

Frye, Northrop. *Fools of Time: Studies in Shakespearean Tragedy* (1967).

Harbage, Alfred, ed. *Shakespeare: The Tragedies* (1964).

Mack, Maynard. *Everybody's Shakespeare: Reflections Chiefly on the Tragedies* (1993).

McAlindon, T. *Shakespeare's Tragic Cosmos* (1991).

Miola, Robert S. *Shakespeare and Classical Tragedy: The Influence of Seneca* (1992).

———. *Shakespeare's Rome* (1983).

Nevo, Ruth. *Tragic Form in Shakespeare* (1972).

Rackin, Phyllis. *Shakespeare's Tragedies* (1978).

Rose, Mark, ed. *Shakespeare's Early Tragedies: A Collection of Critical Essays* (1995).

Rosen, William. *Shakespeare and the Craft of Tragedy* (1960).

Snyder, Susan. *The Comic Matrix of Shakespeare's Tragedies* (1979).

Wofford, Susanne. *Shakespeare's Late Tragedies: A Collection of Critical Essays* (1996).

Young, David. *The Action to the Word: Structure and Style in Shakespearean Tragedy* (1990).

———. *Shakespeare's Middle Tragedies: A Collection of Critical Essays* (1993).

10. The Histories

Blanpied, John W. *Time and the Artist in Shakespeare's English Histories* (1983).

Campbell, Lily B. *Shakespeare's "Histories": Mirrors of Elizabethan Policy* (1947).

Champion, Larry S. *Perspective in Shakespeare's English Histories* (1980).

Hodgdon, Barbara. *The End Crowns All: Closure and Contradiction in Shakespeare's History* (1991).

Holderness, Graham. *Shakespeare Recycled: The Making of Historical Drama* (1992).

———, ed. *Shakespeare's History Plays: "Richard II" to "Henry V"* (1992).

Leggatt, Alexander. *Shakespeare's Political Drama: The History Plays and the Roman Plays* (1988).

Levine, Nina S. *Women's Matters: Politics, Gender, and Nation in Shakespeare's Early History Plays* (1998).

Ornstein, Robert. *A Kingdom for a Stage: The Achievement of Shakespeare's History Plays* (1972).

Rackin, Phyllis. *Stages of History: Shakespeare's English Chronicles* (1990).

Saccio, Peter. *Shakespeare's English Kings* (2nd ed., 1999).

Spiekerman, Tim. *Shakespeare's Political Realism* (2001).

Tillyard, E.M.W. *Shakespeare's History Plays* (1944).

Velz, John W., ed. *Shakespeare's English Histories: A Quest for Form and Genre* (1996).

11. *Love's Labor's Lost*

Especially useful recent editions of *Love's Labor's Lost* have been prepared by John Kerrigan (1982), G. R. Hibbard (1990), and H. R. Woudhuysen (1998).

For readings concerned with stage and television productions, see the Bibliographic Note above, following "*Love's Labor's Lost* on Stage and Screen," and see the material, also above, in Section 4 of this list of Suggested References.

For the play in the context of Shakespeare's other comedies, see above, Section 7.

For a collection of essays on the play, see the title below

by Felicia Hardison Londré. Many important essays, on all aspects of the play (e.g., text, interpretation, production) are reprinted in volumes 2, 23, 38, 54, 64, and 77 of *Shakespearean Criticism.*

For an annotated bibliography, see the title by Nancy Lenz Harvey and Anna Kirwan Carey (1984), which covers material through 1981; for comments on more recent material, see the title by John S. Pendergast (2002), which though not a bibliography comments extensively on virtually all of the useful secondary sources.

Arthos, John. *Shakespeare: The Early Writings* (1972).

Barber, C. L. *Shakespeare's Festive Comedy* (1959).

Carroll, W. C. *The Great Feast of Language in Love's Labour's Lost* (1976).

Gilbert, Miriam. *Shakespeare in Performance: Love's Labour's Lost* (1993).

Harvey, Nancy Lenz, and Anna Kirwan Carey. *Love's Labour's Lost, An Annotated Bibliography* (1984).

Homan, Sidney. *When the Theater Turns to Itself* (1981).

Hoy, Cyrus. *The Hyacinth Room* (1964).

Lamb, Mary Ellen. "The Nature of Topicality in *Love's Labour's Lost,*" *Shakespeare Survey* 38 (1985): 49–59.

Londré, Felicia Hardison, ed. *Love's Labour's Lost: Critical Essays* (1997).

Maus, Katharine Eisaman. "Transfer of Title in *Love's Labor's Lost:* Language, Individualism, Gender," in *Shakespeare Left and Right*, ed. Ivo Kamps (1991).

Pendergast, John S. *Love's Labour's Lost: A Guide to the Play* (2002).

Roesen, Bobbyann. "Love's Labour's Lost," *Shakespeare Quarterly* 4 (1953): 411–26.

Vyvyan, John. *Shakespeare and the Rose of Love* (1960).

Wells, Stanley. "The Copy for the Folio Text of Love's Labour's Lost," *Review of English Studies* 33 (1982): 137–47.

Westlund, Joseph. "Fancy and Achievement in *Love's Labour's Lost,*" *Shakespeare Quarterly* 18 (1967): 37–46.

SIGNET CLASSICS (0451)

The Signet Classics Shakespeare Series:

The Comedies

extensively revised and updated to provide more enjoyment through a greater understanding of the texts

Available wherevver books are sold or at
www.penguin.com

Signet Classic (0451)

The Signet Classic Shakespeare Series: The Tragedies

extensively revised and updated expert commentary provides more
enjoyment through a greater understanding of the texts

Available wherever books are sold or at
www.penguin.com

The Signet Classic Shakespeare Series:

The Histories

extensively revised and updated to provide more enjoyment through a greater understanding of the texts

Available wherever books are sold or at

www.penguin.com

READ THE TOP 25 SIGNET CLASSICS